STUDIES
IN THE
HISTORY
OF
EDUCATION

ESSAYS PRESENTED
TO

PETER GOSDEN

STUDIES

IN THE

HISTORY

OF

EDUCATION

ESSAYS

PRESENTED TO

PETER GOSDEN

EDITED BY

EDGAR JENKINS

Leeds University Press

ISBN 0 85316 165 8

Professor Peter Gosden

CONTENTS

Introduction ix
  Edgar Jenkins

1 Teacher Status and College Culture in the Development of
  a Profession 1
  Peter Cunningham

2 Constructing and reconstructing school technology in
  England and Wales 23
  David Layton

3 English, Australian and New Zealand Prep. Schools: a study
  in degrees of replication 57
  Donald P. Leinster-Mackay

4 The pathos of policy: Adult education as a contribution to
  the British occupation in Germany, 1945–55 85
  Stuart Marriott

5 The power of three: 'Parity of esteem' and the social history of
  tripartism 113
  Gary McCulloch

6 Reporting Academics: A memoir of The Times Higher Education
  Supplement 133
  Peter Scott

7 From local governance to LEA and from LEA to local
  governance: a study of the management and government of
  schools in England from 1839 to 1994 167
  Paul Sharp and John Dunford

8 Illiteracy in provincial maritime districts and among
  seamen in early and mid-nineteenth-century England . . . 195
  W. B. Stephens

A Select Bibliography of works by Peter Gosden 223

Notes on contributors 226

INTRODUCTION

Edgar Jenkins

PETER GOSDEN graduated and trained as a history teacher at Cambridge. After National Service in the RAF, he taught history and religious knowledge in schools in Northwood and Greenford and studied for his PhD on a part-time basis under Eric Hobsbawm at Birkbeck College. He joined the staff of what was then the Department of Education of the University of Leeds in 1960. He was promoted to a Senior Lectureship in 1967, to a Readership in the Administration and Management of Education in 1971 and to a Chair in the History of Education in 1979.

Peter Gosden's research, teaching and publications established Leeds as a major centre for the scholarly study of educational policy and administration. Numerous PhD and other students can readily attest to his skill as a stimulating supervisor and teacher, demanding and securing from them work of the highest quality. His extensive writings about the local and national development of the education service in England and Wales have become the first port of call for any scholar working in this field. His study of educational policy and administration during the Second World War was commissioned in 1968 to fill the missing education element of the official history of this period – and when, in 1989, the then DES wished to mark the sesquicentenary of the establishment of the Committee of the Privy Council on Education, it was Peter Gosden who was invited to deliver an appropriate lecture. In 1967, he co-founded the *Journal of Educational Administration and History*, a highly-regarded publication that continues to be strongly associated with the University and its Museum of the History of Education. Since January 1993, he has been President of the History of Education Society.

These scholarly achievements become even more impressive when placed in the context of Peter Gosden's other contributions, to the work of his department, of the University, and of the wider community. His academic and managerial skills made him the natural choice for the headship of the School of Education when it was established in 1976 from two very different academic units. These skills were equally in evidence when his colleagues asked him to assume the headship for a second time from 1987 to 1991.

Any account of Peter Gosden's wider involvement with the offices of the University of Leeds would précis the recent history and administration of the institution itself and embrace aspects as diverse as Halls of Residence and the Anglican Chaplaincy. He served as a member of the Senate from 1968 until his retirement from the service of the University in 1992, acting as an astute and highly respected chairman of many of its committees. From 1985 to 1987, he served the University with distinction as its Pro-Vice-Chancellor. Beyond the University, Peter Gosden has been closely involved with the government of schools, with the former DES, with other institutions of higher education, with educational matters in the diocese of Ripon, and with the Universities Council for the Education of Teachers, of which he is currently the Academic Secretary. As chairman of the former Joint Matriculation Board from 1988 to 1992, he played a major role in bringing to a successful conclusion the complex and time-consuming negotiations to establish the Northern Examinations and Assessment Board.

The main purpose of this volume is to honour Peter Gosden's contribution to, and encouragement of, the scholarly study of the history of education. The readiness with which other scholars in this field agreed to contribute is an indication not only of the high estimation in which his work is held but also of the warm affection with which he is regarded. If, in addition, the essays serve to stimulate a wider interest in the history of education, no-one would be more pleased than Peter Gosden himself.

CHAPTER
O N E

Teacher Status and College Culture in the Development of a Profession

PETER CUNNINGHAM

Introduction

Peter Gosden's formidable contribution to documenting and interpreting the history of the teaching profession was published in the same year as the James Report, at a critical point in the history of teaching and teacher training. His book marked a significant phase in an unduly neglected aspect of educational history. Donna Thompson had made an early study of the growth and political influence of the NUT,[1] R. W. Rich had reviewed the curriculum and methods of nineteenth-century elementary teacher training[2] and Asher Tropp had considered professional development in the context of the National Union of Teachers,[3] but Gosden offered a more comprehensive and continuous account of the developing profession over a period of 150 years. Subsequent to Gosden's work, a surge of sociological analysis drew on and complemented the historical account. Articles by Purvis, by Parry and Parry and by Eric Hoyle, amongst others, assessed the claims to professionalism.[4] The introduction into this discourse of politics and ideology for example by Gerald Grace, by Jenny Ozga and Martin Lawn, and by Hilda Kean, extended the frame of reference in which teachers as an occupational group had to be considered.[5] In respect of elementary teachers the present paper seeks to explore further two issues suggested by Gosden's work and by certain sociological perspectives.

A triangle of connected themes may be seen to underlie the structure of Gosden's work: first, the level of remuneration (including both salaries and superannuation) and the associated issue of conditions of service; secondly, the associations and unions which teachers formed in order to share and express their collective ideas, with the related aspect of a protracted and unsuccessful drive for some form of professional registration; and thirdly, patterns of training, its institutions and related questions of teacher supply.

Between the points of this triangle may be identified two further issues of importance. Connecting the hard currency of salary levels to the less tangible feature of professional aspiration is the question of teacher 'status' as perceived by society at large – a phenomenon which Asher Tropp had begun to explore. Referring to the 'social position' or 'social condition' of the elementary teacher, Tropp identified status anxiety in the campaigns of the NUT and indicated certain continuing themes in negative stereotyping of teachers. In 1925 the Departmental Committee on the Training of Teachers for Public Elementary Schools turned its attention to the problem of 'low public esteem' for the profession.[6]

The point of professional aspiration is also connected to that of training and supply, and along this side of the notional triangle lies the issue of training college culture. The colleges in which certificated elementary teachers received their formal education and training, had to be flexible in response to changing demand for teachers, but they also imbued their alumni with a sense of tradition and of professional identity. William Taylor in 1969 wrote of a 'distinctive subculture' of teacher training 'to be identified within the broader subculture of English society and education'.[7]

These two features, the popular perception of the teacher on the one hand, and the contribution of training institutions to the professional culture of teaching are themselves interconnected. In our own times this is evident in the campaign of the 'new right' which identifies the source of education's ills in an 'educational establishment' created by the training institutions and which has precipitated yet another critical moment in the development of the profession. The principal concern of the historical study below is with an earlier period of comparable trauma, the 1920s and early 1930s. The period is interesting both for the degree of attention paid in official circles to the quality of teacher training, and for the popular attention to teachers in their struggles with the government over pay. But the account below will also glance forward to the crucial period of the late 1960s and early 1970s about the time of publication of Gosden's book. In conclusion, some points of comparison and contrast will also be made with the late 1980s and early 1990s.

Teacher Status

One source for the perceived status of teachers in society at large is the memories of teachers themselves. Although this source will not be pursued in depth here, a handful of examples gleaned recently at the outset of a new project will offer some idea of the spectrum of response.[8] A teacher who trained in the late 1920s recalled: 'One tried not to mention one's profession. Teachers were confined mentally then . . . it was sad and confining, and for some, lonely', and another trained in the early 1930s remembered: 'When on holiday we tried not to let people know we were teachers or they seemed to retreat'. On the other hand a student teacher who went on to college and qualified in 1930 felt: 'the teaching profession in 1930 was held in high regard . . . we could dress quite well and I believe we were "looked up to" by society in general', and a pupil teacher who eventually achieved certification in 1928 thought: 'the profession carried considerable status, and teachers in general were widely respected. They had dignity and dressed "correctly"'.[9] Such complex and apparently contradictory responses will require more extensive analysis elsewhere. For example, this small sample of four is distinguished by gender, the former female and latter male. As with all oral history, hindsight and response to current educational perceptions also colour these retrospective views, and the later careers of both these men after 1944 took them into the secondary sector, whilst the women respondents had pursued their careers in primary schools.

Contradictory popular attitudes to teachers may also be inferred from the editorials and correspondence columns of newspapers, and in an earlier study I have shown how press views on teacher status were provoked by disputes over teachers' pay in recent decades.[10] Similarly in the inter-war years, it was the issue of teacher salaries which precipitated a hostile campaign by one influential section of the press. Tropp considered that an index of the rise in teachers' status between the wars was increasingly favourable references to them in popular newspapers.

At the *Daily Mail* Lord Northcliffe's journalistic principle entailed 'giving the public what they wanted', one feature of which was the 'talking point' – getting the topics that people were discussing, and developing them. One such topic was 'government waste', and it was in this connection that teachers as public servants became the target of an often quite vitriolic editorial offensive.[11] The *Daily Mail* chose the forthcoming Burnham Committee of September 1924, which was to make its first quinquennial review of teachers' salaries following the historic agreement of 1919, as an opportunity to renew its onslaught on teachers. The attack began on 22 September with a leader comment on teachers' salaries . . . Writing of an 'overpaid profession', the paper at least conceded:[12]

> The elementary and secondary school teachers are an excellent body of men and women who are doing useful service to the nation. But these services, as the *Daily Mail* has frequently pointed out, are distinctly overpaid . . . Teaching in the rate-supported schools is one of the most sheltered of all the sheltered trades. Teachers, male and female, ought to be properly rewarded for their services, but there is no reason why they should be pampered or paid out of all proportion either to their merits or to their exertions. They have mostly sprung from the elementary schools themselves and have passed into the training colleges where, mainly at the public expense they have acquired the moderate accomplishments requisite to teach children . . .

On 25 September it commented further:[13]

> The teachers like to identify themselves with the cause of education . . . In fact the teachers are in many respects a privileged class; and they have come to regard their privileges as really due to their own super-eminent abilities and merits.

The editorial was characterised by disingenuousness. It coupled its attention to teachers with comment on striking railwaymen. And it defended its stance with crude economic argument:

> We are bringing no indictment, of course, against those in the sheltered, or as some hard-hearted economists call them, the 'parasitic' pursuits. Most of them are doing useful and necessary work . . . [but] . . . British manufacturing industry . . . is bled and fleeced for the maintenance of large groups of non-productive workers in sheltered domestic avocations who are too highly paid at the expense of the community and actual producers.

These views provoked a considerable response, and the newspaper printed a number of what it described as 'abusive' letters from teachers. Mostly, these appear as quite reasonable corrections to factual omissions or misrepresentations, with frequent reference to the high accomplishment of many (degree or equivalent), and to the demands of the job (long hours and stress). Two letters from 'contented teachers' were notably from recently retired members of the profession who had benefited enormously from the new Burnham pensions. In the welter of correspondence over the next week, fourteen letters were from teachers in self-defence, two from 'contented teachers' and six in agreement with the paper's strictures.[14] Amongst these last were accusations of poor performance in the low educational standards of elementary schoolchildren, of concealing self-interest behind the 'interests of children', and one from 'A School Inspector', a distant echo of the 'Holmes-Morant circular', alleging that 'the average elementary school teacher is not what can be termed an "educated person"'.

At the opposite end of the political spectrum from the *Daily Mail* lay the *Daily Herald*, by now an official organ of the Labour Party, appealing almost exclusively to the socialist working class and more stolid in style. In a leader column 'From the Workers' Point of View', it replied specifically to the *Daily Mail*'s campaign, under the headline 'We Must Take Care of Our Schools'.[15] It described the *Daily Mail*'s proprietor Lord Rothermere as an 'illusionist' who 'persuades vast numbers of people to buy his papers and boost his immense riches, while doing his best to injure them and put obstacles in the way to their improvement'.

> Yesterday he started a fresh campaign against school-teachers. . . . Most teachers we were told with a sneer, have sprung from the elementary schools themselves. Their accomplishments 'are moderate'.

The *Daily Herald* associated education with civilization:

> Respect paid to those who are forming the minds of the citizens of the future, appreciation of their services, acknowledgement that they are

doing very important work, are proofs that a nation is in a high state of civilization. Wherever teachers have a low place in the social scale, wherever they are grudged the reasonable comfort and ease of mind which they require if they are to do their work well, the standard of civilization is low.

No community can prosper which does not provide sound education; to provide that it is necessary to attract into the service of the schools men and women of character, intelligence and active mind. How could we expect to do this if we treated teachers as Lord Rothermere would have us treat them?

Moreover, the potentially insidious influence of this kind of journalistic defamation was recognised:

> There is, of course, no risk of Lord Rothermere's counsel being followed . . . Yet these ignorant, ungenerous attacks do leave behind them false impressions in many minds. They will in this instance make harder the heavy task of lifting elementary education from the rot in which the present Minister found it.

The *Daily Express* was the chief rival of the *Daily Mail* amongst the popular press. After its rescue by Lord Beaverbrook, by imitating and enlarging on the style of its competitor, its circulation reached one million by 1922. Without referring specifically to the *Daily Mail*'s attack, it was eloquent on 'Our Debt to the School Teachers'. Describing the realities of teachers' modest salaries, and referring to the years of training required, it attributed the drive for economy on Burnham to counties in which public education was treated almost with contempt, and it concluded:[16]

> The contentment of our schoolteachers is of such imperative importance . . . To describe as overpaid a profession requiring such high personal standards and attainments as that of the school teacher . . . is to place the mark of ingratitude upon the services of men and women to whom every home in the State owes the deepest debt.

This opinion was greeted with an 'enormous correspondence' (as the *Daily Express* itself described it) over the following week, largely supportive of, and grateful for, the stance taken. Most of these letters were from teachers themselves, and two referred to what they saw as unnecessary extravagance in educational administration at the expense of the teachers themselves.

The *Manchester Guardian*, too, pursued the theme of a 'Dangerous "Economy"' in the proposed Burnham reduction of teachers' salaries:[17]

> We reward our doctors and our lawyers on a scale the schoolmaster does not dream of; yet a sound education would enable us to dispense very largely

with both of them . . . Further to diminish the teacher's resources is to narrow his outlook, to sour his philosophy, to cramp and twist his attitude to life and as certainly as these things are done they will be reflected in the mentality and spirit of the men of the future who are his charges.

The editorial went on to make its own dismissive reference to the attitudes of the Rothermere press, which 'envisage the teacher as battening upon the famished frame of our industrial life':

> In a life with more kicks than halfpence, the teacher does not often provoke so richly perverse an indictment as this.

Again, it was proposed cuts in teachers' pay that provoked a further public discussion of the merits or otherwise of the teaching profession in September 1931. The *Daily Herald* was vocal in support of the teachers:[18]

> Great Britain has the finest public servants in the world and among these the teachers stand high. They have an exalted sense of duty and it is fitting that it should be so, for they are the custodians of the nation's children.

The main arguments beyond this were the sacrifice of long years in study and 'apprenticeship' and the dedication of teachers in giving many hours outside of school time. One distinct emphasis of the subsequent correspondence from readers was on the interests of the children; six days later the *Daily Herald* reported that 'Letters on teachers' salaries continue to dominate the Editor's huge "protest" postbag and congratulations are pouring in on the *Daily Herald*'s *stand for the nation's schools* [my italics]'.[19] One letter from a redundant weaver, however, envied the teachers their pension rights. A spate of correspondence was also triggered in the *Manchester Guardian* by a leading article on 'The Economies', where the proposed cut in unemployment benefit was coupled with that in teachers' salaries:[20]

> The first is at the expense of the most unfortunate section of the community; the second at the expense of the most important service undertaken by the State.

A subsequent letter written by a works foreman who came of a teaching family dwelt on the short hours, long paid holiday, sick pay and pension:[21]

> Teachers are not harassed by the fear of short time or having to go on the dole; they enjoy the luxury of a 'sheltered' occupation, the 'rainy day' has no terror for them.

The commercial and increasingly competitive press both reflected and informed public opinion. As Gladstone had observed: 'The press, which was formerly the privilege of the educated classes, has become the patrimony of the people'. Of the newspapers cited above, the *Daily Mail* had the leading circulation, nearing two million in 1930, closely followed by the *Daily Express,* and the *Daily Herald* was increasingly a mass circulation paper having crossed the one million threshold.[22] Graves and Hodge felt that the *Daily Mail* was generally laughed at and taken with little seriousness,[23] but it was a popular paper with broad appeal and a high readership in the upper and upper middle classes. The *Daily Express* also enjoyed a wide readership, but with more of a lower-middle and upper working class appeal, and the *Daily Herald* had a solidly working class following. The influence of the newspapers on public opinion is not easy to gauge. P.E.P. suggested in 1938 that the leading article in national morning newspapers was the third most popular item after pictorial features and the main news, and was seen or read by one half of their readers and read completely by one third. However, reader interest declined with income.[24] A Mass Observation enquiry some ten years later found that the Editorial was the main feature enjoyed by 12 per cent of *Daily Mail* and 11 per cent of *Daily Express* readers, in stark contrast to 4 percent for the *Daily Herald*.[25]

Thus the principal negative features of the popular image of teachers in the 1920s were those of an easy and 'non-productive' job, of the modest ability required and the subsidised training received, of teachers' upward social mobility and their hypocrisy in disguising self-interest as educational idealism. They did however find their defenders in a range of newspapers. By the early 1970s, popular perception of teacher status was beginning to be clouded by documentation of 'school failure', for instance with Cyril Burt's statistics in the second black paper purporting to show a fall in educational standards since 1914.[26] Teachers' strikes were another factor discouraging the traditional respect which the *Daily Express* assumed had always been accorded to the profession. The NUT decision to boycott examinations was 'a severe blow to the profession's reputation':[27]

> A great profession – which deserves a career and salary structure that reflects merit, experience and responsibility – is being made to look like a mob, shoving aside those least able to look after themselves.

The *Daily Mirror* set less store by the 'professional' tag, approving of a closer cooperation between teachers and the Trades Union movement in general. But like the *Express* it perceived dedication to the children and to their job as a characteristic of many teachers. With the announcement of the James enquiry, there was comment, too, on the effectiveness of the teachers' training, the *Mirror* noting that colleges had been accused of being out of touch with schools, and Bruce Kemble, Education Correspondent of the *Express* observing:[28]

> Most educationists view this enquiry as more crucial to the future of education in the country's 30,000 schools, than the Plowden, Robbins or Newsom probes . . . For the past 25 years complaints have been made by young teachers about their training.

College Culture

The link between perceived status on the one hand and training on the other was noted early on by Runciman who experienced cultural snobbery towards teachers:[29]

> The standard of culture among teachers is shockingly low, and it is very painful to me to mention the subject at all. I have suffered keenly from hearing the remarks made concerning schoolmasters by ordinary men and women of the upper and middle classes, by clergymen and School Board members of my acquaintance . . . lads and girls are tempted into a profession and fixed for life; then their minds are starved, and they are turned out to endure the mockery of cultured folk, and to perpetuate mental ruin among the younger generation. I have been horrorstruck by seeing the contempt with which teachers are mentioned by the very persons who flatter them to their faces . . .

The infamous 'Holmes-Morant Circular' was merely a reiteration of this apparently common contempt, though in an administratively sensitive and politically charged context, emanating moreover from a noted progressive educationist and perhaps prompted by a complaint from the NUT itself about the overbearing manner of local inspectors.

However Runciman had a solution in mind:

> It is . . . imperative that we should improve the education of the teachers. At present it is the fashion among eager young men who leave the Normal College to employ the evenings in hard study. They work five or six hours per night, deny themselves all pleasures, and finish up by taking their degrees at London. But the man should have his degree before he begins his work as a master: it is monstrous that a professional teacher, trained by the State, should be obliged to toil for years after his 'training' is over before he can call himself an educated man at all.

Gosden pointed to the links between status and training by reference to the long campaign of teachers' associations, and especially the NUT, to lengthen the minimum period of training as a way of claiming parity with the better established professions. But beyond the length of the course lay the culture of the colleges inherited from their Victorian origins, and it was above all the separateness of the colleges that marked out the elementary teacher as distinct from other professionals in her or his training. In a memorandum to the Burnham Committee in 1938, the NUT reiterated its longstanding hope for the day when all teachers would be graduates 'educated not as a class apart, but in free contact with entrants to other professions', and Tropp considered that one factor in the rise of teachers' status was the increasing number of graduates entering the elementary schools in the 1930s.[30] Even general observers such as Graves and Hodge noted a marked improvement during the 'long weekend' of 1918 to 1939, in the quality of both elementary and secondary school teachers, which they attributed to the progressive and devoted administrators of the pre-war Board of Education, and the consequent improved teaching at state secondary schools and provincial universities.

One long letter from a teacher in the *Manchester Guardian* in 1931 related the salary issue to changing status in the quality of training, pointing out that the proposed cut would fall more heavily on the younger teachers[31]

> who received the more intensive and extensive university training, in contrast to the older teacher-training course. Almost all of the older people in the profession were pupil-teachers who had a two years' course at training college, the object of which was to train people to be teachers and not to provide a cultural education. Since the war a large number of competent young people have been attracted to teaching by the offer of a free four years' university course and the seeming fixity of the Burnham Scale.

The writer resented the fact that older men and women who had entered the profession before the war with only low salary expectations had reaped the full benefit of Burnham by retiring in the 1920s.

The importance of the college to a sense of professional identity can be inferred from Ballard's personal experience of Borough Road. The 'culture' that came from the training college itself had a number of aspects and Borough Road College owed its reputation, in his opinion, 'partly to its principles and partly to its principals'.[32] As a Quaker foundation, open to all teachers irrespective of caste or creed, it attracted men of robust minds and independent outlook. And it was led at times by outstanding men, such as Joshua Fitch. The reputation acquired under these eminent principals carried the college through periods of inferior leadership. But there was also the mutual influence of fellow students:

> A college, as the term itself implies, is a collection; not a collection of sticks and stones, but of men. The students themselves are an essential part of

the cultural forces at work. They certainly were so at Borough Road. They educated one another; as indeed was inevitable, coming as they did from all quarters of the realm, with different accents, different social habits, and different intellectual backgrounds.[33]

The women's colleges, by 1920 more numerous than the men's, enjoyed their own distinctive culture. Rev. Stewart Headlam recommended Leah Manning to enter Homerton, having observed in her the makings of a good socialist, despite her 'rather stuffy middle-class family – Methodist and Liberal in politics . . . provided she did not slip back in the atmosphere of a Women's Training College'.[34] Edwards has recently provided a fascinating analysis of the culture of women's training colleges in this period: the academic and cultural opportunities offered were extensive, and many former students testified to the widening of their intellectual interests. This could vary significantly from college to college, particularly in respect of geographical location – the contrast between the opportunities afforded by Avery Hill in the metropolis, Homerton College in the shadow of an ancient university, and Bishop Otter in a quiet cathedral city. At the same time this intellectual stimulus, and the replication of female family roles in the organisation of the college, could work against any incipient feminism.[35]

Of course individual colleges were distinctive in their culture and ethos. Derwent Coleridge, founding Principal of St Mark's, had established a particular reputation for the high cultural atmosphere of his college, and his successor Rev. Cromwell, in evidence to the Cross Commission, considered that in residential colleges students acquire 'something of the same kind of advantages that a boy derives from one of our great public schools'.[36] Despite his strictures on the quality of culture back in the 1880s, Ballard noted that 'in its humbler sphere' Borough Road College, like Balliol, endowed its alumni with 'a tranquil consciousness of effortless superiority':[37]

> To be an Old B. – merely to be an Old B. – is in itself a mark of distinction . . . he cherishes a secret, he radiates an inner joy, and knows in his heart of hearts that he is not as other men are.

Published histories and oral testimony can offer different angles on this phenomenon. Borough Road in the later 1920s saw improvements to students' living quarters, with group studies and a refurnished common room 'in a manner more fitting to the dignity of the college and the standing of the students', according to the Annual Report of 1926; the dining hall was redecorated and its gallery extended to accommodate a small orchestra and an appeal was launched for a properly equipped library. Bartle's history places these developments in the context of a more prosperous governing body and the implementation of a new degree programme, whereas a student of the time attributes them to the personality of the new Principal, F. L. Attenborough, who brought with him the aspirations to Cambridge collegiate culture that he had known as a research fellow at Emmanuel College.[38]

The Oxbridge comparison also appeared in the deliberations of the 1925 Departmental Committee. An objection to training colleges had been their segregation from other institutions of higher education, but an important mitigating factor was seen in the recruitment of students from all parts of the country, resulting in a more stimulating social and intellectual atmosphere. By contrast, the newer universities were often more local in their catchment[39].

> This common life in a residential institution, where students live and where they are taught, is a valuable feature and differentiates the Training Colleges from hostels or halls of residence in universities where students live but have no teaching, and makes the Training Colleges comparable, rather, on this ground, to the colleges of Oxford and Cambridge. To this element may be ascribed the strong corporate sense which distinguishes them, and the continuing effect of the College throughout the teacher's career as a focus of common interest and inspiration.

But it is valid also to generalise about the sector as a whole, and a key to the prevailing ethos of the colleges of the 1920s lies in the structure of the college sector, which a statistical picture can best provide.[40]

	Female	*Male*	*Mixed*	*Total*
Voluntary Training Colleges	36	14	–	50
Municipal Training Colleges	14	3	5	22
Total	50	17	5	72

		Day	*Residential*
Voluntary Training Colleges	Female	2	34
	Male	–	14
Municipal Training Colleges	Female	6	8
	Male	1	2
	Mixed	4	1

Thus the voluntary sector (mostly denominational and predominantly Church of England) was twice the size of the local authority sector, despite the numerous regulations with which the pre-war Liberal administration had sought to secularize all colleges. Mixed sex institutions, in which the University Training Departments had led the way, were introduced in the municipal sector, and marked a considerable change in the character of college life, but in 1917 mixed colleges were still regarded as being 'on trial'.[41] Voluntary colleges were residential institutions on the whole, and more than two thirds of them were for women. On the other hand only four of the municipal colleges were entirely residential – the distinction between residential and day was gradually blurred by the provision of hostels closely attached to the college, but the separation between teaching accommodation and residential did something to diminish the monastic model on which the Victorian colleges had been designed. By 1925 the quality of accommodation was improving as the conditions of grant from the Board of Education required suitable facilities such as a reference library, laboratories, provision for physical training and outside games, and common rooms. Separate study-bedrooms to replace the traditional dormitories and cubicles were becoming the norm with the building of the new municipal colleges. For the Church colleges, Lofthouse has described how they were, in competition with their municipal rivals, reduced to an extended struggle for survival during the inter-war period; the colleges were in desperate need of renovation and reform, but old buildings and traditional methods were generally retained because new solutions could not be afforded.[42]

Some developments in the colleges at this period suggest a distinct improvement. The appointment of Principals being subject to Board of Education approval, British university graduates were becoming the norm, and Heward has discussed the particular significance of this for women.[43] Increasingly the necessity of providing advanced instruction led to the appointment of university graduates in specialist subjects, and the growth of 'tutorial groups' and freedom of 'private study' in some colleges indicated an improved approach to the education of prospective teachers.[44]

On the other hand, many aspects of the traditional isolation remained. There was a strong representation of ex-students, certificated teachers, on the staffs of the older training colleges, which tended to prolong traditional customs and methods. The recruitment of students also encouraged 'in-breeding': voluntary colleges attracted students of their own denomination, even though the religious test could be applied to no more than 50 percent of applicants under the grant regulations.[45] It was financially advantageous to enter a municipal college of one's own LEA, and certificated teachers then proceeded to teach locally – a defect recognised by the Board of Education Report of 1912-13. Even with the older voluntary colleges which recruited nationally a similar situation could arise as many students were guided in their choice of college by the recommendation of a headteacher, thus building up close connections between individual colleges and particular areas of the country. Oral reminiscences often testify to this process.[46]

Further criticisms of college culture included disciplinary arrangements modelled on secondary schools; there were significant gender differences here and a variety of regimes, but despite variations 'the atmosphere of most Training colleges corresponds on the whole to that found in a Secondary School rather than in a University'[47]. The entry condition of signing a declaration of intent to follow the profession of a teacher was also a limiting factor, and this had reverted to a more stringent form in 1922.

Presenting the evidence which they had collected, the Departmental Committee of 1925 saw vocational commitment as a key quality which the colleges were uniquely equipped to convey:[48]

> We agree with the opinion expressed by many of our witnesses that a sense of vocation, a feeling of the dignity of a teacher's work and a conviction that it is worth doing, is vital for Elementary School teachers. We also agree with those who claim that this sense takes time to evoke and confirm. From the sense of vocation, which a good principal and a good staff may inspire, students gain a moral outlook and a point of view which endure when they have forgotten, or ceased to use, knowledge or methods acquired during the Training College course. Students are working in common for a worthy end, under members of the profession which they themselves are entering and favourable opportunities for developing this are presented.

There was also a utilitarian justification for this idealism, as students with a high sense of commitment were considered to be the most effective in getting 'sounder "Three R's"'.

Heward has noted that despite the increasing percentage of graduates, the status of training college lecturers remained low.[49] This fact, and the general reputation of the colleges may in part be due to the powerful influence in élite cultural circles of the criticisms voiced in the journal *Scrutiny*. In its pages L. C. Knights, literary and cultural critic, made the connection between college culture and a popular image of elementary teachers: the college was a 'cross between a barracks and a nursery', and it was consequently 'not hard to see why our schools are tenanted by nervous tyrants whose energies are centred in the problem of maintaining "discipline"'.[50] *Scrutiny*'s success had been such that an editorial notice in the third issue referred to an 'impressive amount of public notice' and to letters from subscribers revealing a public which consciously felt the need of such a review. Its premise was that 'the general dissolution of standards is a commonplace'; and literary criticism could not be undertaken in isolation from what was seen as the current state of cultural degeneration.

> *Scrutiny,* then, will be seriously preoccupied with the movement of modern civilization. And . . . it will direct itself especially upon educational matters . . . It goes without saying that for the majority neither the present drift of civilization nor the plight of the arts is a matter for much concern. It is true that there are many who are interested in one or the other without seeing any connexion between them.[51]

It was also a period in which 'the New Education', informed by various 'progressive' thinkers, was flourishing, and *Scrutiny* acknowledged this in observing that

> Traditional methods of education are being subjected at present to fairly rigorous criticism and a certain amount of overhauling; criticism which sees educational problems as part of the larger problem of general culture is however still necessary.[52]

In a more populist forum, a correspondent to the *Daily Mail* pondered on the nexus between education and culture:

> We are a strangely inconsistent nation; we worship 'education' as the universal cure-all; we cosset the teaching profession as does no other nation; we then revile the BBC for 'highbrow' leanings and bleet for dance music...[53]

The *Scrutiny* attack on training colleges was three pronged: on a 'limited and mechanical curriculum', on 'inadequate staff', and on 'inferior students'. The incessant lecturing which left no time for personal reading and reflection, and indeed the petty restrictions which governed extra-curricular life, constituted the first target; a lecturer who had never heard of Eliot, only just heard of Lawrence, and habitually recommended literary criticism from the *Daily Express* was included in the second; as for the third, a distinct measure of snobbery is evident in quoted responses to questionnaires:[54]

> I should say that for the type of student that enters an elementary teachers' training college the course was adequate, although a minority could have done with something better.
> The students were generally of such low intelligence and so childish

that in most cases excessive surveillance was necessary . . . People made friends because it was easier to hunt men in couples. Almost all of them worked hard keeping each other in the mood when they believed they were having the most wonderful time and it was all just like the 'pictures'. They were the most timid and mild set, absolutely herd-ridden, but they liked to think they were frightfully daring and gay. The men were on the whole boors . . .

Running throughout these comments and *Scrutiny*'s commentary was a hostility to popular culture, as in a sideswipe at a lecturer who referred to the cinema and newspapers as educative forces.

A more constructive approach to the dissemination of high culture through the education system may be detected in the immediate post-war world, and I have discussed elsewhere some connections between the activities of the newly formed Arts Council and the Ministry of Education.[55] Some significant reflections on the culture of training colleges are offered in internal memoranda relating to a scheme for the 'promotion of music in colleges', a proposal for visiting recitalists to perform on Saturday evenings to be followed by conversations with the students on a Sunday morning.[56] It was described as a proposal close to the heart of Sir John Maud, Permanent Secretary and a member of the Arts Council. This was intended as part of a wider Arts Council enterprise to disseminate classical music through the schools. The purpose was to 'gain a general recognition of the importance of music of really high quality as a normal element in a liberal education' and that this process should begin by making contact with the next generation of teachers in Primary and Modern schools. However, in the course of planning, there was some scepticism from HMI who were close to the life of the colleges. One view was that such an initiative would prove more popular with the women than with the men. Doubts were expressed about the likelihood of drawing attendances from students on a Saturday night (and especially so amongst the mature students of the Emergency Training Colleges). There was even the view that the weekend was an important opportunity for students to escape the environment of the college for the outside community.

Again some illuminating comparisons and contrasts may be made with the period of the James Report. For all the changes that had taken place in the colleges over the course of half a century, it is remarkable how many issues raised by the Departmental Committee in 1925 remained unresolved when a Select Committee of the House of Commons in 1969-70 eventually came to review teacher training.[57] The number of local authority and voluntary colleges had more than doubled, and the number of students more than quadrupled. At both points in history, the sector was congratulated on recent improvements both in the quality of entrants and in the academic standing of college lecturers. On the other hand, the twofold function of colleges, higher education and professional training, was still problematic, as was the segregation of students for one specific vocation. Standards, both academic and professional, were still seen as highly variable between different institutions.

The continuing paternalism of the colleges was seen as a strength by officialdom, but physical expansion and cultural change were putting pressure on this traditional regime, which was highlighted by the evidence of the National Union of Students:[58]

> In coping with an urgent need to expand, the colleges have suffered many indignities and their potential as institutions of Higher Education has been jeopardised . . . Contrary to educational theory, colleges of education are still too often small, geographically isolated, single sex, or denominational institutions . . .

A new factor was the 'progressivism' of educational philosophy and teaching method which the colleges were seen to promote. In this sense the colleges were centres of radical culture. As Harry Ree told the committee:

> A tidal wave of new approaches to education is causing a fatal and growing gap of understanding between trainee teachers pushing new methods while those who are settled in school are on the whole practising the old methods . . . Teachers who started ten years ago or earlier are not trained for these new ideas. There is a tendency for them to look rather askance at the 'invaders' from the colleges.[59]

The Black Paper authors focused on this point in their submission to the committee, associating it also with a lack of intellectual stimulation in the college curriculum:

> Nothing can be worse than the unthinking, dogmatic assertion of orthodoxies characteristic of many Colleges of Education.[60]

Cross-questioning of these particular witnesses however elicited the fundamental contradiction of their concerns, wishing as they did for a higher level of personal education at the same time as for a more practical emphasis in training for the classroom.

Conclusion

There are striking similarities and contrasts between L. C. Knights' attack, the strictures of the Black Paper writers of the late 1960s and early 1970s, and the 'new right' critique of the later 1980s and 1990s. For *Scrutiny* the main concern was personal education of the intending teacher, for the New

Right primarily professional competence, and for the Black Paper critics, a combination of these. Recent images of the teacher as radically subversive or professionally incompetent are tied to the perceived quality of training, even though the latter has become more diversified and integrated in the Higher Education sector.

A driving force behind recent government policy on teacher training, the pamphleteers of the New Right highlight the relationship between professional identity on the one hand and the institutions of training on the other. The teaching profession is seen as a closed shop, a restrictive practice, a phenomenon of 'producer culture' which is moreover set to resist any proposed radical changes in curriculum and teaching method. Anthony O'Hear, for the 'Social Affairs Unit' responded to the Government Green Paper of 1988 with enthusiastic support for the 'licensed teacher scheme' including professional training and certification 'on the job', and elaborated his deep scepticism about the value of college training.[61] Caroline Cox and others, the so-called 'Hillgate Group' argued for widespread application of the 'licensed teacher' scheme as an apprenticeship route to Qualified Teacher Status. Their argument is based on the premise that there exists a large number of people, currently barred from teaching in schools, who are better qualified to teach children than many who have been certificated as teachers.[62]

> Critics say that licensed teachers will mean lower standards and a retreat from professionalism. However, proficiency in the classroom is the main criterion for judging teachers, and accountability to the public should be the touchstone of the teaching profession.

Finally Sheila Lawlor, in her pamphlet 'Teachers Mistaught', erroneously represented the institutionalisation of teacher education in the higher education sector as a phenomenon of the 1960s. Here it is the alleged 'progressivism', 'child-centredness' and above all the educational theory offered by the colleges which is the butt of her attack. But it is tied in with a particular image of the teacher which reverts to an old model – the subject specialist who is revered for specialist knowledge and love of the subjects taught.[63]

During the difficult years of the mid-1980s with prolonged industrial action by teachers, the government took advantage of teachers' low popular image, but by the early 1990s the press and public apparently began to show more sympathy for the teachers, as I have discussed elsewhere.[64] Parental support for the teachers' boycott of national curriculum testing, and their reported trust in teachers' assessments offer some evidence of this.[65] As teachers could no longer be the effective demons, then teacher trainers become a useful Aunt Sally – a more obscure target, less well-known to the public at large. Many factors are at work, but there remains a synergy between the reputation of professional training and teachers' popular image. In status and cultural terms teachers continue to be vulnerable to the trap of resentment 'from below' and disdain 'from above'.

References

1 Thompson, D. F. (1927) *Professional Solidarity among the Teachers of England* (New York, Columbia University).
2 Rich, R. W. (1933) *The Training of Teachers in England and Wales during the Nineteenth Century*.
3 Tropp, A. (1957) *The School Teachers*.
4 Purvis, J. (1973) 'Schoolteaching as a Professional Career', *British Journal of Sociology*, vol. 24, no. 1; Parry, N. and Parry, J. (1974) 'The Teachers and Professionalism: The Failure of an Occupational Strategy', in Flude, M. and Ahier, J. *Educability, Schools and Ideology*, E. Hoyle, (1975) 'Professionality, professionalism and control in teaching' in Houghton, V. (and others) *Management in Education*.
5 Grace, G. (1978) *Teachers, Ideology and Control*, Ozga, J. and Lawn, M. (1981) *Teachers, professionalism and class*, Kean, H. (1990) *Challenging the State? The Socialist and Feminist Educational Experience 1900-1930*.
6 Board of Education (1925) *Report of the Departmental Committee on the Training of Teachers for the Public Elementary Schools*, Cmd 2409, pp. 41-42.
7 Taylor, W. (1969) *Society and the Education of Teachers*.
8 'Professional Identity and Teacher Training in the Early Twentieth Century', a research project directed by Peter Cunningham and Phil Gardner 1993-96 and funded by the Leverhulme Trust.
9 'Professional Identity and Teacher Training in the Early Twentieth Century', respondents A6, A1, A21, and A16 respectively. These comments are drawn from the written questionnaire that precedes the recorded interview.
10 Cunningham, P. (1992) 'Teachers' professional image and the Press 1950-1990' *History of Education*, 21, 1, pp. 37-56.
11 see Tropp, A. (1957) pp. 220, 227 and Gosden, P. (1972) p. 52 .
12 *Daily Mail*, 22 September 1924, p. 8.
13 *Daily Mail*, 25 September 1924, p. 8.
14 *Daily Mail*, 24, 25, 26, 27, 29 September 1924.
15 *Daily Herald*, 23 September 1924, p. 4.
16 *Daily Express*, 23 September 1924, p. 8.
17 *Manchester Guardian*, 26 September 1924, p. 8
18 *Daily Herald*, 12 September 1931, p. 6.
19 *Daily Herald*, 18 September 1931, p. 11.
20 *Manchester Guardian*, 12 September 1931, p. 10.

21 *Manchester Guardian*, 14 September 1931, p. 16.
22 P.E.P. (Political and Economic Planning) *Report on the British Press*, April 1938, pp. 114, 125.
23 Graves, R. and Hodge, A. *The Long Weekend*, pp. 58-61.
24 P.E.P. (Political and Economic Planning) *Report on the British Press*, April 1938, pp. 248, 252.
25 Mass Observation (1947), *The Press and Its Readers*, 1949, p. 124.
26 *The Times*, 31 January 1970, p. 3.
27 *Daily Express*, 24 February 1970, p. 8.
28 *Daily Mirror*, 25 August 1970, p. 4; *Daily Express*, 9 February 1970, p. 7
29 Runciman, J. (1887) *Schools and Scholars*, pp. 267-8.
30 Tropp, A. (1957) pp. 227-8.
31 *Manchester Guardian*, 17 September 1931, p. 18.
32 Ballard, P. B. (1937) *Things I Cannot Forget*, p. 35.
33 Ballard, P. B. (1937), p. 40.
34 Manning, L. (1970) *A Life for Education*, p. 35.
35 Edwards, E. (1993) 'The culture of femininity in women's teacher training colleges 1900–50', *History of Education*, 22, 3.
36 Dent, H. C. (1977) *The Training of Teachers in England and Wales 1800-1975*, pp. 13-14; Rev. Cromwell cited by Heward, C. (1993) 'Men and women and the rise of professional society: the intriguing history of teacher educators', *History of Education*, 22, 1, p. 15.
37 Ballard, P. B. (1937) *Things I Cannot Forget*, p. 50.
38 Bartle, G. F. (1976) *A History of Borough Road College*, pp. 71-74; 'Professional Identity and Teacher Training in the Early Twentieth Century' project: recorded interview with respondent A18.
39 Board of Education (1925) *Report of the Departmental Committee on the Training of Teachers*, p. 85.
40 Statistics drawn from Jones, L. (1923) *The Training of Teachers in England and Wales*, Oxford, Clarendon Press.
41 T. Raymont, Vice-Principal of Goldsmith's cited by Heward, C. (1993) p. 17.
42 Lofthouse, M. T. (1992) *The Church Colleges 1918-1939*, p. xvii.
43 Heward, C. (1993).
44 Jones, G. E. L. (1924) *Training of Teachers in England and Wales*, p. 91
45 Jones, G. E. L. (1924) pp. 82-83.
46 'Professional Identity and Teacher Training in the Early Twentieth Century', respondents A18 and A167.
47 Jones, G. E. L. (1924) pp. 78-9, 417-8.
48 Board of Education (1925) *Report of the Departmental Committee on the Training of Teachers*, p. 85.
49 Heward, C. (1993) p. 21.
50 Knights, L. C. (1932) 'Will Training Colleges Bear Scrutiny?' *Scrutiny* vol 1, no. 3, December 1932, p. 258.
51 'Scrutiny: a manifesto' in *Scrutiny*, vol. 1, no. 1, May 1932, pp. 2,4-5.

52 'Scrutiny: a manifesto' in *Scrutiny*, vol. 1, no. 1, May 1932, p. 6.
53 *Daily Mail*, 24 September 1931, p. 10.
54 Knights, L. C. (1932), pp. 254, 258.
55 Cunningham, P. (1988) *Curriculum Change in the Primary School since 1945*, pp. 35, 40, 42.
56 PRO ED 86/264.
57 PP 1969-70 (30-i) x.
58 PP 1969-70 (30-i) x, p. 183 (evidence of Herbert Andrew) and p. 394 (memorandum from NUS).
59 As reported in *The Times*, 31 January 1970, p. 3.
60 PP 1969-70 (30-i) x, p. 523.
61 O'Hear, A. (1988) *Who Teaches the Teachers?* Social Affairs Unit.
62 Hillgate Group (1989) *Learning To Teach*, The Claridge Press.
63 Lawlor, S. *Teachers Mistaught*, Centre for Policy Studies no. 116, p. 7.
64 Cunningham, P. (1992), pp. 51-2.
65 *Times Educational Supplement*, 29 July 1994, p. 1.

Constructing and reconstructing school technology in England and Wales

DAVID LAYTON

Introduction

When, in March 1985, the Department of Education and Science, with the Welsh Office, published *Science 5-16. A Statement of Policy* the response from the science education community was predominantly welcoming. According to *The Times Educational Supplement,* the policy statement seemed 'to be giving science teachers nearly everything they asked for'.[1] All pupils were to follow a broad science programme, suited to their abilities and interests, from their first year in school until the age of 16. The detailed implementation of 'Science for All' was to be based on the experience of the Secondary Science Curriculum Review, itself very much an offspring of the professional organisation of science teachers, the Association for Science Education. Clearly this was not policy emanating as a directive from a remote centre: the statement appeared redolent of the experiences and judgements of reflective practitioners. Breadth, balance, relevance and differentiation were to be leading characteristics of 'Science for All', as indeed they were to be for the school curriculum as a whole.[2] When proposals for a national curriculum were published two years later, science was accorded a place alongside mathematics and English as constituting the core of the new programme.

It is, perhaps, too early yet to judge whether this was the moment when the star of school science reached its political zenith. What is worth noting, in passing, is that before the national curriculum working party on science had completed its deliberations, having been charged by the Secretary of State, Kenneth Baker, to 'take *Science 5-16* as your policy framework',[3] aspects of that policy were being challenged to an extent that enabled the journal *Education* to write of 'Blazing eyeballs between Baker and science chairman'.[4] Faced with the difficulty of fitting its ten foundation subjects into the timetable of years 10 and 11 in secondary schools, confronted by predictions of a shortage of two thousand physics teachers by 1995 and assailed by advocates of the teaching of three separate sciences rather than integrated, co-ordinated or combined science, there appeared to be a danger of a government retreat into 'traditional science for the few' and 'a smattering of science for the many'.

Intriguing though they are, the ensuing vicissitudes of national curriculum science fall outside the scope of this chapter. The government's 1985 policy statement on school science remains a significant point of departure, however, because of what it said and also because of what it failed to say about a related, yet at that time still rudimentary, curriculum innovation, the incorporation of technology as a component of general education for all.

In this connection it is interesting to compare the policy statement with contemporaneous pronouncements on the school curriculum. It was, for example, published in the year in which Her Majesty's Inspectorate formally acknowledged a ninth 'area of learning and experience', the technological, in its list of what should constitute a rounded education.[5] (Earlier HMI listings had included only eight such areas – the aesthetic and creative; the ethical; the linguistic; the mathematical; the physical; the scientific; the social and political; and the spiritual.[6]) Yet, as a friendly critic of the DES policy statement observed, it was disappointingly vague on the important question of the relationship between science and technology.[7] This was all the more surprising because the document affirmed that 'awareness and knowledge' of this relationship were 'objectives of any science syllabus'.[8] True, the statement of policy asserted that links between science and CDT (craft, design and technology) were vital at secondary level and that science and technology formed a continuum at primary level. There was, however, little exploration of the nature of these links and of the structure of the alleged continuum. Repeated references to the technological applications of science, not least because study of them could enhance the understanding of science concepts, did little to dispel the unwarranted, but still persistent, notion that technology was merely applied science. A requirement for the full development of 'scientific competence' was said to be the provision of opportunities for pupils at all ages to bring their scientific knowledge to bear in attempting to solve technological problems. The question of what other kinds of knowledge and skills might be needed for such tasks was largely unaddressed. In the science policy statement there was little discussion of the processes of designing such as featured in the HMI description of the technological area of learning and experience.[9]

March 1985 also saw the publication of the government's overall policies for school education in England and Wales in the White Paper *Better Schools*. Design and technology, deemed vital parts of the curriculum at both primary and secondary levels, were here considered more in the context of 'practical subjects' than as ancillary to science. In discussing the curriculum for 14 to 16 year olds, the White Paper also asserted the need for the curriculum to prepare pupils for employment, making special mention of 'the practical and technological aspects within TVEI courses' as 'elements of a kind which should be in every pupil's programme.'[10] The influence of the government's Technical and Vocational Education Initiative (TVEI) on the development of school technology is considered in more detail below. At this point it is sufficient to note in the White Paper a portent of autonomous school technology, distinct from science, though with each feeding on and into the other. There were also indications of multiple interpretations of what school technology might be and what goals it might serve. Certainly, responsiveness to labour market needs and development of a supply of appropriate skills featured more strongly in *Better Schools* than in *Science 5-16* when references were made to technology. The following year the White Paper *Working Together – Education and Training*, announcing the national extension of the TVEI, was even more explicit. The government's educational aim was 'to give every pupil and student a capability which makes them versatile and sufficiently adaptable for the technological challenges of employment'. To this end, and summarising the curriculum message of *Better Schools*, science, technology and design were listed after 'communication' and 'numeracy' as 'subjects' in which all pupils up to age 16 needed to acquire 'a broad competence'. All this was in accord with government policy for schools which now emphasised 'practical learning'.[11]

In taking the 1985 science policy statement as the starting point for the account of the construction and reconstruction of school technology which follows, it is not intended to imply that the origins of this curriculum innovation do not stretch further back in time. Detailed accounts of earlier attempts to incorporate technology in the curriculum of general education, apart from providing cautionary analyses of failure, illustrate how competing versions of technology were sponsored by diverse agencies and interest groups.[12] The attempted innovations differed in purpose and in their interpretation of the nature of technology, not least how it related to science. No doubt this period, from the Schools Council's pilot project in 'applied science and technology',[13] through the active years of Project Technology[14] and up to the mid-1980s, was a formative one in which stakeholders in school technology, and their opponents, were obliged to clarify their positions and in which experience of teaching technology, especially in secondary schools, was enriched. Even so, a clear policy on school technology, comparable to that attempted for school science in *Science 5-16* was conspicuously lacking. Multiple versions of the subject existed, to an extent which had yielded some one thousand five hundred CDT-related examination syllabuses by the early 1980s.[15] The introduction of the General Certificate of Secondary Education (GCSE) brought some order into this field, but even here it was found necessary to provide three different CDT-related examinations: CDT – Design and Realisation; CDT – Technology; and CDT-Design and Communication. Speaking at a Wembley Exhibition in October 1985, the Secretary of State for Education and Science, Sir Keith Joseph, drew attention to another disturbing feature. 'None of us can be satisfied,' he said, 'with a situation in which 93 per cent of the subject entries in the CDT areas in public examinations at 16+ are from boys and only seven per cent from girls, with the imbalance even greater at 18+ and with a situation in which only two per cent of CDT teachers are women.'[16] In that same year, when a group of leading science and technology educators published their ideas on the nature of children's technological work and the place of technology in the curriculum, these appeared under the title *In Place of Confusion*.[17] In fact, the hope so expressed remained unrealised and the forms and purposes of school technology continued to be contested in even more strident manner in the years following.

Technology for TVEI

Throughout the 1980s and prior to the inauguration of the national curriculum in England and Wales, probably no single influence was more significant in shaping school technology and enhancing its curriculum status than the government's Technical and Vocational Education Initiative (TVEI).

Announced by the Prime Minister, Margaret Thatcher, in November 1982 and under the supervision of the Manpower Services Commission (MSC), an agency of the Department of Employment, this was an attempt to stimulate the provision of technical and vocational education for 14 to 18 year olds in full-time education. Funding over a five year period for a first round of 14 local education authorities, commencing in September 1983, amounted to some £46 million at 1983/84 prices. Additional pilot projects followed in subsequent years, in all 103 authorities receiving TVEI money, although, unlike the first 14, second and later round projects were cash limited to £2 million over five years. In 1987, the government extended the programme into a national scheme involving all maintained schools and colleges, £900 million being available to support the initiative over a ten year period. TVEI-related in-service training for teachers (TRIST) was also funded through the MSC for a two-year period, 1985-87, at a cost of £25 million. Thereafter, the statutory powers of the Secretaries of State for Education and Science, and for Wales, having been enlarged to permit high levels of targeted funding, in-service training came under the DES's LEA Training Grants Scheme.[18]

It is true that the declared aims of TVEI and the criteria relating to the content of school TVEI programmes made no direct reference to technology as a component of the curriculum. Nevertheless, statements in the aims about pupils 'using their skills and knowledge to solve the real-world problems they will meet at work' and the need for greater emphasis 'on developing initiative, motivation and enterprise as well as problem-solving skills' were frequently interpreted by teachers as warrants for the introduction and/or enhancement of technological subjects. The TVEI data base for the pilot phase indicated that some 75 per cent of the schools involved were offering new subjects in the technology area, by far the largest number of developments falling under the subject title of CDT. Other innovations included modular technology, control technology and robotics. In the first three years of the pilot phase of the Initiative, technological subjects represented the largest group of all new courses.[19] When the first director of the MSC's TVEI Unit, John Woolhouse, addressed the 1985 annual conference of the School Technology Forum at Trent Polytechnic, he spoke of technology as 'a central theme of TVEI'.[20] Two years later, as the Initiative moved into its extension phase, a TVEI Consultancy in Science and Technology was established at the same institution under the direction of Professor Geoffrey Harrison. Whilst the formal position was that 'technology in TVEI' related only to the school curriculum for those aged 14 years and over, evidence from the TVEI curriculum evaluation, undertaken by a team of researchers at Leeds University, indicated that TVEI equipment and enhanced staffing made possible the expansion of technology teaching to non-TVEI students aged 14 and over, and also to students in the lower forms of the schools. Frequently the new courses were found to attract students of high ability and the teacher who described his involvement in TVEI as transforming him from a teacher of CDT to the least able to a teacher of technology to the most able was by no means exceptional.[21]

It has sometimes been said of TVEI curriculum developments that the prevailing philosophy was to 'let a thousand flowers bloom'. Whilst the evidence of the Initiative's curriculum evaluation does not support such an extreme judgement, diversity of aims, content, organisation and styles of delivery were certainly characteristic of the technology component. Reporting in July 1989 at the end of a three-year period involving extended visits for observation and data collection in schools in 27 projects, and drawing on a further sample of 18 schools selected because of their developments in technology education, the evaluation team concluded that 'the nature of school technology is still a contestable topic. The distinction between design and technology, for example, is not always clear. The "knowledge content and concepts" of technology are problematical.'[22] It was also their sense, however, that teachers were much closer to consensus than they had been in the early years of TVEI.

Unquestionably, a major contributory factor in this move towards a clearer vision of what school technology might be was the establishment in many projects of working groups of technology teachers. Initially, many of these groups were set up to cope with the task of planning technology courses within the short period of time between acceptance of an LEA's TVEI submission and the actual implementation of the teaching programme in the schools. Thereafter, the panels continued as meetings where experiences could be shared and all manner of problems concerned with content, teaching approaches and assessment could be thrashed out. The collaborative working between teachers in such panels was one of the most positive outcomes of TVEI, valued by those involved as stimulating and useful almost without exception.[23]

It is perhaps understandable that school technology developed within the context of TVEI should have been interpreted largely as a technical subject with the emphasis on a somewhat narrow version of technological capability. The TVEI focus on initiative, enterprise and problem-solving skills influenced the kinds of technological work in which pupils were engaged, though the extent to which technological tasks were truly reflective of the world of work was often questionable. Ambitions for TVEI programmes introduced at age 14 could be severely frustrated by weak foundations laid in the earlier years. This was often the case with problem-solving activities in technology, work of this nature being for the most part uncommon in the practical courses in the first three years of secondary education, at least on the evidence of the national evaluation sample. This lack of progression between 11 and 14 placed limits on the scope of open-ended technology project work within the subsequent TVEI programme.

It was also the case that value considerations relating, for example, to the purposes of a technological activity, the means employed and the consequences ensuing were largely absent from the teaching of technology in TVEI programmes. This is not to say that values were not implicitly communicated: a strong message appeared to be that technology was itself 'a good thing' and was essentially about meeting human needs, despite much everyday evidence to the contrary. A critical dimension to pupils' thinking about technology, its impact on their lives today and in the future, was rarely encouraged. In short, technology was not located in human culture.

Related to the issue of value considerations was that of gender imbalances. In its criteria, TVEI placed strong emphasis on the availability of equal opportunities to young people of both sexes and experimentation with a variety of teaching and learning approaches was undertaken by projects to satisfy this requirement. In simple numerical terms it appeared that some progress had been achieved, the proportion of girls in year 10 studying design and technology increasing from 32 per cent in 1988/89 to 44 per cent in 1989/90. However, in some projects, technology in year 10 was obligatory and the national evaluation interviews with girls on such courses frequently revealed their firm intention to abandon technology at the first opportunity. The figures need to be interpreted with caution. More radical approaches, locating the deficiency in the technology courses rather than in the attitudes of girls, whilst talked about, were rarely implemented in TVEI pilot programmes.[24]

Few schools in the national evaluation sample had used TVEI resources to support a major restructuring of the 14 to 16 curriculum. For the most part, technology courses were accommodated within conventional core plus options structures and timetables of 30 to 40 periods per week. Typically a technology course would occupy four periods per week, taken as two double periods, with the same teacher taking a group throughout the two years of the course. In such an organisational context, opportunities for developing strong industrial links and/or cross-curricular technology were severely constrained.[25]

Where departures from this organisational pattern occurred, they included cross-curricular projects and also the provision of technology education by way of contributions made by a range of different subjects across the school curriculum (Technology Across the Curriculum – TAC). In the first of these, mini-companies might be set up and there was evidence that the project work did 'generate realism, and hence relevance, motivation through a sense of real purpose, and an appreciation of the team approach needed in the real world'.[26] However, such work did not always have a strong technological dimension, the efforts of teachers being frequently directed towards the development of students' inter-personal and social attributes. An evaluation of a British School Technology project, Technology Across the Curriculum (TAC), involving project work in both TVEI and non-TVEI schools and colleges, ten in all, found the same lack of a technological focus in students' work. On the positive side, the degree of collaboration between teachers from different subject departments, a unique experience for most of them, was judged to be a promising foundation for future projects with a stronger technological orientation.[27]

A general point arises here. Much technology education which took place within the context of TVEI needs to be seen in developmental terms over a time-scale of several years. Furthermore, over the same period, the Technical and Vocational Initiative itself underwent changes of focus, notably when the pilot scheme moved into the extension phase in 1987 and, later, when the framework for implementation of the national curriculum became clear. In connection with the former, TVEI advisers met in the early months of 1987 to produce a paper setting out the main issues relating to technology in the curriculum. The resulting publication, circulated to all LEAs and TVEI schools, analysed emerging patterns of technology in TVEI pilot projects and drew lessons for the benefit of those embarking on the extension in which all pupils would 'engage in technology up to the age of 16 and become increasingly technologically aware, up to the age of 18'.[28] Examples were provided of subjects working with technology, not only obvious ones such as science, but also others such as business and media studies. The conclusions emphasised that 'technology is essentially a co-operative activity'. Drawing on the experiences of TRIST, the MSC-funded in-service training scheme, a supporting document, *Technology for All across the Curriculum*, was published at the same time.[29] It would be going beyond the evidence to suggest that a TVEI view on technology education as necessarily cross-curricular was hardening at this time. The advisers' document fully acknowledged the diversity of school technology and the predominance of structured courses leading to a recognisable public examination. However, by the summer of 1988 the TVEI Unit had begun to refocus the aims of the Initiative, its remit then going across the total curriculum for all students 14 to 18 and, by 1992, all schools and colleges. As Anne Jones, Head of Educational Programmes, expressed it, 'TVEI has now spread across the whole curriculum. There is no subject or activity which is not enhanced by being set in a real context, with real examples, provided if possible by adults other than teachers.'[30] On a previous occasion, when arguing for the complementarity of TVEI and the subject-structured national curriculum, she used a matrix with the ten national curriculum subjects along one axis and the TVEI aims and requirements such as industry links, problem solving, economic awareness and technology along the other. The latter, it was claimed, permeated each of the former to their mutual enhancement.[31] As technology alone featured on both axes, a clearer endorsement of its centrality in the curriculum for tomorrow's world would be hard to imagine. Its cross-curricular nature, many subjects being able to contribute to the development of technological understanding and capability, was also implied.

Technology for the national curriculum

The concept of 'technology for TVEI' was overtaken by 'technology for the national curriculum' in April 1988 when the Secretary of State, Kenneth Baker, announced the setting up of a Working Group for Design and Technology. Design and technology were said to be 'of great importance for the economic well-being of this country', making it essential to press ahead quickly in establishing them within the national curriculum. The Group was asked to advise on attainment targets and programmes of study for technology within the national curriculum for secondary school pupils. A Science Working Group, appointed the previous year, was already preparing recommendations about technology for primary school pupils.[32]

   The separate reference to design in the title of the new Working Group requires comment. As far back as the mid-1970s, a DES-funded project undertaken by the Royal College of Art's Design Education Unit had provided an authoritative statement on the nature of design. It was described as a broad field of human activity relating to configuration, composition, meaning, value and purpose in man-made phenomena. Design, it was argued, should be used as a term analogous to 'the humanities' and 'the sciences'. Furthermore, the capacity for design was said to involve a fundamental human ability for dealing with ill-defined problems by use of a distinctive mental attribute, cognitive modelling.[33] Le Corbusier's phrase was 'intelligence made visible'.

Something of this message as applied to the school curriculum was taken up in the late 1970s by the Design Council, originally the Council of Industrial Design founded by Winston Churchill's wartime government in 1945. Its report on *Design Education at Secondary Level* (the Keith-Lucas report) attempted to identify the principles on which good design education in schools should be based and argued for design as an essential component in the education of children at all stages of secondary education up to the age of 16. According to one commentator it attracted 'a host of conflicting opinions. CDT teachers saw it as too art and craft oriented; the art teachers as too CDT. The Royal College of Art's Design Education Unit felt it dealt more with the careers development side than with general design education for schools.'[34]

The school teaching of design attracted further attention when, in January 1982, Mrs Thatcher held a much publicised seminar on design at 10 Downing Street. Summing up, she asserted that: 'Design is too often taught in secondary schools as an art subject. It is rarely taught as it should be – as a practical, problem solving discipline that is ideal for preparing young people for work within the constraints of user needs and the market. Its status as an O or A level subject is dismal . . . Teachers themselves are often not fully aware of the real scope of the subject. Syllabuses are arranged to give greater merit to "pure" art than to the practical application of design.'[35]

This predominantly economic interpretation of design education was not to everyone's taste, but it is clear that design came strongly onto educational agendas in the 1980s. At a meeting between representatives of the MSC and the Engineering Council in October 1987, it was reported that the Engineering Council and the Design Council had been working together to persuade the government to incorporate design as part of technology in the school curriculum. They had also collaborated with the Secondary Examinations Council in preparing a joint paper on design in the curriculum.[36]

The compound title of the national curriculum Working Group appointed the following spring reflected these concerns for the importance of design which, as the Keith-Lucas report had recognised, was unlikely, for practical reasons, to secure a place in an already overcrowded school curriculum as a new subject. However, it was possible for the design dimension of children's education to be enlarged through subjects such as art, home economics and CDT and the Working Group was enjoined to recommend a framework for design education in all its aspects across the curriculum. Its brief was further extended by a requirement for attainment targets and programmes of study for information technology, as distinct from design and technology.

The potential for confusion arising from these multiple tasks and especially from the proliferation of terminology – technology, design, design and technology, information technology – was considerable. An editorial in *Education* described the terms of reference as a farrago and the *Independent* under the heading 'Design fault in the curriculum brief', highlighted apparent contradictions and inconsistencies by reporting an interview with a fictitious member of the Working Group who finished his interrogation in a state of collapse.[37] Unquestionably, serious problems existed. Consensus on the relationship between 'technology' and 'design' was elusive. For some, design was the larger category with technology being equated with the realisation and making aspects within a design task. For others, technology tended to be seen as the all-embracing activity, with design as a component of this. Yet again, design was regarded as 'the exercise of imagination in the specification of form' with technology as 'the application of theory in the control of both form and action', a third partner being craft, 'the application of skill in the production of form'.[38] The Working Group took the position that 'whereas most, but not all, design activities will generally include technology and most technology activities will include design, there is not always total correspondence.' Its use of design and technology as a unitary concept was intended to emphasise the intimate connection between the two activities by implying a concept broader than either design or technology individually and the whole of which was educationally important.[39]

A different point concerned the Group's title, Design and Technology, and the fact that its main task appeared to be the definition, through attainment targets and programmes of study, of a school subject called design and technology (D and T) on the same footing as other national curriculum subjects. However, the foundation subject specified in the 1988 Education Act was simply called technology and the situation was further complicated by the Working Group's tasks in respect of information technology (IT) across the curriculum. IT could be a part of D and T, supporting pupils' activities in a variety of ways. It could also be an important tool for learning in other national curriculum subjects, but it was not itself one of these designated subjects. The eventual uncoupling of IT from D and T was a later development arising from a future revision of the 1990 Statutory Order for Technology, although this separation was seen by some as giving rise to problems, e.g. 'which subject (IT or D and T) will get control of "control"?'[40] Resolution of the nomenclature dilemma was a more urgent matter, occurring as an outcome of the National Curriculum Council's consultation process on the proposals for technology in 1989. It was decided that, in line with the 1988 Education Reform Act, the subject should be known as Technology and that there should be two distinct components, D and T and IT, each with its own attainment targets and programmes of study.[41]

The terms of reference of the Design and Technology Working Group stated that technology was to be viewed 'as that area of the curriculum in which pupils design and make useful objects or systems, thus developing their ability to solve practical problems'. A range of subjects would need to be drawn upon, notably science and mathematics, as well as the principles and practice of good design and a repertoire of practical skills for working in wood, metal, plastics, textiles and other materials. Accordingly, technology was an activity which went 'across the curriculum', drawing on and linking in with a wide range of subjects. Design was 'an essential part of technology'; the designing processes were to be applied 'to real life tasks within typical constraints (time, money, etc.) with due regard to cost, marketability, social, environmental and other relevant factors'. In supplementary guidance further detail was provided on links with other subjects. The co-ordination of D and T activities with work in science lessons, especially those dealing with materials, energy and power, was particularly stressed, and reference was also made to links with art, home economics and business studies.[42] In retrospect, the latter can be seen as a harbinger for a recommendation in the Working Group's final report, that the teaching of D and T should involve the co-ordination of activities currently undertaken in art and design, business studies, CDT, home economics and IT, a grouping that became known as 'the famous five'.

A significant consideration here was that, of these five subjects, only art had been included in the list of ten subjects in the national curriculum. Teachers of other subjects, especially of CDT, home economics and business studies, were understandably concerned about the prospects for survival of their subjects under the new curriculum regime. D and T appeared to offer them the chance of, if not a place in the sun, then at least continued useful existence. There was, however, a price to pay. New ends were being served and some loss of autonomy was inevitable. Transformation of current practices might be entailed and the scope of the subject might be curtailed. Of the five subjects, CDT seemed most secure as a contributor to D and T, although for some of its more craft-oriented practitioners a traumatic process of adaptation might be required. Also, as noted earlier, CDT had been predominantly a subject for boys taught by men, whereas D and T in the national curriculum was to be for both boys and girls across the full range of abilities and motivations. In the case of the reshaping of home economics, components such as textiles and food could, without too much difficulty, be adapted to the requirements of D and T, but others such as child care were more problematic and might need to be relocated elsewhere, for example, as part of personal and social education. The prospect of dismembering their subject in this way clearly did not find favour with all home economics teachers. Business studies was different again. A relative newcomer to the school curriculum, it had made greatest headway in post-16 provisions. However, the association of D and T at all levels pre-16 with considerations of cost and marketing offered an opportunity to business studies for a significant expansion downwards. A danger here was that territorial ambitions might encourage the subordination of D and T to business studies, the former providing contexts for the development of the latter, whereas the requirement was for the latter to service the former.

The Working Group produced an Interim Report in November 1988 and its final report was published in June 1989 as the Secretaries of State's proposals for *Design and Technology for Ages 5 to 16*. The Group met on nineteen occasions at venues around the country, as well as receiving both written and oral evidence from a wide range of individuals and organisations. Shortly after its fourth meeting its remit was extended by the addition of primary school technology, the proposals of the Science Working Group on this topic having been largely drawn up before the terms of reference of the Design and Technology Working Group were announced. The recommendations of the Science Group were to be noted, but the Design and Technology Group was now free to develop a framework common to the full age range 5 to 16.[43]

Reaction to the Interim Report was, for the most part, strongly supportive from both politicians and educational interest groups. School subject associations took the opportunity to reiterate their claims for a firm place in the provisions for D and T and to correct what they took to be misrepresentations of their possible contributions. The Crafts Council, for example, took issue with 'the narrow definition of crafts' it claimed had been adopted by the Group.[44] Both the Secondary Science Curriculum Review and the Association for Science Education felt that the parallels between science and technology had been underemphasised as a consequence of the report's stress placed on 'the distinctiveness of design and technology and its differences from science'. The Association of Advisers in CDT welcomed the liberation of D and T from applied science, but feared the cross-curricular aspects of the proposals would lead 'to superficiality or even triviality', so threatening the newly won and hard-acquired higher status of CDT. A lengthy and detailed critique of the knowledge domains of D and T capability, as outlined in the report, was offered by the School Technology Forum; the concern so identified was taken up by other respondents. The National Association of Advisers and Inspectors for Business and Economic Education welcomed 'the new curriculum area of Design and Technology which establishes a role for Business Education in the curriculum 5-16', although it was worried that the proposals might be interpreted as 'CDT in a variety of contexts'. A plea was made for a stronger representation of Business Education in the proposals: 'to rely . . . on the "Design and Make" process for a business dimension contribution . . . would be to sell Business Education short'. In a lengthy, two-part response, the National Association of Teachers of Home Economics recorded its view that the report was 'exciting and challenging', home economics being 'ideally placed to provide a range of contexts, that ensures the development of a variety of transferable skills'. An accompanying example of a pupil activity (how to use spare accommodation in their school to satisfy a community need for pre-school facilities) was, however, less convincing as, indeed, was an attempt to demonstrate the inter-relationship between terms used in the report and in home economics teaching. The Yorkshire and Humberside Consortium of Home Economics Advisers similarly expressed anxiety 'about the hard impersonal terms "artefact" and "systems"' which were thought likely to cause some difficulties of interpretation. Amongst the several voices speaking for home economics, there appeared to be differences of opinion about the extent to which the subject in its present form could enable children to achieve the proposed attainment targets of D and T. At this stage there was little evidence of concern about an issue which was later to prove divisive, i.e. whether 'food' was a proper material for designing and making activities.

Prefaced by an expression of hope that its contents would not be thought too critical, the Design Council's response to the Interim Report emphasised the need for 'clear definitions of the nature and the curriculum aims of design and technology'. These were presently lacking and the Working Group's attention was directed to the Council's own reports on design in primary and secondary education; its own definition of design was offered as one which 'will bear frequent repetition'. The interpretation of design in the Interim Report was also deemed to be too restrictive, the situation not being helped by exemplary material being drawn too exclusively from CDT.[45]

Many of these critical points were taken up by the Group in its subsequent deliberations. None of the evidence from subject or other interest groups suggested that the broad approach of the Group was in need of serious modification and there were some very positive endorsements of the progress made so far. In oral evidence, representatives from organisations including the Engineering Council, the CBI and the TVEI Unit all commended the approach outlined in chapter 1, those from the Department of Trade and Industry finding it 'a joy to read'. As might be expected, the Royal Society and the Fellowship of Engineering both stressed the importance of co-ordinating pupils' work in mathematics and science with their work in D and T. The Royal Society thought the approach adopted would help 'to dispel the idea (associated with CDT) that design and technology is only for the less able'. The Interim Report had convinced the Society's Education Committee that all secondary school pupils needed 20 per cent of curriculum time for science if they were to do justice to themselves in D and T![46]

A particularly thoughtful and informed response came from the Royal Fine Art Commission, Art and Architecture Education Trust chaired by Lord St John of Fawsley.[47] This argued for the addition of 'environments' to 'artefacts' and 'systems' as the products of design and technology activity, the education of young people 'in relation to planning, landscape, urban design, architecture, building and interior design' being a prime concern of the Commission. The Working Group adopted this suggestion, a similar point having been made by the Royal Institute of British Architects. Another reflective and constructive paper came from a consortium of voluntary agencies working in the field of overseas development.[48] This provided a valuable reminder, with examples, of the need for any technological development 'to fit into a system [which] contains social, cultural and environmental factors'. The role of values and value judgements in design and technological activities was to retain a prominent place in the Working Group's thinking. Not unrelated to this theme was the formidable problem of achieving equal opportunities for girls, as well as boys, to experience and learn D and T. In its comments on the Interim Report, the Equal Opportunities Commission chided the Working Group for not focusing more on the particular difficulties for single-sex girls' schools in which there was often little or no provision for the acquisition of craft skills. In the Commission's view, this was unlikely to be rectified by the adoption 'of a nebulous cross-curricular approach'. It was also important that girls and boys had the same experiences throughout; 'there should be no way in which the Group advocates the adoption of attainment targets which can be reached by teaching design and technology in different ways to boys and girls'.[49]

The final report of the Working Group described programmes of study for D and T under sixteen sub-headings covering the knowledge and skills which pupils would need to be taught in order to achieve the attainment targets. The latter had been reduced to four in number, in sharp contrast to science which had seventeen and mathematics which had fourteen. The D and T attainment targets were:

AT1: Identifying needs and opportunities.

Through exploration and investigation of a range of contexts (home; school; recreation; community; business and industry) pupils should be able to identify and state clearly needs and opportunities for design and technological activities.

AT2: Generating a design proposal.

Pupils should be able to produce a realistic, appropriate and achievable design by generating, exploring and developing design and technological ideas and by refining and detailing the design proposal they have chosen.

AT3: Planning and making.

Working to a plan derived from their previously developed design, pupils should be able to identify, manage and use appropriate resources, including both knowledge and processes in order to make an artefact, system or environment.

AT4: Appraising.

Pupils should be able to develop, communicate and act constructively upon an appraisal of the processes, outcomes and effects of their own design and technological activity as well as of the outcome and effects of the design and technological activity of others, including those from other times and cultures.[50]

A broad and challenging approach to D and T had been adopted in an attempt to make the subject stimulating to the most able, whilst providing opportunities for all children to demonstrate some level of capability. The breadth resided in several dimensions. It was implied by the nature of the products of D and T, i.e. artefacts, systems and environments. A stage set for a theatrical production and an environment for a hamster in a primary classroom were as valid D and T outcomes as an electronic view data system for school news or anti-theft device for a bicycle. Breadth was entailed by the range of contexts – home; school; recreation; community; business and industry – in which tasks might be identified and also by the scope of the attainment targets. AT1 necessitated 'problem construction', an activity which was new for many pupils and often their teachers. AT4 had broad implications for the range of value considerations to be taken into account during appraisal; as with other ATs, there was an important historical and multicultural dimension involved.[51]

In accordance with the requirements of the Education Reform Act, the report went forward in June 1989 as the Secretaries of State's proposals to the National Curriculum Council (NCC) in England and to the

common. If the inertia of past meanings was allowed to take over, anxieties could be dissipated.

In secondary schools where, as HM Senior Chief Inspector of Schools had observed in his annual report for 1989-90, the cross-curricular planning needed for national curriculum D and T was 'a longstanding difficulty',[61] there was considerable diversity of practice. Schools were confronting technology from very different starting points. Much depended on a school's previous involvement in curriculum development and collaborative teaching; on the extent of TVEI influence and funding; on the available equipment and the geography of accommodation; and, by no means of least importance, on internal school and departmental politics and interpersonal relationships. There were valid criticisms from some teachers that the form which technology was taking in their school had so far involved their de-skilling and the redundancy of hard won expertise, especially craft skills. Recording and assessment in D and T were also proving problematical.

Based on their inspection of 438 secondary and 25 middle schools, and observation of 422 year seven D and T lessons in the first year of implementation, HM inspectors concluded that 35 per cent of the lessons were satisfactory, 17 per cent were good and 7 per cent very good, i.e. a total of 59 per cent satisfactory or better. In 33 per cent of the lessons seen, the standards of work were unsatisfactory and in 8 per cent, poor. The inspectors also visited 398 primary schools, nearly half of which were chosen because it was known they were making progress with the introduction of technology. Of 443 lessons with Key Stage 1 pupils, 58 per cent were satisfactory or good, 10 per cent were judged as very good, 26 per cent were unsatisfactory and a further 6 per cent were poor. Of 461 lessons with Key Stage 2 pupils, 62 per cent were satisfactory or good, 8 per cent very good, 25 per cent unsatisfactory and 6 per cent poor. Few of the primary schools had a policy document or teachers' guidelines for D and T; most of the work focused on ATs 2 and 3, to the neglect of ATs 1 and 4, and involved the making of artefacts, rather than systems or environments. In relation to both primary and secondary schools, the inspectors concluded there had been a decline in making activities and recorded as a matter of concern that, in secondary schools, 'standards of D and T work were low compared with non-national curriculum work in years 8 to 11'.[62]

The latter reference was presumably to craft and CDT work which, in the later years and for some pupils, would lead to GCSE examinations in CDT-related subjects. If so, it might be argued that like was not being compared with like. The CDT work was well-established, often with experienced teachers and pupils who had opted for it, and supported by a developed subject culture. In contrast, national curriculum D and T involved teachers in an innovation of considerable, if not unprecedented, magnitude. In the words of the chairman of the NCC, it was 'a radically new and exciting subject which represents a major challenge to previous understanding and practice'.[63] There was a need to create a new subject culture and clearly this would take time, especially as the in-service support available to teachers had been insufficient, a point which the inspectors themselves acknowledged. It was also a subject being taught to all pupils, girls and boys, including those with special needs. Whilst the HMI observational snapshot no doubt justified the comment about lower standards of work in D and T, this needed to be interpreted with caution. In the context of a request from the Secretary of State in November 1991 to the NCC for advice on the case for revising the Technology Order, the comparison was rich material for others who were attacking D and T. In a savage indictment of current practice published by the Engineering Council a day before the NCC's response became public, it was stated that 'Her Majesty's Inspectors are reporting that the standard of work in secondary schools, where national curriculum technology has been running for five terms, is actually declining (in contrast to the other subject areas where improvements have been noted).'[64]

The Engineering Council's report, *Technology in the National Curriculum. Getting it right*, written by Alan Smithers and Pamela Robinson and rich in soundbites, opened with the damning words, 'Technology in the national curriculum is a mess.' In fact, the report addressed only D and T at Key Stages 3 and 4 and said little about primary schools or about girls and technology at any of the four key stages. Its data base was limited: seventeen 'interviews' and six school visits. As teaching of D and T was not due to begin at Key Stage 4 until August 1993 and the report was published in May 1992 when GCSE criteria were not yet available, much was made of syllabuses which had been offered as a bridging arrangement. The assumption that these, and the materials and approach of an entrepreneurial organisation, the so-called National Design and Technology Education Foundation (NDTEF), could be regarded 'as making the nature of national curriculum technology explicit'[65] was one that few others could share and was unwarranted by subsequent events.

In brief, the argument was that D and T was 'invented' without any clear progression to higher education in mind; it lacked identity and needed rescuing. Present interpretations of it as 'generalised problem solving without a specified knowledge base' did not correspond to 'technology as it is commonly understood, that is, inventing or improving things through the application of science and maths'. The subject needed to be delimited as a practical organisation of knowledge and skills. The present attainment targets should be differentially weighted to give greater prominence to planning and making. Alternatively, they should be reduced to two or even one. The suggestion in the report for the analytical study of artefacts of proven success was eminently sensible and nothing in the existing Order prevented teachers from doing this. The examples given, however – the Kenwood food mixer, the electric hover mower, the personal stereo and the fork-lift truck – did not encourage belief that such a D and T programme could overcome gender stereotypes, attract able pupils and contribute to the higher curriculum status of practical capability. The 'cure', as outlined in the report, could well turn out to be more disastrous than the alleged complaint. The NCC 'noted with interest' the report and judged it 'a useful contribution to the debate'. The Council's own conclusions, however, were said to argue 'for a more balanced approach'.[66]

The Engineering Council was not the only 'big gun' firing at D and T from outside the education system. Researchers from the National Institute of Economic and Social Research (NIESR) were severely critical of the way in which D and T had displaced practical subjects such as motor vehicle studies, metalwork, technical drawing and engineering workshop theory and practice from the secondary school curriculum. A series of reports published by the Institute, many associated with the name of Professor S. J. Prais, had compared technology (and its precursors such as CDT) in English secondary schools with vocational courses on the continent.[67] The focus was almost exclusively on pupils aged 14 to 16 and no attempt was made to consider progression in technology education throughout the eleven years of compulsory schooling. The NIESR researchers sought to explain the lower productivity of manufacturing industry in Britain, compared with its western European competitors, by a shortfall in vocational qualifications on the part of British workers particularly at the intermediate level (e.g. craftsmen, technicians and qualified administrative staff). It appeared that the foundations for future vocational training which were being laid in secondary education were not strong enough. Viewed from this perspective, national curriculum D and T was deficient: it was said to lack a sharp focus in relation to materials and skills; too much emphasis was being placed on designing activities at the expense of making; and craft skills were being neglected to an extent that caused children with a practical cast of mind to lose motivation.

Similar points were made in a widely-publicised Channel Four television programme, *Every Child in Britain,* reporting the findings of a Channel Four Commission on Education established to identify needed reforms in the education system. The five commissioners were Professors A. H. Halsey, N. Postlethwaite, S. J. Prais, A. Smithers and Dr Hilary Steedman (NIESR). They asserted that school technology had been 'intellectualised' within the national curriculum. 'Academic drift' had transformed it into a study in which 'no specific materials are prescribed, nor is a degree of accuracy specified in the making of objects (comparable to the 0.5 mm typically prescribed in woodworking classes in Germany).' The rise of technology as a school subject had been at the expense of practical subjects: pupils who may excel in executing practical work could become dispirited in 'verbalising "design briefs"'.[68]

The validity of these criticisms has been challenged,[69] but what is not in doubt is their effect in contributing to a sense that national curriculum D and T was on the wrong track and a second look was needed. The advice of the NCC to the Secretary of State in May 1992 was that fundamental revision of the programmes of study was required and that the statements of attainment should be rewritten. The main aims were to reduce complexity, clarify meaning and introduce greater precision in the specification of concepts and skills to be developed in pupils.[70] In launching the review, to be undertaken by HMI, John Patten, the Education Secretary, emphasised additionally the need to increase teachers' expectations of children's abilities, the greater emphasis to be given to 'the practical element of the subject' and the importance of improving the manageability of the D and T curriculum in the classroom.[71]

The remarkable coincidence, if indeed it was, of publication of the Engineering Council's attack being followed within days by the NCC advice and then the long-delayed HMI report allowed the press to have a field day at the expense of D and T. 'Blue Peter' activities in technology lessons, involving cardboard, paper and egg boxes, were said to be putting Britain's industrial future at risk.[72] Denis Filer, Director-General of the Engineering Council, in welcoming the review as a positive response to the Council's own report, claimed that: 'This should put an end to the Mickey Mouse Technology that has manifested itself in schools.' Whilst acknowledging that implementation was not without its problems, others interpreted events differently. 'We are in great danger of diluting or abandoning one of the century's most ambitious and well thought out innovations,' John Eggleston warned. The apparent 'crime' of national curriculum D and T, in his view, was of trying to make the intellectual and expressive aspects of technology available to all children, an ambitious, brave and difficult endeavour which, if successful could have radical implications for the social order 'by producing too many chiefs and not enough Indians'.[73]

To assist them in their review, Her Majesty's Inspectors issued a questionnaire to representatives from education, industry and business. This was accompanied by a statement entitled 'Characteristics of Design and Technology in Schools' intended to help respondents. To the considerable extent that this reflected the original approach of the

Working Group, there was reassurance, but hints of curtailment and a narrower perspective on D and T activity were also present. 'The quality of the outcome [of D and T activity],' readers were informed, 'is judged in terms of function, safety, reliability, efficiency, appearance, economy and the effects on the environment. Balancing these often conflicting demands will require pupils to make judgements based on values, appropriateness and the merits of different solutions. But, the ultimate measures of success are essentially pragmatic: is it effective; does it work?'[74] Morality, it seemed, had been jettisoned: provided the thumbscrew, the gas chamber or the bug worked well, we were dealing with high quality D and T. From 128 questionnaires distributed by the review team, 90 replies were received, plus a further 90 from the Engineering Council which had circulated the form to its members. Some 70 unsolicited responses were also taken into account. Unfortunately no clear consensus emerged to guide the reviewers and they had to report 'considerable variation in respondents' views on the nature of D and T and what it should contain'.[75] In one sense, this added to the complexity of their task; in another, it increased their freedom to adopt priorities according to their own judgements and the guidance they had received from the Secretary of State.

Their report, published in December 1992 as the proposals of the Secretaries of State, was sent forward to the NCC for another round of consultation. The principal measures included a reduction of the attainment targets from four to two (designing and making, weighted 40 per cent and 60 per cent); a reduction in the number of statements of attainments from 117 to 59; a restructuring of the programmes of study into two core sections (designing and making) and five supporting sections outlining the knowledge and skills to be applied when designing and making (construction materials and components; food; control systems and energy; structures; business and industrial practices); and the limitation of the sections on 'food' and 'business and industrial practices' to Key Stage 2 onwards and Key Stage 3 onwards, respectively. The principal means of teaching the programmes of study was to be by Design and Make Tasks (DMTs) which were specified in number for each key stage. Many of the programmes of study statements were cross-referenced to the Orders for art, mathematics and science. Gone were all references to artefacts, systems and environments, and to the five contexts specified in the original Order. For Key Stage 4, a particularly difficult aspect of the review group's work, there were proposals for both a full course and a variety of short courses which could be aggregated into a GCSE qualification or linked to vocational extension courses. In submitting the review group's report to the Secretary of State for Education, the Chief Inspector maintained that 'the emphasis on making a manageable range of high quality products, and the specification of the essential knowledge and skills should help to ensure pupils' work is rigorous and intellectually demanding'.[76]

The detail of the NCC's consultation, undertaken in the early months of 1993, need not be examined here. Both the NCC and the School Examinations and Assessment Council (SEAC), the latter responsible for assessment arrangements, found the new proposals 'a distinct advance' on the present D and T curriculum, but nevertheless in need of 'substantial further work'.[77] However, in April 1993, the Secretary of State had asked Sir Ron Dearing, newly appointed as chairman of both NCC and SEAC, and from October 1993, of their successor body the School Curriculum and Assessment Authority (SCAA), to conduct a major review of the manageability of the whole national curriculum and assessment framework. Clearly, any further revision of the technology Order needed to be informed by the emerging conclusions from this. Accordingly, though work continued by NCC officers to further reduce the load on teachers and enhance the clarity of any future Order, a decision on technology was postponed.[78] In the meantime, schools were bound by the 1990 Order and had to continue to teach the existing technology curriculum at all key stages.

In its dying days, the NCC sent forward a further set of proposals for national curriculum technology, agreed by the Council at its final meeting.[79] Endorsement of the text was not sought because it had been agreed by then to conduct a review of all national curriculum subject Orders to render them less prescriptive, to reduce the statutory component of programmes of study and to make the Orders more readily understandable by teachers. Even more firmly than the HMI review group, the nettle of a clear definition of school technology had been grasped. The inspectors had pronounced that: 'Design and technology involves applying knowledge and skills when designing and making good quality products fit for their intended purpose.' In the light of consultation, the NCC had amended this to read, 'Technology is the creative application of knowledge, skills and understanding to design and make good quality products.'[80] Reflecting a concern of the Engineering Council, a new section had been incorporated into the programmes of study entitled 'products and applications'. Under this, pupils would study already existing technological products and processes. At Key Stage 4, for example, the functions and workings of products should be related by pupils to the intended purpose of the product, the components available for use in it and how far manufacturability and maintenance requirements were met.[81] This was something less than consideration of how a product had affected people's work, life styles and values, and what unintended consequences had arisen. Such issues, like those of recyclability and disposability, even financial and environmental cost, seemed to have dropped down, if not from, the agenda.

Instead, there was a significant turn of the vocational screw. The White Paper, *Choice and Diversity*, in noting that 'no other western country had given such prominence to technology in the curriculum for all pupils of compulsory school age', linked technology to the government's policy of securing parity of esteem between academic and vocational courses. It was to be 'a central bridging element' of the curriculum for all pupils. As such, it had to be taught 'as a subject with clear practical objectives', and its vocational application was therefore 'as important as its academic grounding'.[82] It was the NCC's view that more work was needed to ensure that the final Order provided a sound basis for further vocational as well as academic study.

The SCAA working group on D and T, one of eleven subject groups established to advise on slimming down the national curriculum, was chaired by an assistant chief executive of the Authority and included a majority of serving primary and secondary school teachers and heads. The outcome of its deliberations, in the form of yet another version of programmes of study and attainment targets, was sent forward to the Secretary of State in March 1994 and immediately accepted as the basis for a further statutory consultation.[83] Although the two attainment targets, Designing and Making, had been endorsed for assessing and reporting D and T, the plethora of detailed statements of attainment had now been replaced by level descriptions, ten for each attainment target. These were synoptic portrayals of performance against which the work of pupils was to be compared by teachers in order to determine 'best fit'. The proposals no longer attempted a definition of technology, but the programmes of study for each key stage included the statement that 'Design and technology capability requires pupils to combine their designing and making skills with knowledge and understanding in order to design and make products'. Previous references to the quality of products were transferred to the programmes of study, but it was not until Key Stage 3 that this strand of 'knowledge and understanding' involved judging a product in terms of 'its impact beyond the purpose for which it was designed'. Also in each programme of study was a clearer prescription than before for the range of activities in which pupils should engage; these included:

1. assignments in which pupils design and make products using a range of materials and components;
2. focused practical tasks in which they develop and practise particular skills and knowledge; and
3. activities in which pupils investigate, disassemble and evaluate simple products.

A gain in time at Key Stage 3 to 63 hours (compared with 45 hours per year for other foundation subjects) was intended to create sufficient time for the practical activities of D and T. However, the statutory requirement at the critical Key Stage 4 was a short course only. This extraordinary decision was sharply at odds with the assertion in Sir Ron Dearing's final report that: 'In the case of technology, as a nation we have a distinguished record in scientific discovery and a proud record among the world's Nobel Prize winners, but we have suffered from an inability to translate scientific discovery into wealth-generating industrial and commercial products. This has weakened the whole economy. We need to develop our commitment to technology.'[85] True, a school was free to extend the statutory short course (5 per cent of available curriculum time) into a full course (10 per cent), but this would be in the face of competition from science (a statutory 12½ per cent whereas many students followed a double course of 20 per cent), history and geography (which were to become non-statutory and optional at Key Stage 4), a second foreign language and other non-national curriculum subjects such as home economics, classics, economics and business studies. The recommendation amounted to clear devaluation of D and T as a component of general education and a lost opportunity for all children, boys and girls, to develop their practical capability up to the age of 16. The seal was set by a recommendation for a moratorium on further major changes to national curriculum Orders for a period of five years.[86]

The making and shaping of policy for school technology

By and large, the recommendations of the Dearing report were well received by the teaching profession as a needed contribution to the reduction of their workload, the simplification of the legal requirements of the national curriculum and the reassertion of confidence in teachers' professional judgement. From a more strategic perspective, others were severely critical, seeing the changes as 'a calamitous and shameful capitulation to professional pressure'.[87] The judgement of a former senior chief HMI was that 'sadly, we have not given the national curriculum a serious go. We are ducking out of it beyond the age of fourteen and reverting to an older pattern that we know failed many people, as well as serving ill the nation.' Essentially, beyond Key Stage 3, the national curriculum had been deconstructed.[88]

As for the specific proposals for D and T, the Design and Technology Association (DATA), representing teachers, found much to welcome in them and the Engineering Council similarly voiced approval, though regretting the cut-back at Key Stage 4.[89] Teachers of CDT certainly could draw reassurance that they continued to have a major contribution to make. Because 'textiles' and 'food' had survived the review as materials and 'areas of study' at Key Stages 1, 2 and 3 (though 'food' was optional at Key

Stage 3), teachers of home economics also retained a foothold. The contribution of business studies, however, appeared to have been severely curtailed.

The most remarkable aspect of the developments, however, was that, from a situation in 1985 when the very idea of a policy for school technology comparable to that for school science was foreign, and in less than a decade, technology had become not only a significant, if contentious, component of a national curriculum, but also an important element in the government's overall education policy.

In 1986 Kenneth Baker had announced the establishment of a network of City Technology Colleges (CTCs) in urban areas.[90] These were not answerable to LEAs, being in receipt of government direct grant. Their promoters were expected to make a substantial contribution towards costs and education for pupils was to be free. A strong bias to technology, science and mathematics would characterise their curriculum, so giving parents 'a new choice of school', fifteen in all being established. Later, in 1991, a Technology Schools Initiative was introduced to promote good technology teaching and vocational developments at Key Stage 4. Each LEA was invited to select the best two bids from interested secondary schools; separate bids were made by grant maintained (GM) and voluntary aided (VA) schools. In the first round, capital grants to GM and VA schools, or borrowing approvals for county schools, totalling some £25 million were made to 100 schools. A second round a year later brought in 122 more schools.[91] A further initiative followed in 1993 whereby GM and VA schools could appoint sponsor governors, as permitted under the Education Act 1993, and form partnerships with the private sector. The curriculum of these Technology Colleges would emphasise technology, science and mathematics. In justification of this development, the Education Secretary John Patten stated, 'there can be no doubt that Britain needs more of its citizens educated in the understanding of technology, with more workers trained in technological skills'. (In passing, it would seem that the second, rather than the first, of these needs had been the greater influence on the shaping of national curriculum D and T.) He continued: 'The development of specialist markets is of great importance to a medium-sized country such as ours, and in no sector more so than in manufacturing industries which depend on skill and high added value . . . [It has been estimated that] by the turn of the century more than two-thirds of all jobs will be knowledge based, requiring "cerebral" rather than manual skills – a complete reversal from fifty years ago.'[92] This statement seemed strangely at odds with the priority given to 'making' in the revised attainment targets for D and T.

School technology, then, for reasons not always free from contradictions and despite lack of consensus on what technology actually is, had come to acquire a significant place in the government's attempts first, to increase diversity of provision and hence parental choice of schools and, secondly, to increase vocational components of the curriculum, post-14, on a par with academic studies. It was also the subject of comment in the White Paper on science, engineering and technology, *Realising Our Potential*, in 1993. Changes to the school curriculum were here said to 'ensure, for the first time, that all pupils, girls as well as boys, will study a broad and balanced programme of science and technology right through to the age of 16.[93] In relation to technology, something less than this at Key Stage 4 was a consequence of the Dearing proposals.

The procedures by which policy for school technology had been made involved the interplay of influences at the macro-level of national politics with those at the micro-level of the school and the workshop/classroom. At the macro-level, it is clear that economic concerns and the professional interests of the engineering community had played a major role. Little evidence exists to suggest the importance of alternative factors such as increasing the representation of girls and women in technology and technology education, or ensuring a technologically literate public alert to the consequences of technological developments and able to monitor critically decisions of a technological élite. The version of technology education enshrined in the 1994 D and T draft Order was also a far cry from that favoured by those who saw technology, because it entailed practical action, as a moral enterprise. It is true that, as one of the initiators of the DATA special interest group on Values in Technology Education argued, crucial aspects of implementation of the Order depended on textual interpretation and there were still some grounds for supporting the development of a critical understanding of technology as part of D and T capability.[94] However, it would be easy, and probably more likely, for the subject to become narrowed to 'the technical and economic aspects of designing and making products for the consumer market'.

Throughout all the debates and consultations, little if any serious attempt had been made to provide an epistemological warrant for technology as a unique cognitive mode associated with a symbolic world which children should be empowered to construct and control. Smithers and Robinson in their attack on national curriculum D and T included a brief section on the nature of technology, drawing on a dated analysis of 'forms of knowledge'. They concluded that technology was 'a practical organisation of knowledge' functional in relation to some delimited class of problems.[95] This appeared to ignore much recent philosophical work which explored the characteristics of technology as a distinctive form of knowledge in its own right.[96]

At the classroom level, many of the factors which influenced the manifestations of D and T were difficult to disentangle from the implementation of the national curriculum as a whole. The context in which teachers worked was a powerful determinant of their responses: the wider range of pupils learning D and T, deficiencies in material resources as well as in teacher knowledge and skills, and the nature of accountability and supervision experienced were all factors which determined teacher reaction. A sense of working continually under the threat of unpredictable curriculum change only added to their difficulties. The TVEI model of technology across the curriculum and the original Working Group's cross-curricular approach for teaching D and T were obvious casualties of the context of both primary and secondary schools. Collaboration between secondary school teachers of different subjects, especially when engaged in the assessment of pupils' D and T coursework, tended to expose value differences across subjects and, often, encouraged retreat into curriculum territory where they felt more secure.[97] The time needed to talk through differences and begin to construct a new subject culture was never available to teachers of D and T: review overtook them before the process of clarifying differences, much less negotiating consensus, had got under way.

In conclusion, it has to be said that policy for technology education has emerged in an unplanned way by a process of action and reaction, involving initiatives and proposals from a variety of stakeholders in this new curriculum area. No systematic identification and detailed consideration of policy issues was attempted, unless the Interim Report of 1988 can be so regarded, and several components of a comprehensive policy, notably teacher training and supply, have received only limited and belated attention. Others, such as progression in learning across the years of compulsory schooling, were constructed and reconstructed 'on the hoof', drawing on a diverse and slowly accumulating body of teaching experience. No one would pretend that the last word on this had been said in the 1994 draft Order. As for the issue with which this chapter began, the relationship between school science and school technology, the 1994 Order is reticent. Cross-references to the science Order have disappeared and the presumptions seem to be that the science of science lessons is ready made for use in D and T tasks, and that technology teachers will embrace this resource. Both are questionable.[98]

A final word concerns school technology as an instrument for the achievement of other educational policies such as making pupils' experience of schooling more 'practical' and related to the world of work, breaking down the divide between academic and vocational studies, and contributing to the supply of technological skills essential to the economy. Such demands on technology education are not in short supply: collectively they represent an impossible burden on any one school subject, however well established and resourced. On one which is as yet not fully grown and still questing after a clear identity, the consequences could be fatal. It would be sad if an exciting and radical curriculum innovation, potentially of great significance, should collapse under the weight of the unrealistic responsibilities being placed upon it.

References

1 *The Times Educational Supplement,* 29 March 1985, 4.
2 *Better Schools* (1985), 14-15.
3 National Curriculum Science Working Group, *Interim Report* (1988) Annex B, para. 28.
4 *Education,* clxxi (1988), 521.
5 Department of Education and Science, *The Curriculum from 5 to 16. Curriculum Matters 2* (1985), 16.
6 Department of Education and Science/Welsh Office, *The School Curriculum* (1981), 6.
7 P. Black, 'What more do you want?', *The Times Educational Supplement,* 29 March 1985, 4.
8 Department of Education and Science/Welsh Office, *Science 5-16: A Statement of Policy* (1985), 18.
9 DES, *Curriculum from 5 to 16,* 35-6.
10 *Better Schools* (1985), 23.
11 *Working Together – Education and Training* (1986), 4.
12 e.g. D. I. R. Porter, *A School Approach to Technology* (1967); G. B. Harrison, 'Technology in Schools', in D. Layton (ed.) *The Alternative Road. The rehabilitation of the practical* (1984), 75-87; D. Layton, *Interpreters of Science* (1984), 254-78.; G. McCulloch, E. Jenkins, D. Layton, *Technological Revolution? The politics of school science and technology in England and Wales since 1945* (1985).
13 Schools Council, *Technology in Schools* (1966).
14 McCulloch *et al., Technological Revolution?* 143-80.
15 M. Rose, 'Craft, Design and Technology', in K. Selkirk (ed.), *Assessment at 16* (1988), 166-85.
16 K. Joseph, Speech at Wembley Exhibition, 22 October 1985. DES Press Release.
17 P. Black, G. Harrison, *In Place of Confusion. Technology and science in the school curriculum* (1985).
18 J. Curtis, *Technical and Vocational Education Review* (1990), 8-11.
19 'Submission to National Curriculum Design and Technology Working Group' in TVEI, *Technology in TVEI and the National Curriculum. A report of three consultative conferences* (1988), 83.
20 J. Woolhouse, 'Technology – a central theme in TVEI', *School Technology Forum Conference Report* (1985), 1-3.
21 D. Barnes, G. Johnson, S. Jordan, D. Layton, P. Medway, D. Yeomans, *The TVEI Curriculum 14-16. An interim report based on case studies in twelve schools* (1987), 43-6.

22 D. Layton, P. Medway, D. Yeomans, *Technology in TVEI. 14-18. The range of practice* (1989), 3.
23 Layton, Medway, Yeomans, *Technology in TVEI*, 113-4.
24 See e.g. G. Harrison, 'Technology in TVEI' in J. Cross (ed.) *TVEI Developments 1* (1986), 64-5; Layton, Medway, Yeomans, *Technology in TVEI*, 49.
25 Layton, Medway, Yeomans, *Technology in TVEI*, 106-12.
26 Layton, Medway, Yeomans, *Technology in TVEI*, 111.
27 British School Technology, Carlton, Unpublished evaluation report: Technology across the Curriculum Project (1987).

British School Technology (BST) was launched on 1 April 1984 with a pump-priming grant from the Department of Trade and Industry and the MSC, the intention being that the organisation should become a self-financing operation in three years. The creation of BST brought into partnership two separate centres which had been leading providers of in-service training for teachers of technology and prominent agents in the development of school technology: the National Centre for School Technology, Trent Polytechnic and the Ampthill Centre established by Bedfordshire Local Education Authority, later BST Carlton.

A later report and evaluation of a follow-up project, Technology for All across the Curriculum (TAAC), is: D. Patrick, *TAAC. Technology for All Across the Curriculum. TVEI developments 12* (1990).
28 TVEI, *Technology for TVEI* and *Appendices* (1987).
29 P. Dutton, *Technology for All Across the Curriculum. A reflection on TRIST experiences* (1987).
30 Anne Jones, 'The real aims of TVEI', *Education*, clxxiii (1989), 352.
31 Anne Jones, 'Take the initiative', *The Guardian*, 24 May 1988.
32 DES Press Release, 136/88, 29 April 1988.
33 Royal College of Art, *Design in General Education. Part One: Summary of findings and recommendations* (1976).

See also: P. Roberts, 'The place of design in technology education', in D. Layton (ed.), *Innovations in Science and Technology Education. Vol. 5* (1994), 171–79.
34 R. Rogers, 'The design and fall of Britain', *The Times Educational Supplement*, 29 April 1983, 22.
35 M. Thatcher, *The Times Educational Supplement*. 29 April 1983, 22.
36 Engineering Council, Action Notes of the meeting held between representatives of the Manpower Services Commission and the Engineering Council on 23 October 1987.

Government responsibility for design became centred in the Department of Industry, so confirming Mrs Thatcher's view of it as contributory to economic regeneration.
37 *Education*. 6 May 1988 and *Independent*, 12 May 1988.
38 B. Archer, 'Design and the fundamentals of learning'. Lecture at the Annual Conference of the Association of Advisers in Craft, Design and Technology. 26-29 April 1988.

39 DES/Welsh Office, *Interim Report of the National Curriculum Design and Technology Working Group*. Nov. 1988, 2.

40 J. Eggleston, 'Technology teachers and the new revisions of the technology curriculum: responses of DATA members'. *Design and Technology Teaching*, xxvi (1994), 15.

41 C. Monson, Presentation by representative of the National Curriculum Council, *School Technology*, xxii (1990), 8.

42 DES/Welsh Office, *Interim Report*. 85-95.

43 DES, NC/DTWG(83)34, Kenneth Baker to Lady Parkes, 29 July 1988.

44 The responses of the Crafts Council and of other professional bodies to which reference is made are printed in *School Technology* xii (1989), 8-62.

45 Design Council, Ivor Owen to Lady Parkes, 20 Jan. 1989 and Response by the Design Council to the Interim Report.

46 The Royal Society, 401002.W401/JAN/CD, Professor L. Crombie to Lady Parkes, 12 Jan. 1989. The Fellowship of Engineering, VB/JSCD/1800, Miss V. E. Budd to Mr S. Jardine, 11 Jan. 1989.

47 The Royal Fine Art Commission, Lord St John of Fawsley to Lady Parkes, 17 Jan. 1989 and Response by the Royal Fine Art Commission to the Interim Report.

48 O. G. Thomas, Submission to the Design and Technology Working Party from a consortium of voluntary agencies working in the field of overseas development, 12 September 1988.

49 Equal Opportunities Commission, Lynda Carr to Stephen Jardine, 12 Jan. 1989 and Design and Technology Group Interim Report – Comment of the EOC.

50 DES/Welsh Office, *Design and Technology for Ages 5 to 16. Proposals of the Secretary of State for Education and the Secretary of State for Wales* (1989), v.

51 D. Layton, *Technology's Challenge to Science Education* (1993), 20-22.

52 National Curriculum Council, *Technology 5-16 in the National Curriculum. A report to the Secretary of State for Education and Science on the statutory consultation for attainment targets and programmes of study in technology* (1989).

53 *Education*, clxxiv (1989), 408.

54 *Education*, clxxiv (1989), 299.

55 *School Technology*, xxii (1990), 4.

56 *School Technology*, xxii (1990), 4-5.

57 *School Technology*, xxii (1990), 5-6.

58 Standing Conference on Schools' Science and Technology, David Bloomfield to A. E. D. Chamier, 18 Jan. 1990.

59 British Management Data Foundation, Anthony Cowgill to John MacGregor, 16 Jan. 1990.

60 Angela Anning, 'Factors affecting design and technology capability at Key Stages 1 and 2', *Design and Technology Teaching*, xxiv (1992), 11.

61 DES/Her Majesty's Inspectorate, *Standards in Education 1989-90* (1991), 9.

62 DES/HMI, *Technology. Key Stages 1, 2 and 3. A Report by HM Inspectorate on the first year. 1990-91* (1992).

63 NCC, David Pascall to John Patten, 8 May 1992.

64 A. Smithers, P. Robinson, *Technology in the National Curriculum. Getting it right* (1992), 5.
65 Smithers and Robinson, *Technology in the National Curriculum*, 8.
66 NCC, David Pascall to John Patten, 8 May 1992.
67 S. J. Prais, E. Beadle, *Pre-vocational Schooling in Europe Today* (1991).
68 A. H. Halsey, N. Postlethwaite, S. J. Prais, A. Smithers, H. Steedman, *Every Child in Britain* (1991), 14-15.
69 D. Layton, 'The revolution in technology education: views from below, above and abroad', in R. Baker (ed.), *Education. The National Curriculum* (1993), 33-5.
70 NCC, *National Curriculum Technology: The Case for Revising the Order* (1992).
71 DES, Press Release 168/92, 2 June 1992.
72 *The Sunday Times*, 31 May 1992.
73 John Eggleston, 'Editorial', *Design and Technology Teaching*, xxiv (1992), 3-4.
74 DES, V. Green, Staff Inspector for Technology, to Design and Technology Review Group Respondents, 24 June 1992.
75 DES/Welsh Office, *Technology for Ages 5 to 16 (1992). Proposals of the Secretary of State for Education and the Secretary of State for Wales* (1992), 4-5 and 47.
76 Stewart R. Sutherland to John Patten, 4 Nov. 1992. Printed in DES/Welsh Office, *Technology for Ages 5 to 16 (1992)*, v.
77 NCC, Sir Ron Dearing to John Patten, 28 May 1993.
78 NCC, Press Release, NCC Issues Interim Report on Technology, 2 July 1993.
79 NCC, *Technology in the National Curriculum. Technology programmes of study and attainment targets: Recommendations of the National Curriculum Council* (1993).
80 NCC, *Technology in the National Curriculum* (1993), 5.
81 NCC, *Technology in the National Curriculum* (1993), 30-1.
82 DFE/Welsh Office, *Choice and Diversity. A new framework for schools* (1992), 45.
83 SCAA, *Design and Technology in the National Curriculum. Draft Proposals* (1994).
84 SCAA, *Design and Technology in the National Curriculum*, iii.
85 R. Dearing, *The National Curriculum and its Assessment: Final Report* (1993), 45.
86 R. Dearing, *The National Curriculum and its Assessment*, 39.
87 J. Clare, 'The strange case of the vanishing curriculum', *Daily Telegraph*, 10 Jan. 1994.
88 E. Bolton, 'Divided we fall', *The Times Educational Supplement*, 21 Jan. 1994, 17.
89 J. Eggleston, 'The new order – DATA's response', *DATA News*. No. 24, June 1994, 1 and 4.
90 DES, *City Technology Colleges. A New Choice of School* (1986).
91 Office for Standards in Education (OFSTED), *The School Technology Initiative 1992-1993* (1994).
92 DFE, *Technology Colleges. Schools for the Future* (1993), 3.
93 Chancellor of the Duchy of Lancaster, *Realising Our Potential. A strategy for science, engineering and technology* (1993), 53.
94 R. Conway, Special Interest Group: Values in Technology Education Newsletter (June 1994), 1.
95 Smithers and Robinson, *Technology in the National Curriculum*, 13-14.

C

96 See e.g. E. T. Layton, 'Technology as knowledge', *Technology and Culture*, xv
    (1974), 31-41; J. M. Staudenmaier, *Technology's Storytellers* (1985), especially
    chapter 3, 'Science, technology and the characteristics of technological
    knowledge'.
97 C. F. Paechter, 'Power, Knowledge and the Design and Technology Curriculum'
    (unpublished Ph.D. thesis, University of London, 1993), 117-55.
98 D. Layton, *Technology's Challenge to Science Education* (1993).

CHAPTER
THREE

English, Australian and New Zealand Prep Schools:
a study of degrees of replication

D. P. LEINSTER-MACKAY

Dealing mainly with either boys' prep schools[1] or with prep schools recently co-educational, this *Festschrift* essay, like ancient Gaul, is roughly divided into three parts. It examines, in a historical perspective, preparatory schools in each of the Commonwealth countries and aims to determine to what extent preparatory or junior schools in Australia and New Zealand have replicated those in the mother country.

The English preparatory school today

Keeping in mind the Heraclitean premiss that everything in this sublunary world is subject to change – including presumably preparatory schools – there is a need to recognise first the changes that have occurred amongst English preparatory schools during the past decade or so, before looking at the historical perspective of prep schools in all three countries.

In 1994 the English prep school sat on the cusp of educational change as it continued to assimilate the 120 girls' preparatory schools which became part of the new IAPS (Incorporated Association of Preparatory Schools) in January 1981. Having held strongly to a previous tradition of membership being wholly for male heads of boys' schools and for a few heads of recently transformed co-educational schools (formerly boys only), the IAPS took the giant leap and incorporated the Association of Headmistresses of Preparatory Schools into its organization. A male cynic might observe that when, in 1994 the President of the IAPS is the Baroness Cox of Queensbury, the Chairman is Mrs C E Prichard (Warwick Preparatory School) and the *Prep School* editor is Mrs Anne Kiggell, it has not been so much an 'incorporation' as a 'take-over'. These three women hold prominent, significant, and one could argue the most important, positions in the modem IAPS.

Partly because of the influx of women into the IAPS, **heterogeneity** is the modern characteristic of IAPS schools today. To quote from the *Independent Schools Yearbook 1992-1993:*

> IAPS schools include boys', girls' and co-educational; boarding, day and mixed; urban and rural. The size varies from over 400 to under 100 pupils, with the majority between 150 and 250. Most schools are charitable trusts. Some are limited companies and a few are proprietorial. There are also junior schools attached to senior schools, choir schools, schools with a particular religious affiliation [shades of Australia!] and schools which offer some specialist provision.[2]

This has not always been so. Any student of the history of the English preparatory school will recall the preponderance in the nineteenth century of the private preparatory school: small, buried deep in the English countryside, and therefore boarding, with loose affiliations with the Anglican Church, more often than not run by a clergyman, and giving instruction mainly in the classics.[3]

Such a light thumbnail sketch by no means does justice to the English prep school, any more than do pejorative references to prep schools to be found in English literature and English journalism. It was Roger Mortimer, a former racing correspondent of the *Sunday Times*, who after four years in Colditz declared that his enforced stay there had not been 'as bad as [his] prep school.'[4] Such pointed badinage is not unfamiliar when past *alumni* have referred to their prep schools through the light of hindsight (of which light none can be more blinding!). General Sir Ian Hamilton, for example, who attended Cheam Prep School when R. S. Tabor was headmaster (1855-1890), once averred that 'at twenty to plunge into the most furious battle was as a game of skittles . . . when compared with going as a ten-year-old to the study of RST on a Monday morning'.[5] Such has been the adverse publicity from professional writers like 'George Orwell', Cyril Connolly and Robert Graves[6] that English preparatory schools have experienced the same kind of obloquy as that suffered by the English public school, and often from the same authors. Such continuing obloquy, from prep school to public school, at least serves to emphasise the articulated nature of the system of education which is peculiar to the English middle and upper classes.

Antecedents

Delving more deeply into the historical context of the English preparatory school, it should be clearly recognised that it was essentially a phenomenon of the Victorian age, even though some schools such as Cheam[7] were founded earlier. By 1900, the **private prep school** had become an integral part of the English **public school** infrastructure. Yet the English prep school emerged from an array of different types of private school[8] and, like them, had a specific purpose: theirs being to prepare young boys for the rigours of the English public schools and to prepare some of them for entry as midshipmen into the Royal Navy.

The English preparatory school: yesteryear

There are two complementary ways of building up a composite picture of the English preparatory school. The first is to examine their institutional antecedents; the other is to look at the stereotypical individuals who contributed to its development.

Institutional antecedents

The institutional antecedents need to be identified. These are first, the eighteenth-century or early nineteenth-century **private classical schools** which were not originally confined to the younger age group (8-13) but were in rivalry with the English Public School in sending boys to Oxford and Cambridge. The Rev Charles Burney (1757–1817), a Cambridge graduate, kept such a private classical school successively at Hammersmith (1786-1793) and at Greenwich (1793-1813).[9] Burney's school did not survive beyond the period of the Napoleonic War but similar private classical schools such as Twyford, Temple Grove, Cheam and Eagle House continued into the mid-nineteenth century to become **classical preparatory schools.**

The nineteenth-century **rectory school** was another major institutional antecedent of the modern English preparatory school. Much more numerous than the private classical school, the rectory school was often the means whereby indigent Anglican clergy achieved 'outdoor relief' from their relative poverty and provided, at the same time, a means of a classical education for their sons. They were a veritable exemplification of the Smilesian dictum: 'Heaven helps those who help themselves'. Whilst many Anglican clergy in their spacious rectories coached candidates for university entry, or, after the Northcote-Trevelyan reforms of the 1850s, for entry into the Indian civil service, many coached young boys for entry into the public schools. Such rectory schools were usually quite small, educating perhaps up to fifteen or twenty boys at any one time including the sons (and possibly daughters) of the schoolmaster-cleric. The Rev Henry Moule (1801-1880) of Cambridge University and Vicar of Fordington, was, *inter alia,* a sanitary scientist but he also conducted a rectory school attended by his eight sons. There were only fifteen pupils all told at any one time at Fordington. Although rectory schools continued to exist throughout the nineteenth century, they gradually gave way to schools of the full-time professional prep schoolmaster. Typical of this translation from rectory school part-time schoolmaster to full-time preparatory schoolmaster was the Rev John Furness who, as curate of Newbold-on-Avon, kept a rectory school in 1856. He was a skilful schoolmaster and successfully coached boys for entry to Rugby School. When Dr Frederick Temple became headmaster of Rugby in 1857, Furness resigned from his curacy and acquired two houses in Rugby itself and began a private preparatory school called 'Oakfield'. Such then was the modest beginning of a later very prosperous Warwickshire prep school for 130 boys.[10]

There were a few **private commercial schools** whose owners realised that offering a classical education in preparation for boys to enter a public school offered greater economic promise than continuing to run a commercial academy. This change of role from commercial to preparatory school-owner was much less in evidence, simply because of the incompatibility of commercial subjects with the classics. One, however, who did manage this transmogrification was J. V. Milne, the father of the children's writer, A. A. Milne. Milne senior had kept a commercial school in Kilburn but, having decided that his prospects would improve by his becoming a classical prep schoolmaster, he sold up and went to Westgate-on-Sea in Thanet, Kent, where he set up Streete Court for the education of the sons of gentlemen. He was then far removed from 'trade'.

A very different institutional antecedent of the English private prep school has been the **choir school.** The Choir Schools Association (1919) consists of first, schools that are both secondary and preparatory in character, such as King's School, Rochester, allegedly founded in A.D. 604. The majority of choir schools, however, are purely preparatory schools such as Llandaff Cathedral School, refounded by Dean Charles J. Vaughan, ex-Head of Harrow, in 1880. Today these choir schools form a discrete sub-set of IAPS schools. They have their counterparts in Australia and New Zealand respectively in St Andrew's Cathedral School, Sydney, and the Cathedral Grammar School, Christchurch, New Zealand, founded in 1881.

A fifth and final institutional antecedent of the modern English prep school has been the **naval academy.** Stubbington House (1841), founded by the Rev William Foster at Fareham in Hampshire, is the best example of such. This aspect of prep schools is now largely overlooked but there were as many as 230 'IAPS' schools preparing boys for the Royal Navy as well as for public schools in 1924. The practice was finally abolished in 1948 by which time Stubbington House had produced very many future admirals for the Royal Navy. Such then have been the **institutional antecedents** of modern English prep schools.

Stereotypes of school leadership

When attention is given to the **stereotypes of individuals** who have added themselves to the ranks of prep school headmasters, there appear to be a wide range of them. In the nineteenth century, most were indigent clerics, who ran their rectory or parsonage schools on a very *ad hoc* basis, depending on their familial needs. Others more ambitious, especially in the early part of the century, had conducted, as already indicated, larger and even nationally recognised private classical schools. Cheam School had established a national reputation long before Charles, the present Prince of Wales, attended.

One very significant group of prep school headmasters were those who had been assistants in a public school, and for one reason or another,[11] had set up their own preparatory schools. These 'translated' public schoolmasters often became leaders in their newly found fraternity. Both the Rev Herbert Bull of Wellington College and Wellington House School and Mr Edward D. Mansfield of Clifton College and Lambrook School became chairmen of the Association of Heads of Preparatory Schools (AHPS), the forerunner of the IAPS. Other good examples of such translated public schoolmen were Rev Lancelot Sanderson (see note 11) of Harrow who refounded Elstree School in 1869 and the Rev John Hawtrey, of Eton, who set up, in the same year, Aldin House, at Slough, to prepare boys for entry into Eton. Such men had one enormous advantage over other prep school owners: they had very close ties with the schools for which they were preparing many of their boys.

Another major group of individuals who contributed to the composition that was the nineteenth-century English preparatory school, were the women who ran dame preparatory schools. In 1994 there is seemingly no prohibition on women in any area of the preparatory school world. As already observed, the citadel of the male presence in English prep schooling has been surrendered. But this is a complete turnabout for the IAPS. The formidable Mrs Charles (Grace) Malden, Principal of Windlesham House from 1896 to 1927, and therefore head of a leading English prep school for over thirty years could not attend meetings of the AHPS because dame prep school heads were barred. She had to be represented at such meetings by her brother-in-law, Mr H. M. S. Malden. Despite this blatant, if then normal, gender discrimination there were very many dame prep schools in the nineteenth century which prepared boys for entry into public school. Some were very prominent ones such as Summer Fields, Oxford, which Mrs Archibald Maclaren, wife of Oxford University's appointed gymnastics director, opened in 1864. Mrs Maclaren had firmly established her school when it was passed on to her son-in-law the Rev Dr. C. E. Williams in 1897, who thus converted a leading dame prep school into a leading classical preparatory school.

Other dame prep schools acquired a measure of fame retrospectively by having boys who later became famous. The young Joseph Chamberlain attended the dame prep school run by the three sisters Misses Pace in Camberwell Grove, South London, whilst young Winston Churchill was, from 1884 to 1888, at the dame prep school, Brunswick House School, Sussex, run by the Misses Thomson, before he went to Harrow.

If, in the nineteenth century, the indigent clergyman, the translated public schoolman and the self-employed dame were the main recruits to prep school leadership, in the twentieth century the list can be extended to include the non-Oxbridge graduate, the training college or college of education diplomate, the otherwise unqualified head with his IAPS Diploma and finally, ex-army officers and others of that ilk.[12]

The foregoing examination of the English prep school would not be complete without some generalisations about discernible trends in English prep school management today. Reflecting the amalgamation in 1981 with the Association of Headmistresses of Preparatory Schools, with its membership of 120 schools, there are now as many as 526 IAPS schools. Because of the past tendency for the Parents National Education Union (PNEU)[13] to be associated with girls' schools, the PNEU schools, previously pre-prep for boys and both primary and secondary for girls, are now full-scale participants in the boys' prep school world. Eton End PNEU School in Datchet, for example, even though its boys are aged only from three to seven, is now a full member of IAPS. This accession of schools for very young boys to IAPS status through the female line so to speak, has been a general characteristic of the English prep school world since 1981.

Membership of IAPS is determined by a process of accreditation from the Independent Schools Joint Council after a head's school has been inspected by an ex-HMI, using the same criteria as applied by the Department of Education and Science,[14] before departmental inspection was withdrawn.

During the last ten or twenty years there have been several deep-set changes that have taken place in the conduct of English prep schools. Several tendencies are now clearly discernible. First, there is the tendency for parents to choose prep schools for their boys within a radius of fifty or sixty miles of home. Parents are thus able to reduce travel time and avoid long journeys between home and school. This 'localization' of both prep schools and public schools has a tendency to make them less exclusive[15] as the ancient process of gentrification bites deeper into the social fabric but with less efficacy. This process of localization ties in with a second major tendency: parents are able to take their sons away for a weekend twice or three times a term[16] so that the schools and pupils are more in touch with the outside world than formerly. Moreover, day schools predominate, so that there is a tendency for many fewer boarders, especially those of very tender years, compared with day boys. The atmosphere in many English prep schools is far less authoritarian than even twenty years ago. Great efforts are made in many schools by the use of female staff, both matrons and teachers, and by the provision of a homely ethos, to make boarding school life less stressful. The curriculum tends to be more scientifically orientated with computers playing a not inconsiderable part in the boys' education. Constitutionally almost all schools in Britain are now charitable trusts and it is not uncommon to find girls being catered for in former wholly boys' schools in the late twentieth century.

But there are other ways in which the schools are accommodating themselves to the late twentieth-century economic pressures. Cothill

House, for example, a now leading Oxfordshire prep school, has capitalised on (a) the general recognition of greater integration with Europe and (b) the relatively inexpensive cost of buying French property by purchasing a *château* near Toulouse. Such an arrangement, whereby older boys spend two of their final terms at the *château,* gives a huge stimulus to students whose life has been bound up, since perhaps the age of six, with compulsory foreign languages.[17]

As for another aspect of foreign languages – overseas pupils – it is a source of increasing schools' incomes:

> 'Teffle!' one bursar told me [Martin Weyer] 'Teaching English as a Foreign Language. Marvellous. If they don't speak it when they got here, we charge them an extra £258 per term'.[18]

This process of cashing in on foreign students is also gathering momentum in Australia.

Preparatory schools in Australia

In the consideration thus far of the origins of the English prep school there has been one glaring omission – the prep school which is the *ad hoc* junior school of an English public school. This omission has been deliberate in order that it may be considered in the context of the Australian preparatory, or more accurately, 'Junior School' (of that term, more later).

Although those English prep schools which are junior schools of English public schools represent a relatively large percentage of the total number of preparatory schools (82 out of 526 = 15.6%) compared with other sub-groups such as choir schools; boys' schools owned or run by women; schools owned or run by clergymen; the figure is slight when compared with the total of boys and boys'-mixed prep schools only. Nevertheless, if the former girls' schools (120) were subtracted from the overall total, the percentage of boys' junior schools compared with the rest of the boys' prep schools would be still no more than (406) 20.2%. It can be seen, therefore, that although the junior school in the United Kingdom is not uncommon, by the same token it is by no means the norm. One cannot say this of Australian 'preparatory schools' [the term is advisedly in inverted commas] for in Australia the number of schools that are modelled on the British norm (private independent prep schools) number no more than a handful or two and most of those are in the state of New South Wales.

This then is the major difference between English and Australian preparatory schools: the Australian schools are mainly junior schools and *ad hoc* to a complementary senior school. In most English prep schools, on the other hand, boys are prepared for a number of schools (the *ad omnia* principle)[19] and the Common Entrance Examination (CEE) and scholarship examinations are the instruments whereby they are distributed amongst English public schools[20] at a twice-yearly-held examination at 11+, and 12+ and a thrice-yearly-held examination at 13+. There is no common entrance examination in Australia although individual schools, in some cases, do hold their own entrance examinations. This difference must be seen to arise from Australia's largely 'mono-transfer' system compared with England's 'poly-transfer' system. It really is a chicken and egg situation. Notwithstanding the difficulties of Australia's state system, with each state having its own curriculum, one might ask: Is the absence of a common entrance system in every state responsible for the Australian preparatory school 'system' or does the system of *ad hoc* relations with junior and senior schools dictate the absence of a CEE in all the states? Whatever is the case these two aspects are complementary.

In the absence of similarities amongst Australian 'prep schools' with English prep schools other than the junior schools of English senior schools – in other words there is an absence of the rich variety to be found in England – it becomes necessary to establish an alternative way of categorising Australian schools. One way of doing it, adopted here, is to examine the quality of the constitutional nature of each prep or junior school to determine its degree of autonomy. In this way three levels of autonomy can roughly be discerned: the fully autonomous school, the semi-autonomous school and the mainly or fully integrated school. It may be revealing at this juncture to note that the Australian equivalent of IAPS is JSHAA, the Junior Schools Heads Association of Australia (including girls' schools), with the emphasis being very much on **Junior** schools. Even in cases where the nomenclature of the junior school is 'preparatory' as at Christ Church Preparatory School, Perth, or Guildford Preparatory School in nearby Guildford, Western Australia, it is a case of Shakespeare's 'a rose by any other name'. These schools are the junior schools of Christ Church Grammar and Guildford Grammar School, respectively.

In addition to this major difference between English prep schools and Australian junior schools, there is another major difference which arises from the tendency of Australian independent secondary schools to be organised largely on denominational lines in each state. Australian junior schools naturally follow the same strong denominational pattern as their senior counterparts. Table 1 shows the denominational divide of junior schools in each state:

With regard to this table a major caveat needs to be issued apart from 'beware DPL-M's statistics!' This table is based on membership of the JSHAA and does not contain junior schools that may have been recently

Table 1

	Anglican	RC.	Uniting Church (including Continuing Presbyterian)	Jewish	Other Non-Conformist Schools	Non-Denominational Schools	Total
NSW	17	5	5	1	1	10	39
Qld	4	2	1	1	–	–	8
S A	3	4	4	–	–	–	11
Tas	2	2	1	–	1	–	6
Vic	17	4	8+1	1	1	3	35
WA	3	5	2	1	1	–	12
Totals	46	22	22	4	4	13	111

created, mainly in the Anglican tradition, and have not become members of JSHAA to my knowledge. For example, the Anglican Church in Western Australia, under the aegis of the Most Reverend Dr Peter Carnley, Archbishop of Perth, has been pursuing a policy in recent years of founding Anglican schools whose fees are much lower than those of the orthodox corporate Anglican schools.[21] But to return to the schools included in the above table, it may be beneficial, for the sake of clarity, to make observations on Australian prep schools on a state by state basis.

(a) New South Wales

In New South Wales there are two extant prep schools dating back to the nineteenth century: St Andrew's Cathedral School (1881) – the only choir school in Australia – and Tudor House Prep School (1897). St Andrew's Prep is more of a department within the Cathedral School than a discrete prep school as are so many of the English choir schools. Of these two nineteenth-century schools only Tudor House can be said to be in the normative mould of the English preparatory school being for a long while privately owned and situated in the heart of the country.

Although Tudor House today is part of the infrastructure of King's School, Parramatta,[22] it has not lost its earlier constitutional character. For all intents and purposes it has a high degree of autonomy but because its headmaster is finally answerable to The King's School Council, it must be seen as a good example of an Australian semi-autonomous or perhaps 'near autonomous' prep school. Certainly it was never intended that boys from Tudor House should go automatically to The King's School. This is a common enough assumption, however, amongst pupils of other Australian junior schools.

A good example, on the other hand, of a fully integrated junior school, in New South Wales, is Waverley College Junior School, owned by the Christian Brothers. It is a boys' Roman Catholic day school with a total population of more than 1200 boys, having begun in 1903 with only twenty-two boys and five Christian Brothers. In such an integrated constitution there has been only a 'teacher-in-charge' (rather than a headmaster) of the junior school. The College Board has been responsible for the general running of the junior school, for the enrolment of pupils, the hiring of teachers and the discipline of the students. This pattern of subordination by the current director of the junior school, Mrs Helen Newman, is very typical of many Australian junior schools.[23]

In contrast, Mosman Church of England Prep School is closer to the normative English prep school, and this despite its overtly denominational orientation. The founder of Mosman, Mr A. H. Yarnold, is a good example of a former assistant master of a public or corporate school becoming a successful prep school headmaster. Yarnold had been an assistant master at both The King's School, Parramatta (1896), and at Sydney Church of England Grammar School, commonly known as 'Shore'. He left 'Shore' to set up his own prep school in October, 1904, with twenty-four day boys. He was headmaster of Mosman until 1944 during which time he earned a reputation as the 'Australian Mr Chips' because of his longevity at Mosman. But the important point is that, notwithstanding the close ties of his school with 'Shore', Yarnold kept his autonomy despite rumours that his school was part of the Shore infrastructure; in theory it may have been, in fact, it was not.

Two prep schools which, constitutionally, form part of Sydney Grammar School (1854) are Sydney Grammar Edgecliff Preparatory School (1911)[24] and Sydney Grammar St Ives Preparatory School (1954). They exemplify the Australian concept of a prep school as being an *ad hoc* rather than an *ad omnia* institution. Any boy attending either school has a right[25] to go on to Sydney Grammar, a most prestigious Australian corporate school. Yet despite this nexus between the prep schools and Sydney Grammar School, there is a surprising degree of autonomy enjoyed by the junior schools, achieved partly by distance from the parent school and partly by deliberate policy. Mr John Maffey, former head of St Ives and a very experienced headmaster, for example, until he retired recently, believed that his school had the greatest measure of autonomy possible.

Amongst the Uniting Church schools a similar situation exists of two semi-autonomous prep schools serving Newington College: Wyvern House (1938) and Lindfield (1957). Both are **fully day** schools which is another feature that has been, and continues to be, widely adopted in Australia. Because Australia is a country of dense urban living, as well as a continent of vast desert spaces, there is a tendency not to have many, if any, boarding places in corporate schools. Boys, living in a metropolis, can travel to school daily. Perhaps the most interesting of NSW schools is that of Coogee Prep School (1914) at Randwick Junction in busy south-east Sydney. It is another wholly autonomous school with a distinctly nineteenth-century atmosphere. Old fashioned though it appears to be, it is immensely successful. It has at least two features reminding one of some English nineteenth-century prep schools: first, in eighty years, it has had only two principals: Mr W. M. Nimmo, the founder (1914-1964) and Mr A. N. Brown (1964–). Secondly, it is still a small school of just over a hundred and twenty boys as were so many English nineteenth-century prep schools. No English prep school, however, rents its premises from the local Presbyterian church and conducts its business in rooms above the church itself!

(b) Queensland

Despite the enormous size of Queensland (667,000 sq miles) – it is equal to 5.5 times the size of the British Isles[26] – it had only eight JSHAA member schools in 1986. One possible reason for this paucity of independent primary or junior schools has been the lack of independent secondary schools arising from the efficacy of Queensland's Grammar Schools Act (1860) which established state secular grammar schools. With such state competition it has been difficult for independent schools to flourish in Queensland. By the end of the nineteenth century, only Nudgee Roman Catholic College (1891), among extant schools, existed to compete with Queensland State Grammar Schools.

The earliest Anglican sally into providing prep schooling in Queensland was that by the Rev Canon Horace H. Dixon[27] who founded a prep school in 1901 which eventually became Southport Preparatory School to service Southport School. The master of the preparatory school is responsible to the headmaster for the day-to-day administration and general conduct of the school. He is not responsible, however, for the financial aspects of the school nor does he attend meetings of the school's governors, but he is on various advisory committees of the board of governors. This constitutional relationship of the prep school with the senior school is typical in Australia.

By far the most important prep school in the history of Queensland's education provision is Toowoomba Prep, which is the only fully autonomous prep school in Queensland. It is not constitutionally linked with any senior school, not even Toowoomba Grammar School. Moreover Toowoomba Prep is probably one of the best examples of an Australian prep school that developed very much on English lines. The school was founded in 1911 by E. A. Gill, an assistant master at Toowoomba Grammar. As such he was in the tradition of Lancelot Sanderson of Elstree and John Hawtrey of Aldin House, both of whom were translated public schoolmen from Harrow and Eton respectively. Gill began with thirteen day boys and four boarders and steadily built up his numbers. But the man responsible for building up the reputation of Toowoomba Prep as being one of Australia's leading preparatory schools was Norman Scott ('Boss') Connal. He was headmaster from 1929 to 1958. When he began in 1929 there were forty day boys and twenty-seven boarders. When he retired in 1958 there were 160 boarders and eighty-three days boys. Connal turned Toowoomba into one of Australia's most celebrated prep schools.

The other school of major importance among Queensland schools is the Church of England Grammar Prep School (1912) founded by the Rev W. P. F. Morris, a Christian Socialist who had spent a little time with Samuel Barnett at Toynbee Hall. He was also a proponent of Muscular Christianity being influenced by Charles Kingsley and, more quixotically, by the prowess of Viking rowers, as indicated by the school coat of arms chosen by Morris. Morris's ambition was to set up a senior school which he was encouraged to do by the Brisbane Diocese. From 1915 onwards both prep and grammar school worked in tandem. Although the present head of 'Churchie' prep school[28] is styled 'Headmaster of the Preparatory School', the two schools, senior and prep, function as an integrated unit. The present headmaster of the prep school regards his relationship with the senior school to be semi-autonomous, with his being responsible for the day-to-day administration of his school as well as for the syllabus and extracurricular activities.

(c) South Australia

Amongst the six Australian states, South Australia distinguishes itself with being the only one without a history of convicts. It was settled in the 1830s largely by nonconformist migrants so that one well-known history of the early years in South Australia is Douglas Pike's *Paradise of Dissent* (1957). In such circumstances one might expect to find a preponderance of nonconformist schools in the state. In fact there are just as many Roman Catholic corporate secondary schools in South Australia as there are nonconformist ones: four in each case. Moreover the jewel in the crown would be St Peter's College, an Anglican school modelled on St Peter's,

Westminster, and founded in 1847. Such an acknowledgment, however, might be hotly contested by those associated with Prince Alfred College, the flagship of the Uniting Church in South Australia.

To return to the world of prep schools there is only one extant prep school in South Australia that dates back to the nineteenth century. That school is St Andrew's School, founded in 1850. But although it is a member of the JSHAA, it is not a school in any way influenced by the English prep school. It has more in common with an Anglican parish school. From the beginning it was co-educational and during the twentieth century it began to adopt some Australian prep school characteristics. For example, during the rectorship of the Rev Cecil F. Eggleton (1944-1964), it became customary to appoint as head teachers, men from the independent secondary schools such as Mr Neville Pickford (1958-64) from Scotch College. The Rev Eggleton was in favour of small classes, too, so that his school had more in common with English prep schools than with parish schools. Boys began to win scholarships to St Peter's School so that St Andrew's, if not becoming a *de jure* prep school, became a *de facto* one. Moreover, the school in 1967 was renamed St Andrew's School rather than St Andrew's Church Day School, thus attempting more of a prep school ethos. School fees, a school badge and motto and school uniforms completed the transformation. Although St Andrew's is not a prep school in the English sense, it is sufficiently like one as to be recognised as a 'quasi-prep' school. Be that as it may, by its membership of the JSHAA it is an Australian junior school *per se*.

St Peter's College Prep School is of much later foundation than St Andrew's. The relationship between St Peter's prep school and Collegiate school has been one of the subordination of the former to the latter. The Rev Henry Girdlestone was the Collegiate headmaster (1894-1919) who established the prep school in 1910. Since then a series of prep school traditions has been established including the holding of a separate chapel service each morning[29] and a prefect system within the prep school. The latter measure was seen as a preparation of prep school boys for responsibilities in the Collegiate school. Other measures were taken to separate the activities of the senior and junior boys. The prep school held a separate swimming gala (1928) and sports day (1935). Masters-in-charge of the prep school from 1910 to 1953 were all former masters of the senior school but despite the close cultural and geographical proximity, it can be claimed that the prep school enjoys a semi-autonomous relationship with the Collegiate school. It would seem that, as with so many Australian junior schools, St Peter's Prep School is responsible for the day-to-day running but questions of overall policy are in the hands of the senior school headmaster.

Amongst Adelaide schools Prince Alfred College (PAC) is the great rival to St Peter's but the former is nevertheless somewhat socially inferior to the Anglican school. The PAC prep school was opened in 1911 as a device to boost numbers at the senior college. Throughout the depression period the Prince Alfred Prep School always had problems of recruitment which were reduced by the building of a new Spanish-style PAC prep building in 1937. Looking at PAC constitutionally, from 1911 to the 1980s, there have been only seven individuals responsible for the prep school. All of them have been styled 'master-in-charge' so that the headmaster of PAC in the 1980s expected 'to be informed of significant occurrences before the event and no autonomy [was] granted to the prep school master-in-charge regarding the appointment or release of staff'.[30]

This position of close integration between junior and senior school was replicated in yet two other South Australian schools: in the relationship between Scotch College and Scotch College Junior School (1919). From the beginning, Scotch College was proprietorial about the boys in its preparatory school. The purpose of the prep school was to prepare boys solely for Scotch College. As the school magazine declared quite explicitly, 'it is not the policy of the school to prepare boys for other schools'.[31] This forthright statement of subordination marks the school as quintessentially Australian in its eschewal of the conventional English private preparatory school policy of servicing several public schools. As far as Scotch was concerned, however, this integrated model of prep schooling did not continue after the Second World War. The late Mr Robert (Bob) Gilchrist was appointed master-in-charge in 1948 but from then on he toiled to change the constitutional position of the prep school *vis-à-vis* Scotch College. From 1950 onwards, when new school buildings were provided, Scotch College Prep School began to be less integrated and won a degree of autonomy. By 1954 Gilchrist was delivering his own headmaster's report[32] and had instituted a prep school prefect system. Gilchrist was helped in his push towards semi-autonomy by the change of head of Scotch College. Mr Gratton, of the old Australian mould who regarded the prep school as an integral part of his Scotch College, was replaced by P. C. W. Disney, an Englishman educated *inter alia* at the Dragon Prep School. Gilchrist and Disney together increased Scotch College Prep School's degree of autonomy, so that Gilchrist became truly a headmaster with almost total responsibility for the running of his school.

All this changed when Disney died suddenly in 1961 and the Hon. Charles Fisher succeeded as headmaster of Scotch and proceeded to clip Gilchrist's wings.[33] If generalisation is permissible from this instance, it could be observed that in the matter of autonomy of prep schools much depends on the personality and character of the prep school head and especially of the head of the senior school. During his time at Scotch (1962-69) Charles Fisher restored the former integrated character of Scotch College and Scotch College Prep School.

(d) Tasmania

The Hutchins School (1846) and Launceston Church Grammar School (1846), Tasmania, are two of the oldest corporate schools in Australia. Launceston Church Grammar School claims to be the oldest boys' public school in Australia with a continuous unbroken history.[34] It perhaps might be borne in mind that the Australian tendency to produce *ad hoc* links between independent 'secondary and primary' schools is likely to be accentuated in the relatively sea-girt state of Tasmania where, for example, in Hobart, Hutchins prep school boys are very likely to go to **The Hutchins** school. Given that circumstance, the record of both The Hutchins School and Launceston Church Grammar School is one of close co-ordination between their respective senior and junior schools.

It would seem that Launceston Grammar did not acquire a prep school until 1931 when it took over a recently defunct dame school in Launceston. According to the school's historian, Basil W. Rait, Mrs F. S. Nightingale[35] ran the newly acquired prep school as an integral part of the senior school. It prospered and new premises were provided in 1935 for the burgeoning school. Known as 'Little Grammar', the school passed on its pupils at the age of ten to the senior school. Rait describes it as being 'now an integral part of the school's jurisdiction'.[36] Earlier Rait had suggested that the prep school was a 'fine nursery for the big school'.[37] In 1955, however, there was a movement towards a modest separation of the schools' activities so that for the first time the junior school had its own speech day. This chimed with the more recent developments of separate chapel services, assemblies, athletics sports and swimming carnivals.[38]

The degree of integration between senior and preparatory school was much the same at The Hutchins School, Hobart. It would seem that awareness of the presence of junior boys at The Hutchins School occurred earlier than at Launceston. In 1887 the existence of a 'Lower School' was acknowledged when the Lower School 'worked for two hours on Saturday as a preparation for the Higher School'.[39] Such a reference by the school's later historian, Dr Geoffrey Stephens, is a little vague but there was nothing vague about his reference to a dame prep school in the 1890s run in Hobart by a Miss Paten which by 1899 was 'a preparatory section of Hutchins.'[40] By 1919 a fully operational junior school was established next to the senior school.[41] During the 1950s the junior school was moved, from Macquarie Street where the senior school was sited, to Sandy Bay, where it preceded the removal of the senior school to that site. But as Geoffrey Stephens has observed, it was 'an integral part of Hutchins'.[42]

Both The Hutchins Prep School and Launceston Church Grammar Prep School could be said to be conforming to the Australian norm of either a semi-autonomous or fully integrated existence. A glance, too, at the history of the Friends' School in Hobart confirms this trend of integration where – although two prep schools were set up in 1925 at Sandy Bay and at Lindisfarne – they were 'planned as feeders for the main school',[43] i.e. they were as much a means to an end as they were ends in themselves. Although the examination of Tasmanian prep schools has been a little perfunctory, the normative trend of Australian junior schools still comes through.

(e) Victoria

In so far as Melbourne regards itself as the most sophisticated and cosmopolitan city in Australia, notwithstanding the claims of brash Sydney, it could be expected that its system of independent schools would reflect that sophistication or superiority, and it does. Victoria is the only state that has had an inherent class system for some time amongst its independent schools. This 'class system' is seen clearly, despite Australia's egalitarian reputation, in the two levels of independent school in Victoria, each of which is served by its own schools' association. The élite group of eleven schools is called the Associated Public Schools of Victoria (APSV 1877)[44] whilst members of the second group are known as the Associated Grammar Schools (1920s).

Looking first at the APSV prep schools, the established pattern has been one of little autonomy for the prep schools even when they are sited apart. Scotch College Junior School (1862) is a typical example of this institutional integration with both schools on the **same** site. But even when the prep schools are on different sites from their parent school, the degree of autonomy is very measured. Wadhurst (1886) and Grimwade House (1918), the two feeder schools of Melbourne Church of England Grammar School, experience only a limited measure of autonomy. Such concern for their respective lower schools in Australian corporate schools is understandable since their own future institutional health is at stake.

Geelong College (1861), the leading Uniting Church School in the state, had a similar background of integration. Geelong College Preparatory School was not founded until 1921 under the aegis of the college's energetic and distinguished headmaster, the Rev F. W. Rolland (1920-1945) and its *raison d'être* lay in 'feeding' the senior school with a stream of young boys. As was customary in Australia, the first two individuals to be made responsible for Geelong College Prep School were styled 'master-in-charge', but the third incumbent, Mr L. J. Campbell, who was there from 1931 to 1962, became the first 'headmaster' *per se*. Under his guidance, or direction, the prep school moved to a nearby location giving the prep school a degree of topographical distance from the college. The prep began to have separate assemblies from the College in 1942. Geelong College prep school, under L. J. Campbell, is a good example of how a prep school's relations with its senior school can change. Parmenidean permanence is a mirage. As early as 1921 the prep school had its own *Prep School News*. In 1934, during Campbell's headship, the first prep school speech night was held, after which many separate prep school functions were similarly held. Since the 1960s the two schools have operated separately with no 'staff sharing'. Today there is a principal at Geelong College who, with the College Council, controls and administers both the senior and the preparatory schools. The two schools share the same constitution but, according to Mr E. C. McLean, the College archivist, there has been a trend at Geelong College for greater prep school autonomy. Both the senior and the prep school have their own headmasters who report to the principal. The principal has the ultimate say on staff selection, but the prep school head has a large say in the appointment of his own staff.[45]

Similar shifts in degrees of autonomy occurred, too, at Wesley College, where L. A. Adamson, a major Australian Arnoldian, was headmaster from 1902 to 1932. During Adamson's time the prep school was very much part of the senior school. As the 1908 school prospectus stated: [the prep school is] 'an integral part of the college and the boys [are] made to feel that they [are] members of a big Public School'.[46] After Adamson retired, however, the Wesley Prep School, under Mr Edward A. Wells as headmaster from 1936 to 1965, began to enjoy a great measure of autonomy. Admittedly the Second World War helped this process when the two schools were deprived of their respective school buildings to allow them to be used for the war effort. During the headship of Wells the junior school was run almost as a separate school, enjoying a great degree of autonomy.

Both the case of Geelong College Prep School and Wesley Junior School show that the historian of education has to display caution in assessing the degrees of autonomy amongst prep schools. Two cogent points can be made:

(i) A prep or junior school can enjoy a degree of autonomy from the senior school despite close physical proximity. More depends on the personalities of the two heads; and

(ii) Neither hegemony nor autonomy are static categories. There is constant movement with the trend in the 1980s/1990s being towards greater devolution and freedom of decision.

One major characteristic that is typical of Victorian schools is the tendency for the corporate schools to run not one but two feeder prep schools. Examples of such an arrangement are to be found with Caulfield Grammar School (1881) and Malvern House (1961) and Wheelers Hill (1981); Melbourne Grammar School (1858) with Wadhurst (1886) and Grimwade House (1918); Xavier College (1878) with Burke Hall (1921) and Kostka Hall (1937); Haileybury Grammar (1892) with Castlefield (1969) and Newlands (1975). But the best example of this Victorian tendency is that of Geelong Grammar which not only has two boys' prep schools in tow, Glamorgan at Toorak (1887) and Highton (1924), but also embraced co-education in the early 1970s at both junior and senior levels. These, together with the Geelong experimental year at 'Timbertop', made Geelong Grammar School a unique scholastic empire. The relatively large size of the Victorian preparatory or junior schools compared with their English counterparts constitutes another chief characteristic of these schools. They tend to be large feeder schools ensuring a steady supply of boys (and girls) into the corporate schools as the following table shows.

Table 2

Junior School Populations in 1984

Geelong College Junior School	467 boys and girls
Combined Geelong Grammar Junior Schools	680 boys and girls
Combined Haileybury Junior Schools	840 boys
Combined Melbourne Grammar Junior Schools	820 boys and girls
Scotch College Junior School	465 boys
Wesley College Junior School	728 boys and girls
Xavier Preparatory Schools	736 boys

Even the junior schools of Associated Grammar Schools, though relatively small themselves, in typically Australian fashion have junior or prep schools that by English standards are still very large. For example, in 1984, Yarra Valley Anglican Junior School had 407 boys; Mentone Grammar Junior School had 480 boys and Kinnoul de la Salle Junior College had 486 boys. There is a tendency, too, in these Associated Grammar Schools to divide the school up into three parts as do Ivanhoe Grammar School and Camberwell Grammar School, the prep school being the equivalent of the English pre-prep stage (grades 1-3) and the junior school the next stage (grades 4-6).

The impression given so far about Victorian schools is one of almost uniform subordination of the prep or junior schools to their senior schools: the very essence of Australian prep schools. But it has been suggested that this may vary according to the personalities of individual heads or even of individual councils. By and large, however, the Australian pattern of prep schooling is very discernible.

One school in Victoria that stands out in all this is Christ Church Grammar School which despite its nomenclature is a prep school without a corresponding senior school. It is, therefore, fully autonomous. It is the only one in Victoria. 'Grammar School' it may be styled, but its intake is from kindergarten to year six, i.e. from three years to eleven plus. Moreover it was run by a Mrs Edna Bingham ([?] to 1958) when it was conducted by a Mrs Josephine Oldham. It has been, therefore, a twentieth-century dame prep school. Today, whilst remaining in the JSHAA, Christ Church Grammar School is the only parish primary school in Victoria. If it were in England, it would probably be subject to 'voluntary aided' status, yet in England voluntary aided primary schools are not 'feeders' of public schools. Australia is not just the home of exotica such as the platypus and the kangaroo!

(f) Western Australia

To return to the less exotic, the prep schools of Western Australia have a uniformity about them with regard to their constitutional position *vis-à-vis* their respective senior schools that form a fitting conclusion to the examination of Australian prep schools. They are uniformly normative, that is they are all junior schools of their respective senior schools and without exception are located on the same site as the senior schools. Moreover, apart from the head of Christ Church Preparatory School, whose title is 'Master of the Preparatory School' and the head of Newman College Junior School whose title is 'Headmaster', the title of the other nine prep school heads is 'master-in-charge' which as we have seen is the signal for little autonomy being enjoyed by the junior school. But if that generalisation is largely valid, it is not so in all cases. Much depends, as suggested previously, on the personalities involved. It is worth noting that at Christ Church the headmaster of the senior school, Mr Jeremy Madin, gives the 'Master of the Preparatory School' wide discretionary powers with regard to the prep school, that is, if the comments of two unnamed but intelligent and perceptive parents have any validity.

This concludes the observations to be made on Australian preparatory schools. We now turn to the prep schools of New Zealand and are struck immediately by several differences between the two antipodean systems.

Preparatory schools in New Zealand

One might begin this third part with a paradox about New Zealand schools *vis-à-vis* Australian junior schools. Whereas there are, *pro rata*, more *ad omnia* prep schools in New Zealand, approximating more closely to the normative English nineteenth-century preparatory school, than in Australia (where, as demonstrated, the majority are *ad hoc* junior schools), some of the New Zealand schools show decidedly idiosyncratic features. In other words, although the British and New Zealand schools have much in common, some of the latter, for example, St Michael and All Angels' Church Day School, Christchurch (1851), are very different, showing closer approximation in this case to the English voluntary primary school system. But the majority of New Zealand schools do show a close resemblance to various types of English prep school, and this despite the evident influence of Scotland on New Zealand (especially in the South Island). Of twenty-one New Zealand prep schools only seven could be said to be attached formally to secondary schools. Four of those seven are Presbyterian schools[47] and are therefore denominational, replicating the Australian senior-junior school nexus. The other three prep schools linked with seniors are: Cathedral School, Christchurch, which has first year secondary boys only and is therefore much more of a prep school than an all-age school. This leaves only St Peter's, Cambridge, (1935) which began life as a normative English-style prep school and Dilworth (1894) which is a peculiarly New Zealand prep school and has a strong whiff of charity about it. The remaining fourteen New Zealand prep schools have the *ad omnia* character of English prep schools of not being attached to any particular secondary school.

But not only do New Zealand prep schools have more in common with English prep schools compared with Australian junior schools but also, paradoxically, they are more heterogeneous than either of the other systems, and it is this **heterogeneity** which will form the cynosure of the rest of this study.

Nelson College Preparatory School (1856) is perhaps the most divergent of all New Zealand prep schools and, *a fortiori*, of other schools in England and Australia. Its uniqueness lies in the fact that at Nelson a quasi-prep school charging fees for twenty-six boys and twenty-six girls exists officially attached to a state secondary school which is what Nelson College now is. This prep school arrangement consists of **two** prep schools, one for girls and one for boys and each consists of two forms only. Each form contains exactly twenty-six scholars so that at any one time there are fifty-two pupils on scholarship. This unique arrangement is an accident of history.[48]

The **Cathedral Grammar School, Christchurch,** like Christ Church Grammar School, Melbourne, may have the nomenclature of a Grammar School but is nevertheless largely a prep school. As such, it strongly exhibits New Zealand heterogeneity. **Hereworth School (1882-1901)** is dated thus to signify that it is a school that like Stoke-Brunswick in Sussex, England, is an amalgam of two schools: **Heretaunga** (1882) and **Hurworth** School (1901). Both Heretaunga and Hurworth were in the English tradition.

Dilworth Prep School (1894) distinguishes itself, as already noted, by being the New Zealand prep school, which apart from the four Presbyterian prep schools, most approximates to the Australian junior school model. It also has had an unusual history by being concerned with importing orphans from Ireland since Dilworth School is based on a very generous benefaction, administered by a Trust Board. **Huntley School** (1895) founded a year after Dilworth is positively orthodox by comparison, having developed along English nineteenth-century lines. It was founded as a private prep school by two expatriate Englishmen, one a Rugbeian, the other a Wykehamist. **King's School, Auckland** (1896) is the largest New Zealand prep school and is the flagship of those institutions, preparing boys for both King's College and for Auckland Grammar School. It is a large school, too, of more than 500 boys and therefore much larger than most English prep schools.

The New Zealand schools considered so far were all founded, with the exception of Hurworth (1901) in the nineteenth century. Consideration will now be given to twentieth-century foundations, in chronological order. **Waihi Preparatory School,** founded by an old Salopian, Joseph R. Orford in 1907, is distinguished by being the only New Zealand prep school which is still 100 per cent boarding. Furthermore, it has another nineteenth-century English feature: it is very small. It had only ninety-six pupils in 1988. Moreover in 1988 it had had since 1907 only four heads including the present head, Mr Peter Prosser. A greater contrast with the day school King's with more than 500 boys cannot be imagined. Orford, the foundation head, was both a distinguished scholar and athlete having gained a triple Blue at Cambridge, 1st class honours in *Literae Humaniores* and the coveted Porson prize for Greek. The most significant aspect of Orford's school in the South Island is its total independence of any senior school.

Southwell Prep School (1911) is another New Zealand prep school founded by an expatriate Englishman, Cecil E. Ferris. It began very humbly with one pupil but today it is one of the leading prep schools in New Zealand. It was the first New Zealand prep school to be elected to the Incorporated Association of Preparatory Schools which is very appropriate since it is so redolent of a traditional English prep school.

Wellesley College (1915), just outside Wellington, despite its nomenclature, is a preparatory, and not a secondary, school. It also has a most complex history, involving four schools, too involved for inclusion in this study. Suffice it to observe that the antecedents of Wellesley College are to be found in both an early twentieth-century dame prep school and a similarly early secondary commercial school. Today Wellesley College is distinguished for its 'progressive education' image arising from the imaginative regime of Mr Graeme Dreadon. It is a mark of his progressivism that although many of his boys go on to independent secondary schools such as Scots College, Wellington College, Wanganui Collegiate School and Rathkeale, the **majority** of its leavers go to local state schools, particularly Hutt Valley High. What English prep school sends most of its leavers to a locally maintained school?

There are some prep schools in New Zealand, however, that are 'orthodox' in their practice. **Scots College Primary School** (1916), for example, has from its beginning been fully integrated with Scots College. In 1987, for example, 95 per cent of the 230 boys went on to the college. For New Zealanders, such a performance is unorthodox. **St Andrew's College Preparatory School,** Christchurch (1917), however, is similar to Scots College Primary School, Wellington, in its being integrated with the senior school. Perhaps it is the preponderance of a Scottish tradition or a cross-Tasman tradition that prevails in these two clearly Scottish orientated schools.

St Mark's Church School (1917), Wellington, is not unlike St Michael and All Angels' School, Christchurch, in that it is a 'co-educational preparatory Church day school' charging fees. In English terminology it would be seen, apart from the fees, to be a voluntary aided primary school. But St Mark's and St Michael's are good examples of New Zealand unorthodoxy or idiosyncrasy.

To return to a more English style prep school, **Medbury** (1923) is the only New Zealand prep school that has shown any dynastic tendency[49] as did so many English prep schools in the nineteenth century. Such a tendency at Medbury has been brief but the school **has** been governed by more than one generation of Chennells: Eric Chennells and his son Frank Chennells. The school itself was run from 1923 onwards like any autonomous private prep school in England.

St George's Prep School, Wanganui (1927) is yet another example of New Zealand heterogeneity in so far as it was a purpose-designed school, designed to replace the closure of Hurworth School in that year.[50] St George's was in close association with Wanganui Collegiate School but despite its close association was not constitutionally linked, any more than West Downs, a purpose-designed English prep school, conducted at one stage by Lionel Helbert,[51] was in any way constitutionally linked with Winchester to which it sent some of its boys.

The foundational headmaster of St George's, Wanganui, was a Mr Maurice Fell, an Oxford graduate, who ruled his school with a quixotic hand from 1927 to 1947. He was a strong disciple of Miss Charlotte Mason and her Parents National Education Union (PNEU) which was based on principles of authority and obedience. Fell, 'an almost Blimp-like figure', was a great upholder of English middle-class values in the antipodes.

St George's has, since its inception, changed its focus and charter. In 1927 it was constituted as a boys' boarding prep school. Today it is a co-educational day school. Since 1979 it has been preparing about a third of its Form 2 pupils for **state** schools.[52] This is, of course, a very significant departure from the purpose of orthodox prep schools. Constitutionally St George's is very unusual since today it is a co-educational day school feeding Wanganui Collegiate School, a boarding school for boys only. The two schools are governed by the Wanganui College Board of Trustees: the college directly, the prep indirectly. There is, however, a management committee responsible for the running of St George's, consisting of four main board members and four parent representatives. Compared with many English prep schools, St George's constitution is very unusual.

But if St George's constitution is strange to English readers, the constitution of **Hadlow School** (1929) is even more unusual. Hadlow began as a private preparatory school owned by Mr Alexander Don in 1929 but survived into the 1960s only by being taken over by the Trinity School Trust in 1954.[53] The Trinity School Trust consists today of St Matthew's Collegiate School, a private school for girls and younger boys; Hadlow Prep School, and Rathkeale College for Boys (1964). In 1971 Hadlow School became a co-educational prep school thus becoming preparatory to both Rathkeale College for Boys and St Matthew's Collegiate School for Girls.

It can be said that there is no English equivalent to such a constitutional arrangement, the most comparable being the group of Downsend schools consisting of Downsend, a boys' day prep school and five other associated prep schools.[54]

St Peter's School, Cambridge (1935) (see p. 77) is an all-age boys' day and boarding and girls' day school operating under St Peter's School Trust Board. It began as a boys' boarding school, the creation of Mr Arthur Broadhurst, a wealthy Englishman and an alumnus of West Downs Preparatory School, run by Lionel Helbert (see note 51). There is no need to rehearse the several constitutional changes which St Peter's has undergone.[55] In recent years (1985) Mostyn House in Cheshire has experienced a similar metamorphosis in so far as it now has boys, in addition to those of normal prep school age, from the age of thirteen to sixteen, thus having a preparatory and senior school combined. *Pace* this Mostyn House development, St Peter's own constitutional development is most un-English.

Two further prep schools require some brief attention before this survey of New Zealand schools is completed. **Lindisfarne College** (1953) is a Presbyterian boys' day and boarding school but only the two lowest forms are of prep school age. It is a school following the Australian denominational paradigm. Finally, **St Kentigern School** (1959) is the prep school of St Kentigern College (1953), educating boys from five to thirteen. Because it is in a different location it has a very considerable degree of autonomy. The senior forms of the prep school share some of the senior school's facilities. But only 40 per cent of the school's pupils go on to the college. Some 45 per cent go to Auckland Grammar whilst another 10 per cent go to King's College. The remaining 5 per cent go on to state high schools. Because of this diversity in transfer of boys, St Kentigern's School is more like many English prep schools than the normative Australian junior school with its *ad hoc* arrangements.

From this very brief survey of New Zealand prep schools it can be seen quite clearly that the chief characteristic of New Zealand prep schools is their **heterogeneity.** Their founders have often been enthusiastic Englishmen like J. R. Orford of Waihi or A. J. B. Broadhurst of St Peter's. Southwell, Medbury and St George's, Wanganui, too, all exhibit this strong English influence. Heterogeneity is very evident, likewise, in the background of Wellesley College and in the history of Hadlow School of the Trinity Trust.

Conclusion

New Zealand prep schools have shown the same *ad omnia* principle which, in the nineteenth century, had been normative for most English prep schools. Australian schools on the other hand have widely practised the *ad hoc* principle in which senior schools have close oversight of their junior schools. New Zealand prep schools whilst approximating more closely to English prep schools, on the other hand, have displayed the greatest degree of heterogeneity.

Australian and New Zealand prep schools, therefore, whilst sharing the same origins of the mother country have developed differently – which phenomenon is not uncommon in families! Finally, it might be observed that since 1981 English prep schools, as a whole, have taken on a similar characteristic of heterogeneity (cf. Mostyn House *et al.),* which has hitherto been *sui generis* to New Zealand schools.

References

1 *The Rise of the English Prep School* (1984) was concerned only with boys' prep schools and following that precedent this essay, in the main, is similarly concerned only with boys' schools. Moreover the term 'prep' has been used interchangeably and frequently with the term 'preparatory'.

2 *Independent Schools Yearbook 1992-1993*, A & C Black, p. 799.

3 cf. Donald Leinster-Mackay, *The Rise of the English Prep School*, The Falmer Press, 1984, *passim*.

4 Jeffrey Bernard, *The Spectator*, 27 March 1993, p. 49.

5 I. S. M. Hamilton, *When I Was a Boy*, Faber & Faber, p. 104.

6 See *Such, Such Were the Joys, Enemies of Promise* and *Goodbye to all That*.

7 Cheam was founded in 1645 as a private classical school but it was not till 1855 that it became officially a prep school, i.e. preparing boys between 8 and 13 specifically for public school. This occurred when the new headmaster, Mr R. S. Tabor, decided to concentrate on the preparation of younger boys for public school.

8 See Donald Leinster-Mackay, *The English Private School 1830-1914 with special reference to the Private Preparatory School*, Vols. 1-3, Ph.D, Durham University, 1972.

9 Such was the renown of his scholarship that his library was bought up by the British Museum Library.

10 See obituary on the Rev J. M. Furness, *Prep Schools Review*, Vol. 3, No. 20. December 1901.

11 The Rev Lancelot Sanderson was advised by his headmaster at Harrow, the Rev H. Montagu Butler, to seek his fortunes elsewhere because his 2nd class honours degree would probably diminish his chances of his being a housemaster at Harrow.

12 See Philip L. Masters, *Preparatory Schools Today: Some Facts and Inferences*, Adam and Charles Black, 1966, p. 23.

13 The Parents National Education Union (PNEU) was founded by Miss Charlotte Mason (1842-1923) of the House of Education, Ambleside, in 1903. Its aim was to assist the home in laying the foundations for the sound education of young children. This sound education was based on several premisses one of which was the infinite attention span.

14 *Independent Schools Yearbook*, 1992-1993, p. 799.

15 Rugby now has about 30 per cent of its pupils drawn from the Midland area. Martin Van der Weyer 'Marketing the Old School Tie' *The Spectator* , 4 September 1993, p. 21.

16 This, of course, does vary with individual schools.

17 *The Spectator*, 4 September 1993, p. 21.

18 Ibid.

19 This author can remember the terms 'ad hoc' and 'ad omnia' being used extensively at the History of Education Society Conference in December 1968 by Mr John Stocks when speaking on 'Scotland's *ad hoc* authorities 1919-1930'. At this same conference, Dr Peter Gosden gave a paper entitled 'Technical

Instruction Committees'. Both papers were later published in the volume entitled *Studies in the Government and Control of Education Since 1860*, Methuen, 1970.

20 Winchester conducts its own examinations and does not, therefore, participate in the Common Entrance Examinations.

21 See Clem Wright, 'Financial Foundations, Other Christians, and Outer Suburbia: the development of independent secondary schools in Western Australia since 1945'. The University of Western Australia M.Ed. Dissertation 1988. Appendix 1.

22 The relationship between The King's School and Tudor House is changing. Tudor House boys are being encouraged to enter King's School as boarders but since the numbers at Tudor House have been down in recent years because of the recession, the impact has not been great. The boarding numbers at King's in 1993 were only 55 per cent of the possible capacity. [I am grateful to Peter Yeend of The King's School for this information.]

23 Other prep schools in NSW that *inter alia* have similar constitutional ties with their senior schools are: The King's School Preparatory School, ('Gowan Brae' since 1955); St Aloysius College Junior School (1908); Barker College Junior School (1944).

24 Edgecliff Preparatory School is a good example of an Australian dame/prep school. The school was owned by a Miss Isobel van Heuckelum, who retired in 1956 in her mid-eighties.

25 The same does not apply at The King's School. Neither from Tudor House nor the TKS Prep School have the boys the **right** to enter the senior school. Admittedly very few are rejected but rejection is possible. [I am grateful to Peter Yeend for this affirmation.]

26 *Whitaker's Almanack*, 1983, p. 718.

27 He had been a housemaster at Warkworth House School in Cambridge and was an experienced schoolmaster.

28 The Church of England Grammar School, Brisbane, has been known for generations as 'Churchie'.

29 *St Peter's College Magazine*, No. 103, May 1920, p. 19.

30 From answer to questionnaire (1986) in my possession.

31 *Scotch College Magazine*, Vol. 2, No. 2. First term, 1922, p. 2.

32 Having gained the title of 'Headmaster' of the Prep School in 1950.

33 Gilchrist no longer delivered his own headmaster's report but had it incorporated in the report of Scotch College itself.

34 H. Vernon Jones, *The Story of the Launceston Church Grammar School 1946-1971*. Launceston, 1971, p. 1. Though an older school, King's School Parramatta's history is not unbroken.

35 Miss Nightingale ran the prep school from 1931 to 1946 with much distinction and part of the school is named after her.

36 Basil V. Rait, *The Story of the Launceston Church Grammar School 1946-1971*, Vol. 4, Launceston, 1946, p. 197.

37 Basil V. Rait, *The Story of the Launceston Church Grammar School 1946-1971*, Vol. 1, Launceston, 1946, p. 82.

38 H. Vernon Jones, *op. cit.*, p. 38.

39 Geoffrey Stephens, *The Hutchins School 1846-1965*, Hobart, 1979, p. 121.

40 Ibid., p. 148.

41 Ibid., p. 225.

42 Ibid., p. 339.

43 W. N. Oats, *The Rose and the Waratah, The Friends' School, Hobart, 1832-1945*, Hobart, 1979, p. 239. Despite the title of this book the Friends' School in Hobart was not founded until 1885.

44 The eleven members of APSV are Melbourne Grammar, Geelong Grammar, Wesley College, Scotch College, Xavier College (1901), Geelong College (1908), St Kevin's College, Brighton Grammar, Carey Grammar, Caulfield Grammar and Haileybury Grammar.

45 From interview with Mr E. C. McLean on 19 August 1986 with Dr Ian Wilkinson, research assistant.

46 Wesley College Preparatory School Prospectus 1908, p. 36.

47 St Andrew's College (1916); Scots College (1916); John McGlashan College (1918) and St Kentigern (1959).

48 See D. P. Leinster-Mackay, *Prep Schools Down Under*, Chapter 9, soon to be published.

49 In Australia, where the opportunities for scholastic dynasticism are many fewer because of the overall characteristic of *ad hoc* junior schools, one good example of dynasticism is Mosman Prep School, Sydney. Yarnold's son-in-law succeeded him at Mosman Prep and he was succeeded in turn by his son-in-law before an outsider was appointed.

50 H. E. Sturge, an old Wykehamist, was the owner-headmaster of Hurworth Prep School in Wanganui. He left Wanganui in 1927 to link up with Heretaunga School and form Hereworth school.

51 See D. P. Leinster-Mackay, *op. cit.*, p. 139. For a full treatment of Helbert see Nowell C. Smith, *Memorials of Lionel Helbert*, Oxford University Press, 1926.

52 There is a catch in the statement since it refers to the practice of 80 per cent of the girls going to State schools in the absence of a girls' equivalent of Wanganui Collegiate Boys' School.

53 For details of the tragedy of Hadlow school's first headmaster see D. P. Leinster-Mackay, *Prep Schools Down Under* (to be published).

54 These consist of Downsend Lodge, Ashtead, mixed school for pupils between 3-7; Downsend Lodge, Epsom a school with similar age range; Downsend Lodge, Leatherhead, a similar mixed school; Dowsend Lodge, Rowans – a similar school and Dowsend Lodge, Senior Girls for girls between 7 and 13. See *Independent Schools Yearbook*, 1992-1993, pp. 910-911.

55 See F. A. L. Bull, 'Structa Saxo' (founded upon a rock); the Genesis and Development of A. F. B. Broadhurst English Style Preparatory Boarding School for Boys, St Peter's School, Cambridge, New Zealand, 1936-1978. M.A. thesis. See also D. P. Leinster-Mackay, *Prep Schools Down Under*, (to be published).

CHAPTER FOUR

The pathos of policy:
Adult education as a contribution to the British occupation in Germany, 1945–55

STUART MARRIOTT

Re-educating Germany

This chapter opens as the celebration of a rather inexact anniversary. In Britain fifty years ago numerous agencies of government and the armed services were at work planning how Germany was to be occupied and controlled once the Second World War was over. For some time previously publicists and back-room advisers had been debating what was called 're-education', the idea that future security in Europe would depend on the victorious Allies' being able to bring about a permanent reform of the German national character.[1] Though the notion was controversial, and by no means uniformly well received among the policy élite, a Foreign Office 'Memorandum on the Re-education of Germany' was approved by the War Cabinet in 1944. The task as presented there was conceived in terms of the democratic reconstruction of social and political institutions. But inseparable was the sense that after the war the German people would have to go through a great deal of 'unlearning'; and there seems to have been an assumption that 'adult education' would be called on to play its part in that process.[2]

A Control Commission for Germany was set up in 1944, and within it an Education Branch. It was envisaged that the latter would have eight sections, one of them specifically for Adult Education.[3] In the summer of 1945 Education Branch moved out to Germany, and was very soon provided with a basis on which to construct its activities. This was the inter-Allied Potsdam Agreement, which with misleading simplicity declared that the purposes of control included elimination of Nazi and militaristic tendencies, and supervision of German education so as 'to make possible the successful development of democratic ideas'. This chapter traces the subsequent fate of 'adult education', broadly and narrowly understood, as an element of British occupation policy and practice. The discussion treads a hesitant way among grandiose notions of ideological reconstruction, attempts at the 'cultural export' of institutions, and expressions of the art of the possible.[4]

Education Branch (as it remained until September 1949) counted at its peak some two hundred and fifty staff, though never more than six or seven specialist officers for adult education. (One survivor of that select band recalls that as a young man he was responsible for the educational condition of some two million German adults!) After 1949 the adult education specialists were even fewer. That may seem a slight foundation on which to erect a history, but an instructive story is there none the less.

From September 1945 there was a marked evolution of practice. Among the occupying powers the British began to distinguish themselves by an interventionist, even evangelical interpretation of the Potsdam agreement. A directive on administration, local and regional government was issued, which suggested that through the imposition of British concepts and methods the inhabitants of the zone were to experience a form of mass-training in democratic behaviour.[5]

In education itself the first and intensely practical concern was to organize the schools, to find enough passably intact accommodation and enough passably non-Nazi teachers to get the new scholastic year under way (a theme soon to be repeated with variations in the universities). Even so, a pervasive notion of re-education appears to have determined the climate in which education control officers operated.[6] In November 1945 the Commission codified all the policies which were already operative in a *Directive on Education, Youth Activities and German Church Affairs*. The immediate aim was 'to secure the earliest possible resumption of German educational activity while ensuring the elimination of National Socialist, nationalist and militarist doctrines, principles and methods'. The long-term purpose was 'to endeavour through the German educational system to awaken in Germans, individually and collectively' a sense of communal responsibility, respect for freedom of opinion and speech, and an interest in representative government,[7] a formulation which closely echoed the 're-education' proposals previously considered by government.

Rebuilding adult education

When freedom of assembly for non-political purposes was granted, in September 1945, the door opened for a resumption of associational and cultural life. At almost exactly the same time Educational Control Instructions No 18 (Vocational Education) and No 21 (Adult Education) appeared, requiring German local administrations to set up routines for planning and reporting work in these fields. According to the order issued by Military Government for the Düsseldorf area: 'Where local conditions permit German Authorities will be required forthwith to submit plans for the resumption of Adult Education at an early date ... There is no intention to dictate the lines along which Adult Education should develop in Germany. Nevertheless a form must be adopted at this stage which, while allowing the freedom necessary for healthy development, will permit of adequate control.'[8]

The adult education instruction did in fact involve a significant attempt to dictate, of a piece with the more general policy of requiring Germans to adopt 'democratic' methods. Organizers and teachers were to be strictly vetted (according to standard procedures for eliminating Nazi and militarist influences) but once approved they would have a free hand and there would be no pre-censorship of lectures or textbooks. However, a

D

'local committee' was to be established in each *Kreis* (the equivalent of a small county or county borough in England) 'to initiate and receive requests from interested voluntary organizations for any form of Adult Education'. An instruction was passed down that 'Those responsible should be encouraged to make the committee as widely representative as possible of local interests and to make provision in particular for the representation of women.'[9] That was obviously part of the democratization plan, and it may even have been a trial-run for introducing 'local education authorities' on the British pattern.

Education Branch was pressing at the same time for the appointment of administrators with special responsibility for out-of-school education. Viewing the two initiatives in a single perspective, one suspects that the 'local committee', with its implied separation of governance from administration, was intended as a typically British check on the resort the Germans could be expected typically to favour, that is, placing extensive authority in the hands of specialist officials.[10]

These early British interventions have hitherto not received proper acknowledgement. Hasenpusch, writing in 1977 without benefit of access to the official deposits of British records, inferred that, as soon as the way was open, interested Germans began to set up institutes for adult education. In this interpretation the initiative belonged entirely to *unbelasteten* ('non-guilty') civilians and local administrators, with the military authorities performing the 'negative' functions of security clearance.[11]

If adult education was to be re-established most of the practical effort, of course, had to come from the Germans, and in some areas they did produce a quick and energetic response. The first local committee for adult education appeared in October 1945 at Springe near Hannover, and *Volkshochschule Springe* was the first adult evening institute to open.[12] A surge of interest, voluntary and official, spread across Hannover and Lower Saxony. (Since this was the region to which Hasenpusch confined his research, he was accordingly prone to what one might call a 'patriotic misreading'.) But in the North Rhine region, for example, the voluntary response was weak and the German authorities dragged their feet over introducing the required administrative arrangements. There the result was a certain amount of hectoring from 'Mil. Gov.'[13]

Another 'positive' initiative of these early months was Education Branch's enquiry into women's education, led by Miss Jean Gemmell, who appears to have been responsible for adult education in the 1945–46 period. Although primarily concerned with access to conventional educational opportunities, her committee investigated the potential of women's voluntary organizations and began to press the example of the English women's and rural institutes on the Germans, the aim being, as the official *British Zone Review* later put it, to develop a 'liberal education in citizenship'.[14]

Formal adult education, particularly as organized through district *Volkshochschulen*, was inevitably the central preoccupation, and by March 1946 there were forty-two of these institutes in existence.[15] A zonal adult education conference was inaugurated in April 1946; from it emerged a co-ordinating group which functioned as a sub-committee of the zonal consultative committee for education.[16] Notwithstanding the serious paper shortage, revival of specialist publishing was encouraged. In May 1946, by arrangement with the home Ministry of Education, a small advisory party of HMI was brought to investigate adult education in the Zone and the British Sector of Berlin.[17]

The first eighteen months of the occupation were marked by an increasing tension between the priority which had to be given to 'negative' control and practical problem-solving, and the assumption that the British were surely in Germany to achieve something 'positive'. In February 1946 the head of Military Government circulated a memorandum on 'The problem in Germany', which queried in part what contribution the information and education services were making. Whereupon the director of Education Branch asked his staff 'to consider how far the Adult Education already being undertaken within the framework of the organized German education system was contributing towards the general re-education of the Germans away from their old-time beliefs in aggressive nationalism, militarism and the more recent one of Nazism'.[18]

The response, produced by the forthright Jean Gemmell, seems to have ruffled a few feathers. She pointed to the ineffectiveness of the *Volkshochschulen*, which were her concern; but devoted rather more words to attacking British parsimony and ineptitude in the handling of cinema, radio, newspapers, publicity, book supply and so on, all of which were the business of another department, Public Relations and Information Services Control.[19] Gemmell's memorandum was careless of military and administrative niceties, and also happened to raise awesome questions of what re-education really was, and of who could be expected to do anything about it.

Education Branch was discovering that democratic renewal was no straightforward task. The initiative over local committees for adult education never took off. Six months after the instruction had gone out German authorities were still being chided for slow progress. The HMI who visited in May 1946 concluded that the committees which did exist were in the grip of sectional interests; and some months after that Education Branch acknowledged that official requirements were being misunderstood or even flouted. Eventually it was conceded that the scheme had failed to secure any broadly-based representation of interests and needs.[20]

Another well-intentioned, and entirely abortive move of this early period was the so-called 'ABCA Scheme'. In February 1946, as part of the process of reinstating party-political activity, an item on 'Political Re-education' was added to the existing directive on administration and local government.[21] This led to an agreement within the Control Commission to institute a network of discussion groups, aimed at young adults, and supported by pamphlet publications. It would follow 'the general lines' of the British wartime Army Bureau of Current Affairs (the very successful 'ABCA'). Implementation was to be in the hands of the Germans themselves, subject to control through a small liaison team.[22]

In its inception the plan revealed the difficulty of putting re-education into practice. Political Division saw it as a device 'to bring the political parties out of the realms of abstract discussion and enable them to prove their ability to offer something to youth by showing the way to factual discussion of practical problems', and was anxious that control should be arranged so that any success could be credited to the emerging German political leaders. Education Branch envisaged a longer-term process: German politicians could not yet 'discuss controversial topics objectively', and the management should include 'some educationalists whose training makes them less inclined to be dogmatic'. The visiting HMI were aware of this tension, and not surprisingly supported Education Branch's emphasis on the longer-term process.[23]

As a compromise it was agreed to place the scheme with Information Services Control. There remained problems of finding the one liaison officer and one sergeant-assistant considered necessary to oversee the democratic re-socialization of hundreds of thousands of young German adults, and of securing £300 sterling for purchase of materials in Britain. Eventually the project was redirected into Education Branch, where it made great progress (on paper) for a time, and then foundered among the administrative shoals.[24]

Locating the policy

An interesting question arises about the extent to which those responsible for adult education in occupied Germany can be said to have been pursuing, at however distant a remove, British 'policy'. At this early period the Control Commission in the Zone and Berlin was accountable through the London-based Control Office for Germany and Austria (COGA) to the Chancellor of the Duchy of Lancaster. But it is significant that the deputy military governor, Lieutenant-General Sir Brian Robertson, speaking to a party of visiting parliamentarians in July 1946, described the Berlin headquarters of the Control Commission, with a certain military crispness, in these terms: 'This is the business end of the stick in the sense that it is here that policy is made and advice given to London.'[25]

Major James Mark (the control officer who undertook the first review of the German universities after the surrender) left Germany in the spring of 1946 to return to civilian employment in COGA, where he found the section which handled educational business to be of small significance in the total scheme of things. The officials had little stake in policy matters. Their job (as Mark later put it) was to act 'as intermediaries between people in England with a concern for education . . . and the experienced people in the Zone, who were dealing with education on the ground'. On the other hand, he recalled, there was an impressive level of public concern about German education, and within it 'a considerable ideological interest'.[26] Here lies a clue to that peculiar 'layering' of ideas about how Germany was to be managed, on account of which it so difficult to provide crisp answers to apparently crisp questions about what and where the policy was.

In the highest reaches of policy-making 're-education' was probably never much better than a slogan, never properly defined because of dissent and ambivalence over how such a notion was to be incorporated into British post-war security aims. At somewhat lower levels various lobbies and interest-groups continued to believe that the idea had practical significance. The Labour government, enjoying little leisure for setting out the details of the 're-education of Germany', had to face criticism from its own supporters on the left, from concerned public opinion and the popular press, and from an important Commons Select Committee, over its failure to impose any coherence. There was a dispute within the Labour Party about what some saw as a discreditable lack of concern for social-democratic reconstruction, and an inflammatory internal memorandum of March 1946 found its way out to Germany (where, one can be sure, there were sympathizers among the lower administrative ranks). The paper attacked the reactionary nonentities who were in charge of the Control Commission, and urged that a 'Labour' policy be implemented all the way down through its hierarchies. It accused Senior Officers of making 'no real or positive contribution', and alleged: 'Their only function is to decide as to whether administrative proposals from below conform to "policy" . . . In fact few people among the administrative or executive parts know what this "policy" is or whence it emanates.'[27]

Pakschies, the historian of re-education who uncovered an errant copy of this document in Germany, is surely too stark in identifying it as the source of the disquiet which continued through the summer of 1946.[28] Traces of cause and effect are obscured by the variety of contributions to the argument, and the confusion regarding what was to be done. Furthermore British intentions were in disarray as a result of the economic and political failures of so-called Four-Power control, and uncertainty about how long the occupation would continue.

Amidst all the oppressive difficulties evident by the spring of 1946, the 'educational' justification for the British presence received support from a perhaps unexpected quarter, the House of Commons Select Committee on Estimates. At the end of May the Committee had begun to investigate expenditure in Germany, and in July a sub-Committee visited the Zone and Berlin. Their concern was the circumstance ('probably without parallel in history') that a year after the end of a war the British taxpayer was still contributing £80m to the upkeep of the 'principal adversary'. British adherence to inter-Allied agreements on restraining German industry was producing a 'downward spiral' of morale and economic performance. Reporting in July 1946 the committee observed tellingly: 'If our policy is merely punitive and our desire is to make Germany an economic desert our stay should be as brief and economical as possible. If, however, we regard our stay in Germany as a mission – to change the German outlook and to create a new democratic spirit our expenditure in the building up of machinery for education, culture and moral regeneration will be fully justified.' However, the atmosphere of uncertainty was very damaging, particularly in the way it inhibited recruitment of 'Young, efficient men and women, imbued with proper tradition of service and fired with the moral purpose required'.[29]

Coincidentally or otherwise, shortly after the Select Committee reported Berlin was informed that the Cabinet Overseas Reconstruction Committee would soon be considering 'Re-education of Germany' and that a general statement of policy was required. Education Branch produced a response, and in the first week of September it was passed all the way upwards as a provisional but reasonable basis for 'the next stage of our Occupation'.[30] This was the 'Recommended Policy for Re-education in Germany', the interest of which lies in the attempt – by a subordinate agency of the Control Commission, and not by Westminster or Whitehall – to marshal ideas within some kind of coherent framework. Education Branch proposed extensive devolution to German authorities, and an end to the practice of keeping British-occupied areas isolated from the rest of the world; the time had come, it argued, for more positive and adventurous approaches.

The most ambitious section, and the most interesting from an adult educational point of view, dealt with 'Measures to be taken to combat the ignorance of the German people'. Prominent here were proposals for organizing 'personal contacts' abroad. The first approvals had in fact been given for German educationists to go to Britain, and more were being considered: 'particularly in contemplation are those of prominent Germans engaged in Adult Education . . . to confer with British authorities and see for themselves how work with Adults is organized in England'.

The document also made much of the ABCA scheme, now elevated into a grandiose plan for a publicly-incorporated Bureau of Citizenship, but only a month later Education Branch was to acknowledge that progress was blocked.[31] The autumn of 1946 saw the emergence of a rather different 'Anglo-German' programme in which Control Commission staff were encouraged to take part in German cultural and current-affairs groups. Helen Liddell from the Information Service of the Royal Institute of International Affairs, who visited during 1947, described the British staff as 'a body of able, disinterested and hardworking enthusiasts' particularly devoted to running these Anglo-German discussion groups.[32]

The Bureau of Citizenship was lost, though, not just because of administrative difficulties, but because by the end of 1946 the chance of imposing anything of the kind had disappeared. And if other ideas in the 'Recommended Policy' did now begin to turn into practice, it was because they were found capable of adaptation to a rather sudden and dramatic change in the political situation. This new alignment was brought about by Ordinance 57, which required the setting-up of popularly-elected *Land* (provincial) governments wielding extensive authority over civil affairs.

'Observing, assisting and advising'

Towards the end of 1946 Britain and the United States agreed to merge the economies of their two areas of Germany into the so-called Bizone. The real origin of this move, it has been suggested, lay in the determination of the British Foreign Secretary, Ernest Bevin, to set up defences against the spread of Communism from the East, and to involve the Americans in their construction. One repercussion in the British zone was that devolution of regional government had to be hurried along. To carry credibility the *Länder* now created needed to enjoy significant legislative powers, and educational and cultural affairs were among the obvious subjects for immediate transfer.

This sudden turn provoked severe accusations from educational experts in Britain and the Control Commission that such a transfer of responsibilities was decidedly premature. But it was already too late to resist; their priorities had fallen victim to the mismatch between re-education theory and more concrete political and strategic considerations.

Ordinance 57 is conventionally seen as ushering in a second phase of the occupation, requiring a move from 'control' to what was eventually codified as the task of 'observing, assisting and advising the Germans in regard to the democratisation of political life, social relations and education'.[33] In decreeing this change of course the home government was left with some explaining to do. Thus, at an Anglo-German conference held in London during the summer of 1947 an official spokesman declared that educational reconstruction (the new name for re-education) remained an important part of British policy, and henceforth would be pursued by building contacts between Germany and the rest of Europe.[34]

Some months previously, in a highly visible attempt to deflect accusations of a sell-out, the Foreign Office had devised the post of Educational Adviser to the Military Governor. The first occupant, Robert Birley, came from the headmastership of Charterhouse. The appointment was received with some indignation on the Labour left, but Birley was an acknowledged progressive in the world of the public schools, he was respectful of the German cultural heritage, had bearing and charm, and could be relied on to further the British cause. He immediately set about polishing the image and asserting the purposeful nature of his country's educational presence in Germany. In August 1947 the deputy military governor issued a statement which made clear that the Educational Adviser was engaged in 'work of co-ordination and direction' arising out of what was intended to be 'a bold comprehensive and consistent policy'. Nothing was said about the content of the policy, other than a vague reference to the need to 'exert a good influence' and 'present the British point of view'.[35]

What Birley actually did was to set the tone. He shunned references to 're-education', and made himself the champion of personal contact as the foundation of reconstruction. He did not invent this 'personal' approach. Before his appointment the field-staff of Education Branch seem to have been operating on a basis of partnership with their German clients, and perfecting their notable (to some, notorious) style of working informally and through contact 'on the ground'. Like them, Birley seems to have arrived at a realistic appreciation of what was possible – though in his case it also reflected the leanings of a public-school headmaster who had no taste for structural tinkering, and who placed his confidence in character building, the encouragement of a liberal élite, and the 'inner reform' of relationships and curricula within institutions.[36]

In September 1947, some five months after Birley had taken up office, members of the Select Committee on Estimates were back in Germany. Despite their anxiety to contain spending overseas, they felt able to report that 'if the creation of a new democratic spirit in Germany is to succeed, expenditure on such services as education must be accepted as essential'. The visitors took evidence from Birley, and seem to have been adequately impressed. They declared rousingly, 'Of all the tasks which confront British administrators in Germany, none surpasses that of recasting the German educational system', for this would lay 'a sure foundation for lasting peace'. The education specialists were working in 'an economic setting of universal and chronic shortages, against a dreary background of ruined cities, crumbling industries and general hopelessness'; they needed 'fine sincerity of purpose and strong moral fervour. Theirs is obviously a long-term task.'[37]

The committee reported to the Commons that there was a need for a clear policy, and an ambitious, long-term programme. Yet under Ordinance 57 'the British function can only be to advise and help'; even worse, educational efforts were being blighted by complete uncertainty as to the future. About that time Helen Liddell recorded 'a stultifying sense in the British zone of lack of policy in the highest quarters outside Germany'; enlightened intentions were being frustrated by lack of resources, and government needed to recognize that talk about re-education entailed a substantial and sustained commitment.[38]

Government was preoccupied with what one might call the strategic envelope rather than the detailed contents, and as a result of worsening East-West relations priority began to attach to the reinstatement of Germany, or at least the part not under Soviet control, as a political entity. After mid-1947 Marshall Aid contributed to the process by fuelling the economic recovery of the Western zones.

Birley was briefed by the Foreign Office, and there are hints of how educational matters began to accommodate to emerging political realities. Reporting on the year 1948/49 Education Branch described its overall task as being to present the British point of view, and secure 'the cultural integration of Germany into Europe'.[39] The work took on a cross-cultural aspect, with increasing use of conferences, summer schools, secondments and organized visits, involving Germany with Britain, and sometimes with Switzerland and Sweden. Adult education offered a congenial focus for this kind of work, and it had the added virtue of being clean of controversy. (One of the results of giving the *Länder* a free hand in educational legislation was that in the school sector old political and sectarian controversies continued to flare, and Education Branch did not wish to be singed.)

Inside the zone, reconstruction of the adult education system went ahead. Although there was none of the open conflict which resulted from the cultural imperialism the Americans began to practise once they had decided to remain in Europe and take a 'positive' line,[40] the encounter of British missionary zeal and German self-reconstruction in adult education had its peculiar tensions. The *Volkshochschule* was accepted as the obvious and natural mode of provision, but there were doubts about how it was developing institutionally.

Whether the British were worrying about the 'problematic side of the German character', the need for objective teaching, or the democratization of opportunity, the answer always seemed to lie in the ideas and methods of a genuine adult education movement – according to the current British understanding (and sometimes with a little Nordic garnish added). In two respects the British tried to work across rather than along the grain of German understandings, and in both respects failed. They tried to push the trade unions into adopting structures for general or civic adult education, and the universities into embracing extra-mural responsibilities.

The universities and adult education

In mid-1946 the visiting party of HMI noted that 'It has been one of the best features of Adult Education in Britain that the Universities have assumed some corporate responsibility for the dissemination of sound knowledge'; German universities should be awakened 'to their extra-mural responsibilities' and made accustomed 'to the idea of "Extension" work'. The 'Recommended Policy' which appeared soon afterwards stated categorically that it was proposed 'to require the German university authorities to consider the establishment of some form of regular extra-mural activity . . . in the field of general adult education'.[41] Only a few months later, as the powers of the new *Land* governments were being confirmed pell-mell, the chance of any such requiring had gone; and yet the extra-mural idea continued to play an important part in British advice-giving.

Early in 1947 a delegation from the Association of University Teachers toured the universities of the British Zone, and produced a rather condemnatory and pessimistic report.[42] The members of the Commons Select Committee who visited Germany some six months after the dons had gone home noted that 'the whole system of university education is ripe for overhaul' – adding, interestingly, that 'Extra-mural activities are merely social and do not serve any public need' – and proposed that British experts might be brought in to help.[43] The difficulty, though, was that the AUT report had proved something of an embarrassment;[44] Birley needed a more subtle approach, and he thought he had found it in the idea of an enquiry, not unlike a British royal commission, but entrusted largely to sympathetic Germans.

The membership of the resulting *Studienausschuß zur Hochschulreform* (study commission on reform of higher education) was announced in January 1948. Lord Lindsay, Master of Balliol, was the one British member, and a Swiss professor was included as a disinterested voice. Whatever the reason for choosing Lindsay, the significant point is that the resulting report was coloured through and through by his characteristic thinking: it has been said that much of the English translation reads like 'pure Lindsay', and unwary commentators have mistakenly referred to a 'Lindsay Report'.

The *Gutachten zur Hochschulreform* of November 1948[45] recommended a more socially diverse recruitment to universities, correctives to over-specialization, strengthening of the academic middle ranks as against the professoriate, and greater involvement of lay people in the general governance of institutions. (One German member of the commission sought inspiration in the charter of the University of Leeds, as translated by his local university control officer.)[46]

Lindsay's own concerns were particularly evident in the proposals for raising the esteem of teaching and strengthening social studies, but also unmistakable was his concern for adult education. He was a champion of the voluntaryism and social purpose which defined the 'movement', and had long presided over Oxford University's extra-mural partnership with the Workers' Educational Association. According to David Phillips, during the commission's deliberations Lindsay pleaded that higher teaching should be extended to the whole community through a 'liberal, general political education' designed for adults.[47] In the event a section of the so-called 'Blaues Gutachten' (Blue Book) was devoted to 'Adult Education', interpreted largely as political and social education.[48] The recommendations published there showed a peculiar blend of proselytizing and restraint. They seemed to steer clear of significant structural changes, yet did envisage a departure from the German academic ethos by way of more social engagement, sponsorship of extra-mural teaching, and recruitment of working-class ability through trade-union agencies.

In the succeeding debate, education ministers and university rectors, without actually dismissing the report as an attempt at alien imposition, distanced themselves from it. Specifically they rejected the idea of more institutionalized involvement by and with the lay community.[49] Despite subsequent flickers of interest in the British 'extra-mural department', the enquiry proved no more formative for adult education than for any other area of university organization. The report was engineered and delivered too late, the outstanding example, in Falk Pingel's view, of the dilemma the British faced from 1947 onwards – of how to bring ideas for democratic change into the realm of practical possibility, but under circumstances where the occupying power had debarred itself from imposing anything.[50]

Workers' education

The 'Blaues Gutachten' included recommendations on co-operation between universities and trade unions, the second obvious area in which

Germans declined to follow the example that was offered. From an early date the WEA sought to make a mark on educational reconstruction, with the active encouragement of the authorities in England and Germany. It nearly succeeded in gate-crashing the HMI visit of 1946,[51] and the Inspectors themselves, arguing that a civic emphasis in workers' education depended on freedom from doctrinal methods, observed: 'In Britain the Workers' Educational Association claims to be non-party and non-sectarian in its provision. This is the democratic view of Adult Education.'[52] Education Branch was very alert to signs of separatism and partisan indoctrination among its German charges. It sponsored a meeting at Bielefeld in December 1946, at which the unions were persuaded to declare support for the *Volkshochschule*-system as provider of general education. But in reality there was often a feeling of mutual alienation, and the union side was anyway more interested in developing its own kind of functional training to strengthen internal organizational capacity.

In the summer of 1947 a party of British adult education experts, including a senior WEA figure, visited the Zone and Berlin. They did not find any evidence that workers were being encouraged to join general adult courses; there was a need for something better than paper agreements, and the trade-union and *VHS* movements should establish a joint-committee structure.[53] (It is difficult to resist pointing out here that for the last forty years the 'joint committee' had been the nostrum of English adult education.) The Germans seem to have been consistently resistant to such attempts at cultural lending. The association *Arbeit und Leben* ('Labour and Life'), which originated in Lower Saxony in 1948 to help workers take advantage of existing adult educational facilities, maintained cordial relations with the WEA, but refused to regard itself as the German equivalent.[54]

Lindsay did believe that the Germans ought to have a WEA of their own. He brought to his work in their country an apparently unquestioning belief in the possibility and rightness of cultural *colportage*. Some twenty years earlier, when involved in an enquiry into higher education in India, he had unblushingly written about applying 'the W.E.A. lotion' to Indian universities, and he seems to have taken a similar line in 1948 – Phillips quotes a telling entry in the commission's records: 'For heaven's sake, said Lindsay, Why can't people in Germany for once copy what others have?'[55]

For some months after the report on university reform had fallen flat he kept up the pressure. His last attempt was in May 1949, when he helped to promote a private conference on working-class education at Hamburg, and brought to it representatives of the WEA, and the British co-operative and trade union societies. His contingent attacked the social remoteness of German academia, and seems to have been uniformly convinced that civic education and university reform in Germany would not come except through partnership with a new and independent movement for workers' education.[56] Phillips suggests that if Lindsay's health had not been failing he would have gone on to advance the cause of adult education in Germany well beyond what was hinted at in the reform commission's report.[57] It is just as likely that his colonialist zeal would have found itself in a blind alley.

The dominant view on the German side was that general, cultural facilities were already available for those who cared to use them, and that the special requirement of the Labour movement was a modern system of 'employee education' – something alien, and probably distasteful to most enthusiasts for what in Britain was referred to as 'adult education'. The divergence revealed itself with a kind of terminal clarity, it would seem, during a conference on workers' education sponsored by the British and United States authorities in 1952. The advocates of a WEA-style solution were warned against misrepresenting the possibilities of the German situation in such a way as to give unwarranted plausibility to their own ideological assumptions.[58]

The *Volkshochschulen*

The British also had problems in coming to terms with the revived *Volkshochschule*. Its centrality to adult education in Germany was acknowledged, and yet there was recurrent scepticism about its contribution to building democracy.

In September 1946 Education Branch declared that prevention of dogmatism and encouragement of non-partisan teaching were the key elements of its work. The *Volkshochschule* offered the best prospect of a general education available to all, conducted on the basis of objectivity; for that reason it was the one form of adult education which deserved direct public financial assistance.[59] Seven months previously a 'position paper' by specialists in Education Branch had described the actual situation much more cautiously. The *VHS* was certain 'in the next few years to play a great role'. But for the moment, so long as it was offering a jumble of elementary language classes, miscellaneous vocational training, and pretentious academic courses given by inferior lecturers, 'It would be absurd to assume that such schemes touch even the fringes of the problem of re-education'.[60]

Those comments appeared over the initials of Jean Gemmell. Her few surviving reports suggest a stringent, almost embittered critic of German tendencies. Her notes on the second zonal conference at Bonn commented ruthlessly on the platitudes, weariness and superannuation of those who were coming to the top in the *Volkshochschule*-movement, and on their authoritarian disregard for younger people with new ideas.[61]

This critical reserve seems to have been generally shared in the early period. The rush to found *Volkshochschulen* was interpreted as a somewhat 'inflationary' reaction to the national disaster, without much potential for education in civic responsibility. The visiting HMI of 1946 accused German organizers of 'turgidity and grandiloquence' even in the handling of practical matters. Their programmes revealed a 'tendency to philosophical and emotional "escapism"'. (The language of the HMI report was still being used verbatim in Education Branch's *Brief for Official Visitors* issued in 1948–49.)[62]

Yet the *Volkshochschulen* were the principal means available to British officials on the spot. An extensive survey, undertaken in early 1949, suggests how these institutes were more than a flash in the post-war pan.[63] Ronald Wilson, who served in Germany as an adult education specialist with the Control Commission and its successor bodies from 1947 to 1958 has noted distinct planes of rhetoric and practice in the British involvement with German adult education: on top there was a high-minded, but inappropriate emphasis on the extra-mural and voluntarist models, while underneath field-staff sought to encourage a liberal, pluralist evolution, but a *German* one for all that.[64] Charles Knowles, who had overall charge of adult education in the period 1949–51, warned of the dangerous rift between the educated and the uneducated classes, but believed that the solution had to be an internal one: 'To present the original W.E.A. conception to modern Germany, where social cleavage has deepened into political and ide[o]logical division, may well accentuate the problem . . . The Volkshochschulen are in line with the best German experience and tradition. When a German thinks of adult education he naturally thinks of them.'[65] What was needed, he believed, was to encourage more generous and less dogmatic attitudes within German adult education, by exposing responsible people to helpful outside examples and leaving them to draw their own conclusions.

From control to cultural relations

During 1948–49, after the Soviet attempt to cut off Berlin, the three Western Allies reinstated a central government in Germany in the shape of the Federal Republic. There followed yet more readjustments in British cultural policy. These were based on the assumption of 'normalization', the gradual transition to ordinary 'bilateral' relations with an independent country. In September 1949 the Control Commission became the High Commission for Germany, and Education Branch the Cultural Relations

Division; at the same time the non-military presence began to be run down, and it was envisaged that cultural relations would soon be handed over to the British Council. But the structures which survived over the next few years were also clearly linked to the diplomatic imperative of preserving influence over whatever the Germans might choose to do for themselves.

In June 1949 Unesco mounted its first international conference on adult education, at Helsingør in Denmark, and there Knowles spoke enthusiastically of bringing Germany back into the European family of nations.[66] At the same date there were renewed complaints that too much control was being relinquished too quickly, and that the future of Education Branch was being brought into question just as its task became all the more significant. In March 1950 Knowles briefed Professor T. H. Marshall, Birley's successor as Educational Adviser, on German adult education, emphasizing its persisting immaturity. He specifically noted the excessive academic emphasis and neglect of social studies, the divorce between the *Volkshochschulen* and the trade unions, and the isolation of the universities. But what was to be done at a time of dwindling resources? The Foreign Office must move, Knowles suggested, to alert British experts to the political significance of adult education in Germany, and to encourage professional contacts and exchanges.[67]

The Foreign Office decided that it did need to keep its finger in the pie, and in October 1950 set up a Consultative Committee on Educational Relationships with Germany to advise on a programme of sponsored activities between the two countries. In November a party of British adult education specialists was sent out on a visit; on its return it proposed a stepping-up of professional exchange, through joint conferences, shared involvement in summer schools, secondment of teachers in both directions, and so on.[68] In May 1951 several of the more important people who had taken part in the visit were invited to the Foreign Office to discuss implementation of these ideas. After some preliminary skirmishing over whether additional mechanisms were needed, the senior official present, Chaput de Saintonge, revealed what the meeting was really about: 'the Foreign Office had now agreed that their educational programme for Germany should continue for a minimum period of three years. Originally, one of the main objectives of this programme had been to bring German organisations and individuals into touch with their counterparts in other countries. Now, however, the scope of our work had changed considerably and was an intrinsic part of the overall political programme designed to bring Germany into the Western European sphere and to counter propaganda coming from the Soviet.'[69]

Chaput de Saintonge reassured his visitors that the FO would not concern itself with the details of contact between the two countries. But clearly adult education was being co-opted into an official strategy: 'An informal sub-committee would be useful in advising the Foreign Office on the planning of its adult education programme. The Educational Adviser had agreed that the proposals for 1952–53 should be accompanied by a note on the German Adult Education movement and the particular targets on which visits should concentrate their fire during 1952–53.'[70]

The experts fell in happily enough with the proposal that proper consultation was needed to 'avoid last minute improvisations', and a sub-committee was in existence from November 1951. Its task was to advise on the spending of funds available for cultural relations in the field of adult education, and to supply technical expertise.[71] The underlying purpose, as with the parent committee, was to ensure that relationships with West Germany hewed to the British diplomatic line. And indeed, this was simply the latest version of the idea that 're-education' was an instrument to ensure the political reliability of Germany according to British strategic requirements.

This was a time when adult education in England was experiencing its own internal troubles over political 'reliability',[72] and it is tempting to view the work of the FO Sub-Committee on Adult Education as an auxiliary of the Cold War. A more immediately interesting consideration, though, is that its membership was drawn from the adult education 'establishment'. This was inevitable, given the ideological monopoly enjoyed by the 'movement' in welfare-state Britain, but it also artificially extended the life of rather tendentious views of what was best for German adult education.[73]

Entrusted with the distribution of symbolically significant sums of public money the group was given a top-flight membership; nominally it reflected the diversity of British practice, but was heavily biased towards 'liberal adult education'. When first set up it included two directors of university extra-mural departments (one of whom was also honorary secretary of the Universities Council for Adult Education), the General Secretary of the WEA, and the Education Officer of the TUC. Only one member was from the local authority sector, and he soon moved to a university post. By 1956, when the sub-committee was nearing the end of its useful life, the extra-mural interest was even more dominant.[74]

In November 1951 Knowles in an address to the Universities Council for Adult Education asked for help in keeping alive the idea of reconstruction in Germany, so that 'some educational work may be saved from the wreck' – by which he meant an occupation policy turned inside out by the forces of international confrontation and rearmament. But he also performed the interesting feat of combining an appeal to the British universities with a forthright dismissal of the idea which would most obviously occur to them: 'To demand', he declared, 'that German Universities should follow the

British example would be fatal. The virile Adult Education Movement would be swallowed up in the reactionary University life.'[75]

Here was a contrariety which inflicted British thinking for much of the occupation period. British experts were being asked to support a drive to develop an overall system of adult education for Germany, but what they tended to offer derived more from the current debate over the distinctive character and tradition of adult education in their own country. They preached the virtues of certain treasured institutional arrangements – the extra-mural department, partnership with a voluntary movement for itself and for its links with the trade unions, the non-vocational three-year tutorial class as the touchstone of pedagogical organization – and all of this was in German terms somewhat beside the point.

In November 1951 at a meeting in Hamburg called to discuss Anglo-German cultural co-operation, the group representing British adult education laid particular stress on the social and political responsibilities of universities, and thence came a proposal to mount an Anglo-German conference specifically on that theme. This conference, sponsored by the Universities Council, took place in Oxford at the end of 1952.[76] It was a distinguished gathering, but the only practical outcome was encouragement offered to a small group at the University of Göttingen who were experimenting, against the set of German academic attitudes, with a scheme of *Seminarkurse* for the general public, inspired by English 'tutorial class' provision.

A return fixture promoted a year later by the Unesco Institute for Education at Hamburg was even less helpful to the British cause. The German professors there insisted that any scope for university involvement in providing adult education had been abandoned long since; the *Volkshochschulen* were successful and enjoyed high esteem, and there was no sense in the universities engaging in what would be seen as inappropriate competition. A participant in these encounters, Kurt Meissner, would later draw attention to the peculiar character of what the British had constantly tried to offer: in global perspective, it was surely their idea of extra-mural responsibility which was aberrant, not the tighter academic self-concept of the German universities.

Donald Cameron Watt has suggested that British policy in Germany was vitiated by too much democratic self-satisfaction and too little sociological imagination.[77] These peculiarities were still evident, at least as far as the printed word can reveal, among the English experts who were seconded to work in Cultural Relations during and just after the final years of the occupation. They included Professor G. R. Potter, the Sheffield historian, who was much involved in the UCAE; Werner Burmeister, the former *émigré* who became a leader-writer for the *Manchester Guardian* and then a senior member of the London University extra-mural department; and another prominent extra-mural lecturer and leader of the Tutors' Association, Norman Dees. All recorded comments and comparisons which reveal a tendency, a determination indeed, to judge German adult education from the point of view of a supposedly superior English example. By 1955 the two countries were supposed to be learning to learn from each other, but the impulse was still there to wag the finger at an unregenerate German adult education movement.[78]

Conclusion

Although 're-education' attracted official attention during the final phase of the war, there had been great reluctance to spell out what it might mean in any operational sense. Only the more obvious, and purgative, requirements for controlling German education were incorporated into the planning process. The same ambiguity infected the early years of the occupation itself, and it was later recognized by some who had been involved. James Mark believed that 'there was a policy, but it was not clearly defined'. Con O'Neill, who wrote the 1944 Foreign Office 'Memorandum on the Re-education of Germany', regarded the topic at the time as an important item of foreign policy; some thirty years later he was to look back on it as 'a very vague notion . . . rather a foolish notion' and as an 'ambitious semi-propaganda concept which fizzled out as it deserved to do'.[79]

Even worse, there was no consistency across the different layers of British involvement. In some vague sense the post-war Labour government wanted Germany to be 're-educated', but was preoccupied with other matters. There were strong views within the Control Commission about needful changes in German local government, public administration, schooling and the universities, but neither the means nor determination to push them through. In education the British lost their opportunity, it has been said, by failing to act quickly enough at the start of the occupation. But that was perhaps as much dilemma as failure: balancing the strong views on the need for reconstruction were the conscientious hesitations of people who felt that imposition could not be reconciled with the mission to teach democracy.

Perhaps Re-education was a 'policy' only in a negative sense. At a very general level the British were committed to it – in that they periodically concluded it was not happening. But to have specified the measures necessary to turn it into practice, and to have calculated the cost of implementation, would have immediately revealed its absurdity.

Could matters have been managed any differently in the realm of adult education? In the Soviet Zone socialist and communist sympathizers were put in charge in order to secure its malleability. The British, however, had to live with the consequences of their decision to encourage liberal pluralism. The Germans who achieved recognition under this tolerant regime had their own ideas about the nature and shape of adult education. Fritz Borinski, who returned after years of exile in London to take a leading role, acknowledged his deep respect for the English adult education tradition but took a fiercely independent line over what was needed in his own country.[80] Could bribery have served as a means of implanting novel structures? Large amounts of money would surely have been needed, and they were not available. And, in any case, experience in the US zone showed just how resistant were indigenous German conceptions of *Bildung* – education in the sense of personal cultivation – to merely financial and technical blandishments.[81]

So the British were committed to inspiring the Germans to accept approaches and methods which did not chime with their natural ways of thinking. (And the Germans had an intellectual tradition of their own which gave them a head-start in matters of *Geist* and inspiration.) The dilemma, although only tangentially acknowledged, affected adult education with particular poignancy. If the task was not just to support promising local initiatives, but also to open windows and let in a generous democratic light from outside (as in effect it was from mid-1946), then Education Branch urgently needed to enlist the support of the leadership of adult education at home. But the British experts, because of their own position, values and assumptions, were prone to emphasizing solutions for Germany which those on the spot sensed to be unworkable. There might be elevating talk about the social responsibility of the universities, and the partnership of labour and learning, but those were not the terms in which most on the German side approached the problem.

This chapter has traced the progress of a rather special rhetoric. That rhetoric was a function of the pattern of relations between Britain and Germany immediately after the war, and it was fated to collapse as those relations lost their post-bellum character. It marked, one might say, an exercise in quasi-imperialism. A visitor of 1947, Helen Liddell, observed a marked 'colonial' attitude among the kindly, tolerant but superior British officialdom. Ronald Wilson, once a workaday participant, recalled years afterwards the defining quality as 'eine gewisse, freilich durchaus positive missionarische Haltung' (a certain missionary, though entirely positive attitude).[82] One is tempted to compare experience in Germany to the intense involvement in adult education which occurred in parts of the colonial Empire during the late 1940s and 1950s, also dedicated to preparing subject peoples for democratic self-sufficiency. There was the same confusion about how long the process would require, and the same premature resolution by external political events. There was also the same evaporation of interest once the missionaries had been brought home.

David Phillips has written about the predicament of the British regarding the 'control' of German schools and universities and its sometimes paradoxical, almost farcical aspects.[83] There was something of that in adult education too, where one of the consequences was that out of the failure of missionizing came a kind of success. There have been many comments on how work in adult education turned out to be an especially acceptable and congenial part of British re-education activity.[84] It was the approach – the informality and 'fair play' at all levels of social relations, and the fostering of contacts – and not the ulterior aims which impressed, and which is still celebrated in German accounts of post-war educational reconstruction. That is a generous response, and it leaves a latter-day English writer to ask how the balance, as regards respect for democratic institutions and practices, and public esteem for adult education, stands between the two countries today.

References and notes

1 The literature on 're-education', as the idea developed in Britain and the United States, is extensive. Two sample historical accounts are: Otto Schlander, *Reeducation: Ein politisch-pädagogisches Prinzip im Widerstreit der Gruppen* (Bern/Frankfurt am Main, 1975); and Lothar Kettenacker, 'The planning of "Re-education" during the Second World War', in N. Pronay and K. Wilson (eds), *The Political Re-Education of Germany and her Allies after World War II* (1985).

2 Kurt Jürgensen, 'British occupation policy after 1945 and the problem of "Re-educating Germany"', *History* 68: 223 (1983).

3 Kettenacker, 'The planning of "Re-education"', 66-69; Arthur Hearnden (ed), *The British in Germany: Educational reconstruction after 1945* (1978), Appendix I; Jürgensen, 'British occupation policy after 1945', 231-232. The official title of the occupation authority was 'Control Commission for Germany (British Element)' or CCG(BE).

4 The broad context is provided in David Welch, 'Priming the pump of German democracy: British "Re-education" policy in Germany after the Second World War', in I. D. Turner (ed), *Reconstruction in Post-War Germany: British occupation policy and the Western Zones, 1945-55* (Oxford, 1989); and Pronay and Wilson (eds), *The Political Re-Education of Germany*. The work of Education Branch is dealt with more specifically though not at all systematically in Hearnden (ed), *The British in Germany;* and Kurt Jürgensen, 'The concept and practice of "Re-Education" in Germany 1945-50', in Pronay and Wilson (eds), *The Political Re-Education of Germany.*

5 Wolfgang Rudzio, 'Export englischer Demokratie? Zur Konzeption der britischen Besatzungspolitik in Deutschland', *Vierteljahrshefte für Zeitgeschichte*, 17 (1969); Ulrich Reusch, *Deutsches Berufsbeamtentum und britische Besatzung: Planung und Politik 1943-1947* (Stuttgart, 1985).

6 Ronald H. Wilson, 'Erwachsenenbildung als Re-Education?' in Otto Volker (ed), *Von Hohenrodt zur Gegenwart: Rückblick und Zukunftsperspektive. 40 Jahre Volkshochschul-Verband in Hessen* (Frankfurt am Main, [1986]), 113.

7 Public Record Office, FO 1050/1305, 'Recommended Policy for Re-Education in Germany' recapitulates the aims laid down in the directive of November 1945.

8 FO 1013/2193, correspondence: HQ MG North Rhine Province, 15 Sep 1945; HQ MG Regierungsbezirk Düsseldorf, 27 Sep 1945.

9 FO 1013/ 2193, correspondence 15, 27 Sep 1945.

10 FO 1050/1287, 'Report of His Majesty's Inspectors on Adult Education in the British Zone of Germany and the British Sector of Berlin', Jul 1946, 3; and Armin Hasenpusch, *Der Aufbau des Volkshochschulwesens 1945-1947 im niedersächsischen Raum* (Hannover, 1977), 31-35.

11 Hasenpusch, *Der Aufbau*, 19-29, 31. Hasenpusch based this phase of his research largely on correspondence emanating from the Control Commission which survived in German municipal archives. For accounts of the origins of *Volkshochschulen* in the US Zone see Alfred Knierim, *Die Entwicklung des hessischen Volkshochschulwesens im Zeitraum von 1945 bis 1952* (Frankfurt am Main, 1982) and Renate Krausnick-Horst, *Volkshochschulen in Baden-Württemburg 1946-1986* (Stuttgart, 1986).

12 Since the conventional translation 'folk high school' does not satisfactorily capture the sense, and terms such as 'people's college' and 'popular university' have no contemporary resonance, the German title *Volkshochschule* (*VHS*) is used throughout this chapter. The *VHS*, a programme of activities in a locality rather than a single building, may be thought of as a superior version of what the English used to call the 'evening institute'.

13 FO 1013/2193, correspondence and reports, Jan to Mar 1946.

14 FO 1050/1298, minutes and reports on German Women's Education, Oct 1945- Mar 1946; FO 1050/1302, Review of German Education, May 1945-July 1946; Helena Deneke, 'Die Women's Institutes in England', *Die Sammlung* 3 (1948); *British Zone Review*, 4 Jan 1947, 12.

15 FO 1013/2180, Education Progress Report to Mar 1946.

16 Hasenpusch, *Der Aufbau*.

17 FO 945/141, correspondence Apr 1946; 1050/1287, 'Report of His Majesty's Inspectors on Adult Education'.

18 FO 1050/1320, correspondence: Major-General W. H. A. Bishop to Major-General P. M. Balfour, 20 Feb 1946 ('Secret'); D. C. Riddy to Bishop, 20 Feb 1946.

19 FO 1050/1320, memorandum on 'Re-education of Germany', 20 Feb 1946 and related correspondence. A hint of the peculiar situation within the Control Commission is given by the fact that the director of Education Branch (Riddy) was a senior member of the Education Inspectorate seconded from London, whilst the head of PR & ISC (Bishop) was a major-general, a career soldier.

20 Hasenpusch, *Der Aufbau*, 31, 39; FO 1050/1311, 'Observations by Education Branch on a Report on Adult Education', 4 Oct 1946; Control Commission for

Germany (British Element), Education Branch, *Brief for Official Visitors to Germany. 1st November. 1948* (1949), 31.

21 Rudzio, 'Export englischer Demokratie?'

22 FO 1050/1290, 'ABCA Scheme' [May/Jul 1946].

23 FO 1050/1290, 'ABCA Scheme'; and 1050/1287, 'Report of His Majesty's Inspectors on Adult Education'.

24 FO 1050/1311, 'Observations by Education Branch on a Report on Adult Education', section 6(f); 1050/1305, 'Recommended Policy', section VI/6.

25 House of Commons, Select Committee on Estimates, *Second Report* (1946), Minutes of Evidence, 489.

26 James Mark reported in David Phillips (ed), *German Universities after the Surrender: British occupation policy and the control of higher education* (Oxford, 1983), 142, 152.

27 Quoted in Günter Pakschies, *Umerziehung in der Britischen Zone 1945-1949: Untersuchungen zur britischen Re-education-Politik* (Weinheim/Basel, 1979), 220. Pakschies found this document in the papers of Major T. J. Leonard, a former official in the school textbook section at Education Branch. Leonard seems to have clung on to a large amount of the paper which passed over his desk at the Control Commission. The collection was eventually deposited at the Georg-Eckert-Institut for international research on school textbooks, Braunschweig; and the 'Leonard Nachlaß' proved to be a most useful surrogate at a time when the Control Commission's own records were still closed to researchers.

28 Pakschies, *Umerziehung*, 229.

29 Select Committee on Estimates, *Second Report* (1946), xiii, xxv.

30 FO 1050/1305, 'Recommended Policy'. The associated correspondence shows that the document was completed on or by 4 Sep 1946, a date which has evaded previous authors who have located other copies of this important document.

31 FO 1050/1311, 'Observations by Education Branch on a Report on Adult Education', section 6(f).

32 *British Zone Review*, 28 Sep, 7 Dec 1946, 4 Jan 1947; Helen Liddell, 'Education in occupied Germany: a field study', in Liddell (ed), *Education in Occupied Germany. L'Éducation de l'Allemagne occupé* (Paris, 1949), 129.

33 HQ, CCG(BE), *Policy Instruction No. 40* (Policy in Regard of the Future Organisation of Education Branch and Information Services Division, February 1949).

34 Reported in *Times Educational Supplement*, 25 Jul 1947; *G. E. R. Bulletin* (German Educational Reconstruction), Aug/Sep 1947.

35 FO 945/199, memorandum from Deputy Military Governor, Aug 1947.

36 See Michael Balfour, 'In retrospect: Britain's policy of "Re-education"', in Pronay and Wilson (eds), *The Political Re-education of Germany*, 145; Arthur Hearnden, *Red Robert: A life of Robert Birley* (1984).

37 House of Commons, Select Committee on Estimates, *Eighth Report* (1947), 11, 21.

38 Liddell, 'Education in occupied Germany', 118, 131. It should be added here that there are two policy documents of this period which carried the collective

authority of the four occupying powers, but which add nothing to this
discussion. In June 1947 Control Directive No. 54, 'Basic Principles for
Democratization of Education in Germany', issued from Berlin, probably on the
prompting of the US authorities, who had recently decided to embark on a
restructuring of education in their zone. In August a quadripartite working
party examined the implications for adult education and produced a statement
on 'Basic Principles for Adult Education in Germany', which was eventually
approved as Control Council Directive No. 56, 28 October 1947. (Drafts and
copy in FO 945/281.) Directive No. 54 put the British on the spot (because of
their policy of devolution), but they responded by claiming that it simply offered
'guidance' on how to evaluate proposals coming from the German side. No. 56
was couched in very general terms, and apparently elicited no response, evasive
or otherwise.

39 This evolution of policy is discussed in Pakschies, *Umerziehung*, 249-250.
40 Knierim, *Die Entwicklung des hessischen Volkshochschulwesens*. For the 'cultural
    mismatch' in the United States zone see James F. Tent, *Mission on the Rhine:
    Reeducation and denazification in American-occupied Germany* (Chicago/London,
    1982).
41 FO 1050/1287, 'Report of His Majesty's Inspectors', 16, 34; 1050/1305,
    'Recommended Policy', section IX/8.
42 Association of University Teachers, 'The universities in the British Zone of
    Germany', *Universities Review*, May 1947; translated as 'Die Universitäten der
    britischen Zone Deutschlands', *Die Sammlung* 3:2 (1948), Beilage. See also
    Harold Perkin, *Key Profession: The history of the Association of University Teachers*
    (1969), 154; Phillips (ed), *German Universities after the Surrender*, 163.
43 Select Committee on Estimates, *Eighth Report* (1947), 22.
44 The AUT report has been condemned as superficial and opinionated. One
    former COGA official remembered the delegation as 'a group of somewhat left-
    wing inclined dons' with 'very strong views on education' who wanted to get out
    to the Zone to investigate. According to the *obiter dicta* of some later historians
    the experts embarked on their visit in ignorance of conditions in Germany, and
    were little more than a gaggle of professors seizing the opportunity of a free trip,
    in some cases to pursue their own research interests: see comments reported in
    Phillips (ed), *German Universities after the Surrender*, 152, 162, 163.
45 Control Commission for Germany (British Element), Office of the Educational
    Adviser, *Gutachten zur Hochschulreform vom Studienausschuß für Hochschulreform*
    (Hamburg, 1948); and English translation, Foreign Office, *University Reform in
    Germany: Report by a German Commission* (1949).
46 A. W. J. Edwards in Hearnden (ed), *The British in Germany*, 183.
47 Quoted in David Phillips, 'Lindsay and the German universities: An Oxford con-
    tribution to the post-war reform debate', *Oxford Review of Education* 6 (1980), 98.
48 Foreign Office, *University Reform in Germany*, 60.
49 Falk Pingel, 'Wissenschaft, Bildung und Demokratie: Der gescheiterte Versuch
    einer Universitätsreform', in Joseph Foschepoth and Rolf Steininger (eds),

Britische Deutschland- und Besatzungspolitik 1945-1949 (Paderborn, 1985). See also Harald Husemann, 'Anglo-German relations in higher education', in Hearnden (ed), *The British in Germany*.

50 Falk Pingel, 'Attempts at university reform in the British zone', in Phillips (ed), *German Universities after the Surrender*.

51 FO 945/141, correspondence Apr 1946.

52 FO 1050/1287, 'Report of His Majesty's Inspectors', 28.

53 'Report on Free Adult Education in the British Zone of Germany and the British Sector of Berlin', October 1947, 15. (Copy in the possession of Mr R. H. Wilson.)

54 Fritz Borinski, 'The British influence on German adult education', in Hearnden (ed), *The British in Germany*, and general discussion at 294-295; Ronald H. Wilson, 'Erwachsenenbildung im Nachkriegs-Deutschland: Berlin-Reminiszenzen eines beteiligten Engländers', *Volkshochschule im Westen*, Aug 1981, 314.

55 Drusilla Scott, *A. D. Lindsay: A life* (1971), 202; Phillips, 'Lindsay and the German universities', 97.

56 FO 1050/1058, minutes of private meeting of English and German personalities interested in working class adult education, Hamburg, 18 May 1949. See also Scott, *A. D. Lindsay*, 302-304.

57 Phillips, 'Lindsay and the German universities', 100.

58 See Hearnden (ed), *The British in Germany*, 294-295.

59 FO 1050/1311, 'Observations by Education Branch on a Report on Adult Education'.

60 FO 1050/1320, 'Re-education of Germany'.

61 FO 1050/1287, 'Report: Volkshochschultagung' [Sep? 1946].

62 FO 1050/1287, 'Report: Volkshochschultagung'; CCG(BE), *Brief for Official Visitors*.

63 FO 1050/1059, 1060, surveys of adult education in Lower Saxony and North Rhine-Westphalia.

64 Wilson, 'Erwachsenenbildung im Nachkriegs-Deutschland', 324.

65 FO 1050/1058, 'Adult education and the working class in Germany' [1949/50], 4-5.

66 Unesco, *Summary Report of the International Conference on Adult Education, Elsinore, Denmark 19-25 June 1949* (Paris, 1949).

67 FO 1050/1058, C. I. Knowles's briefing notes on adult education.

68 FO 1050/1228, office note, 9 Nov 1951; see also D. Caradog Jones, 'Relations between British and German adult education', *Tutors' Bulletin* [Association of Tutors in Adult Education], Winter 1950/51, 4.

69 FO 1050/1228, 'Note of a Meeting', 24 May 1951.

70 FO 1050/1228, 'Note of a Meeting'.

71 FO 1050/1228, office note 9 Nov 1951; Consultative Committee on Educational Relationships with Germany, Sub-Committee on Adult Education, minutes 15 Nov 1951.

72 Roger T. Fieldhouse, *Adult Education and the Cold War: Liberal values under siege 1946-51* (Leeds, 1985).

73 Ronald Wilson, 'Erwachsenenbildung im Nachkriegs-Deutschland', 314.
74 FO 1050/1228, Sub-Committee on Adult Education, minutes 15 November 1951, 8 March 1956.
75 FO 1050/1228, C. I. Knowles, 'Address to the British Universities' Council for Adult Education', 1 Nov 1951, 10.
76 The theme of this and the following paragraph is treated more fully in Stuart Marriott, 'Fifty years of an educational mission: The "Tutorial Class" movement in Anglo-German perspective', in Stuart Marriott and Barry J. Hake (eds), *Cultural and Intercultural Experiences in European Adult Education: Essays on popular and higher education since 1890* (Leeds, 1994), 111-113.
77 Donald Cameron Watt, *Britain looks to Germany: British opinion and policy towards Germany since 1945* (1965).
78 Marriott, 'Fifty years of an educational mission'.
79 James Mark, reported in Phillips (ed), *German Universities after the Surrender*, 142; and Sir Con O'Neill, reported by Kurt Koszyk in Pronay and Wilson (eds), *The Political Re-Education of Germany and her Allies*, 130, note 7.
80 Fritz Borinski returned from exile in England to become one of the leading figures of post-war German adult education. For his opinions and publications see Stuart Marriott, *English-German Relations in Adult Education, 1875-1955: A Commentary and select bibliography* (Leeds, 1995).
81 Knierim, *Die Entwicklung des hessischen Volkshochschulwesens*.
82 Liddell, 'Education in occupied Germany', 128; Ronald Wilson, 'Re-education–Educational Reconstruction', *Rundschreiben* (Landesverband der Volkshochschulen Niedersachsen), January 1987, 14.
83 David Phillips, 'British educational policy in occupied Germany: Some problems and paradoxes in the control of schools and universities', in Peter Cunningham and Colin Brock (eds), *International Currents in Educational Ideas and Practices* (History of Education Society, 1987).
84 Erich Weniger, 'Die Epoche der Umerziehung 1945-1949', *Westermanns Pädagogische Beiträge* 11 (1959), 12 (1960) [in four parts]; Martha Friedenthal-Haase, 'Britische Re-education: Struktur und Aktualität eines Beispiels interkultureller Erwachsenenbildung', *Neue Sammlung* 28 (1988).

The power of three: 'Parity of esteem' and the social history of tripartism

GARY McCULLOCH

Peter Gosden's work has richly documented the failure of recent education policies to take heed of historical experience. As he notes, education as a field seems especially prone to a tendency to 're-invent the wheel', with time and resources being wasted as a direct consequence of this. Indeed, he suggests, 'Without some attention to the recent historical background – the collective memory of educational government – adequate evaluation of policy becomes impossible and avoidable blunders will be committed.'[1] The present essay seeks to illustrate this general argument by means of locating current preoccupations with the idea of 'parity of esteem' in relation to historical changes and continuities. In particular, it is in the *social* history of education that many of the most instructive links may be found. This is because the assumptions and interests inherent in such ideals as 'parity of esteem' are often not apparent in legislation or public debates, but are rooted at a more profound level in social, political, cultural and other traditions.

It seems especially important in this regard for us to look beneath the official phrases and 'texts' that are embodied, even embalmed, in legislation or familiar policy documents. For example, as is often forgotten, the Education Act of 1944 did not itself mention the idea of developing three different types of secondary school. Even so, this 'tripartite' division, into grammar, technical, and modern schools, became one of the best known and most enduring images of the reforms of the 1940s.[2] If we are able to inspect the long-term patterns involved in this kind of tripartite division, the ways in which it has often been attempted to identify three kinds of child each with different aptitudes, abilities, and positions in society, we shall begin to illuminate the social history of 'tripartism' itself. 'Parity of esteem' comprises only one particular form of tripartism, although even on its own it has been subject to vigorous contestation over its meaning and implications. It certainly serves to highlight the important connections that exist between long-term patterns and current issues and policies. As a policy goal, 'parity of esteem' was highly fashionable in the 1930s and 1940s, then fell out of favour, and has again become a strong theme of education policy in the 1990s. How can we account for such a pattern, including the revival no less than the fall from grace? What are the similarities and the differences between the education policies of the 1940s, and those of the 1990s? And what are the prospects that the ideal of 'parity of esteem' will be any more successful in the 1990s than it was in the 1940s?

Such questions may be conceived as part of a broader project, that of developing a social history of education policy. In such a project we need to face not only towards the past, but also towards the consequences of current policies in the future. We must confront the myths about the past that often inform, and misinform, contemporary policies. We need also to resist at all costs the temptation to 'raid' the past for easy answers to current issues. It will not be likely to appeal to those who are seeking a 'quick fix' to problems, but it is likely to suggest cultural depth and the longevity of issues that may on the surface appear to be novel. It should convey a sense of the complexity of past dilemmas, as well as of their relationship to wider social, political, economic and cultural changes. Just as a 'sociology of education policy' promises to examine in a critical way the social and ideological bases of the policy process,[3] so a social history of education policy can help us to understand the sources of today's problems, the underlying issues concealed in contemporary nostrums.

Three types of child

In approaching the social history of tripartism, the historical continuities provide us with the clearest overarching feature. The resilience of tripartite divisions over many decades, their continual reconstruction to adapt to changing social and political contexts, attests to the sheer power of this categorization in helping to understand the history of education in Britain. The links between the Taunton Report of the 1860s, the Norwood Report of the 1940s, and the present day have been well noted by historians such as Simon, Lowe, and Goodson.[4]

If we are searching for an 'ideal type' to convey the most important and most durable attributes of tripartism, the example most often cited is that of the Norwood Report on the secondary school curriculum and examinations, published in July 1943. As is well known, Part I of the Norwood Report identified three 'rough groupings' of pupils which, 'whatever may be their ground, have in fact established themselves in general educational experience'.[5] On the basis on this, it proceeded to argue that such distinctions should be acknowledged and cultivated in the future provision of secondary education. In so doing, it hoped, they would provide both a theoretical and practical basis for 'secondary education for all'.

According to the Norwood Report, the first type of pupil was 'the pupil who is interested in learning for its own sake, who can grasp an argument or follow a piece of connected reasoning'.[6] Such pupils had previously been associated with grammar schools, and went on to the 'learned professions' or into 'higher administrative or business posts'.[7] The most suitable curriculum for such pupils, it averred, was one that 'treats the various fields of knowledge as suitable for coherent and systematic study for their own sake apart from immediate considerations of occupation'.[8] The Report concluded that grammar schools should continue to uphold an ideal of 'disciplined thought provided by an introduction to the main fields of systematic knowledge, which is valued first for its own sake and later invoked to meet the needs of life'.[9]

By contrast, the Norwood Report defined the second type of pupil as one who showed 'interests and abilities' that lay 'markedly in the field of applied science or applied art'. Such pupils would be better suited to a curriculum that was 'closely, though not wholly, directed to the special data and skills associated with a particular kind of occupation',[10] particularly in industry, trades, and commerce, and this should be provided in secondary technical schools. At the same time, the third type of pupils identified in the Report apparently dealt 'more easily with concrete things than with ideas', and demanded 'immediate return' from any endeavour: 'His horizon is near and within a limited area his movement is generally slow, though it may be surprisingly rapid in seizing a particular point or in taking up a special line.'[11] For these pupils, it suggested a curriculum with 'a balanced training of mind and body and a correlated approach to humanities, Natural Science and the arts', not with any specific job or occupation in view but in order to 'make a direct appeal to interests, which it would awaken by practical touch with affairs'.[12] The kind of institution that would best meet these needs, it considered, was a new kind of secondary school to be known as the secondary modern school.

It is possible to extrapolate three separate traditions of education derived from the tripartite divisions suggested in the Norwood Report. The first type invoked the élite tradition of liberal education for leadership that had been developed in the public and grammar schools. The pivotal phase of this kind of education had been the Victorian period, when the classical curriculum, emphasis on team sports, and general *esprit de corps* of the public schools fostered their unchallenged role as 'the chief nurseries of our statesmen'.[13] During the twentieth century, the assumptions on which 'education for leadership' was based were challenged from several directions, but the ideal was able to adapt to changing conditions and even to extend its influence into the growing state sector of secondary education.[14]

The second type of pupils, and the kinds of curriculum and school that were associated with them, were closely related to a tradition of technical and vocational education for skilled labour. This tradition also stretched back at least as far as the nineteenth century, from the mechanics' institutes through the Samuelson Commission of the 1880s to the junior technical schools that were developed in the 1920s and 1930s. It was in many ways a much weaker tradition than the first, clearly subordinated and inferior to it in terms of its social status, despite determined efforts to broaden and enhance its appeal such as were made through the Bryce Report on secondary education in the 1890s.[15]

Third and last was a plebeian or banausic tradition of mass education for the working class, once again rooted in the nineteenth century with the monitorial system and elementary schools, and similarly adapting to changing social and political demands in the twentieth century. In the context of rising pressures for mass secondary education from the 1920s onwards, the notion of 'working class secondary education' attained new force. The secondary modern schools that emerged in the 1940s may be interpreted as the final, doomed attempt to work out the implications of this distinctive approach in practical terms.[16]

This highly resilient, deeply entrenched tripartite pattern of the liberal, the vocational, and the banausic in English educational history demands some explanation. In this regard, the two major theoretical frameworks that are most often applied are the Marxist and the Platonic. On the Marxist view, tripartite divisions have been based on social class differences and inequalities between (broadly) the aristocracy, the middle class, and the working class. Such an explanation is socio-economic in nature, positing an inherent conflict between opposing social interests. It is argued that schooling has been designed, if not always successfully, to exploit and increase the productivity of the working class, and to maintain their subordinate position in society. The work of Brian Simon in particular has established this general view as a familiar and widely accepted interpretation of English educational history.[17]

The Platonic version of tripartism, based on the ideas of the Greek philosopher Plato in *The Republic*, would tend to emphasize the distinctions between three different groups in society corresponding to the 'gold', the 'silver', and the 'copper'. The emphasis here is on providing a philosophical and cultural framework to rationalize different capacities and aptitudes, and the different roles in society to which they lead. The first class, associated with gold, was that of the philosophers, from whom the 'guardians' or philosopher-kings of the society would be chosen. The second class was made up of the 'auxiliaries', or skilled merchants and tradesmen, and this was characterized as silver. Artisans and farmers, made up of iron and copper, constituted the third class. The first class would be given a liberal education, while the second class would be given a vocational training. Several commentators have noted the resemblance of twentieth-century English educational patterns to this general ideal. Some, like Richard Crossman in the late 1930s and John Dancy in the early 1960s, have strongly criticized the enduring influence of Platonic educational ideas.[18] Others, like Sir Richard Livingstone, R.C. Lodge and Eric James, have cultivated it no less avidly.[19]

The dominant English tradition of education, based as it has been on inequality and hierarchy, seems closely related to both of these major theoretical frameworks. The tension between them is most promising as a point of departure for a social history of tripartism. Even so, in their finer detail, historical patterns are rarely so neat and straightforward as this might suggest, and they are contested often in subtle and unexpected ways. It can be misleading even to regard the idea of tripartism itself in terms of a static and unchanging typology, for it has been perceived to exist in several different forms and has adapted according to changing social and political contexts. At least five different notions of 'tripartism' have had a marked effect on English educational institutions in the twentieth century. It is in the contestation between these types, involving different groups aligned with rival ideologies and interests, that their significance would appear to lie both in the past and for the present.

In the first type of tripartism, social hierarchy correlates straightforwardly with educational hierarchy, generally with the academic or 'liberal' approach at the apex, the technical or vocational in a poor second place, and the plebeian or banausic coming last. Both Marxists and Platonists would recognize this kind of relationship, although of course for widely varying reasons, and it has been probably the most familiar version which has recurred on many occasions throughout the nineteenth and twentieth centuries. Types of schools have translated immediately into tiers of schools. On the other hand, this clear hierarchical ranking has not been the only type or manifestation of the social distinctions represented in tripartism.

A second type of tripartism has involved social emulation of established, and more prestigious, institutions, curricula, and traditions. The less well-established forms of provision – the technical and the modern – imitated the grammar and public schools. This tendency minimized the actual differences between the different types of institution, and enabled those associated with the technical and the banausic to aspire towards higher things. Unlike in the first type of tripartism, this second version did not assume a preordained position in society for those taking part in the different kinds of school; they no longer 'knew their place'. It also allowed much greater scope for contact and cooperation among the separate forms. However, since norms and ideals were dictated by the already entrenched cultural forms, it also meant a tacit acknowledgement of status differences between the liberal, the vocational, and the banausic.

In a third version of tripartism, these status differences were turned on their head to emphasize that the distinctive qualities of novel institutions were actually superior to those of the old. In the 1940s, for example, it could be argued that secondary modern schools were 'a new and better conception of education for the adolescent, rather than an apish imitation of what in many respects in secondary education has been a failure in the past'.[20] On the other hand, what this 'new and better conception of education for the adolescent' should have been was never worked out in any detail or coherence, certainly not in the secondary modern schools.

These first three types of tripartism all implied strong value judgements about the alternative forms of provision. A fourth type, agnostic in character, tended to place the emphasis on the idea of individual schools and other educational institutions finding their own level, that is, transcending their limitations or overcoming problems and prejudices through their own efforts. This seemed to be the position favoured by the Norwood Report in 1943, despite Sir Cyril Norwood's own often stated preference for grammar schools. Thus the Norwood Report called for secondary schools to offer 'equivalence of opportunity to all children in the only sense in which it has valid meaning, namely, the opportunity to receive the education for which each pupil is best suited for such time and to such a point as is fully profitable to him'.[21]

At the same time, however, a fifth version of tripartism developed that amounted to a much stronger notion of 'parity of esteem' between different types of school. According to this view, each of the alternative kinds of school, whether grammar (liberal), technical (vocational), or modern (banausic), were to be regarded as fundamentally equal or equivalent to each other. They were therefore to be accorded equal respect by pupils, parents, and the community at large. This notion often received official sanction, and yet it rarely became established in practice. In particular, although the White Paper *Educational Reconstruction* (1943) talked of establishing a secondary education 'of diversified types, but of equal standing',[22] the tripartism of the 1940s and 1950s signally failed to bring about parity of esteem.

The appeal of this fifth version of tripartism needs to be addressed and understood in relation to a range of perceptions and intentions in different contexts. The currency of the idea of 'parity of esteem' seems to owe something to administrative convenience, as it provided a straightforward formula for making educational distinctions that avoided uncomfortable social issues and inequalities. At this level, it might be regarded as a polite or official fiction that provided a basis for policy developments, but which was prone to ignore practical realities and conflicting viewpoints. To some extent, too, it probably reflected a pious hope that official indifference to status distinctions could in itself help to eradicate the worst effects of the 'English tradition' in education. More severely, an element of cynicism might also be detected as it sought to obscure the continuing realities of social inequality behind a smokescreen of parity.

Such reflections also help us to discern likely reasons for the persistent failure of the notion of 'parity of esteem' to be realized in practice. First,

E

despite the many channels of influence and control that were at the disposal of the Ministry of Education and related agencies, 'esteem' was not in their gift either to dispense or to withhold. It was, rather, at the mercy of market forces, the more so as parental choice between different kinds of schools became an important issue in the 1940s-50s and again from the 1980s. Secondly, the competing interpretations of tripartism constantly confused and interfered with the ideal of 'parity', making it difficult to maintain this as a clear policy objective over the longer term. Thirdly, it tended to fall victim to the many sceptics who were always ready to ascribe sinister ulterior motives. As political allegiances changed and control alternated between rival factions, parity of esteem was an aim that could be derided within a few years of becoming established as a linchpin of policy, or else regarded with affection and disdain in different quarters at the same time.

Perhaps, too, there was also a more basic or fundamental reason for the failure of 'parity of esteem'. It may be argued that there was no adequate theory to support the idea. On this view, it amounted to little more than a technical fix that ignored the larger forces of culture and history in educational change, and therefore failed to address or solve deep-seated and long-term problems. Neither the Marxist nor the Platonic framework would recognize a theoretical basis for 'parity of esteem'. Indeed, each would tend to regard it as a contradiction in terms. It denies on the one hand existence of social inequalities relating to educational differences, and on the other hand the importance of values or cultural distinctions. Market theory or competitive individualism applied to education would also find it difficult to allow scope for a notion that aspires systematically to 'buck the market'. Arguably, then, it was a policy goal that was essentially hollow and without substance, and this helps to account both for its short-term potency and for its longer-term failures.

There are many aspects in the social history of tripartism that deserve further exploration. The nature of the so-called 'new tripartism' of the 1990s, compared with earlier manifestations, is an obvious example.[23] The relationship between gender and tripartism is another potential avenue for research, both in highlighting the gender distinctions in the different forms of education, and in suggesting how they have challenged, transcended, or tended to break down tripartite divisions. Another key theme would relate to the experience of tripartism, seeking to understand for example the personal and family stigma involved in failing the 11-plus exam, or the sacrifices involved in 'success'. The 11-plus exam also raises the issue of how to approach the coercive technologies of tripartism, the devices that were designed to facilitate and to rationalize clear demarcations between three types of child.

Moreover, it needs to be emphasized that there have been many different manifestations of tripartism in this country besides that of differing types of secondary school. The effects of 'streaming', examinations and curriculum within comprehensive schools may also be related to resilient tripartite divisions.[24] A tendency for institutions of further and higher education to exhibit tripartite characteristics has also been identified, and this similarly warrants more extended treatment.[25] It would be eminently possible, too, to focus in greater depth on the importance of changing social and economic patterns in the twentieth century, and on the changing nature of the 'class society' itself. The decline of the Empire and the rise of popular democracy created new challenges to the idea of 'education for leadership'. The increasing role of the State in education at different levels, and its changing relationship to private, religious and local forms of provision, also established novel contexts for familiar debates. The changing occupational structure of the country, including a marked decline in the proportion of manual workers since the Second World War and an increasingly large suburban and 'middle-class' population, provided a further strong influence on the character and rationale of tripartism, as did the effects of large-scale unemployment.

While remaining alert to these wider and largely unexplored issues, however, it is useful to dwell a little longer on the theme of parity of esteem as a version of tripartism in England in the twentieth century. In particular, the debate over the validity of this idea in the 1920s, 1930s, and 1940s is highly instructive for us to recall. Furthermore, perhaps the most arresting question of all still needs to be addressed in detail: if parity of esteem failed in the 1940s, how and why did it become rehabilitated as a potent influence on education policy in the 1990s?

The rise and fall of 'parity of esteem'

It is important to emphasize that there were many who were sceptical about the idea of parity of esteem even in the 1930s and 1940s, and that it was always highly problematic in its character and role. As has already been noted, it did not coexist comfortably with the several other forms of tripartism that were current. There were also at least two different versions of 'parity of esteem' itself. This was acknowledged in his memoirs by Lord Eustace Percy, who as President of the Board of Education in the 1920s had observed the rapid development of these ideas. The first and more familiar version was that of parity of esteem between different kinds of secondary education. The second, which Percy himself thought had a greater chance of success, was a bipartite notion that reflected a duality between the 'liberal' and the 'vocational'. This, he suggested, offered the prospect of establishing 'parity between two educational "ladders", one leading through the secondary school to the university, the other through the senior and technical schools to the college of technology, with ample facilities for changing from one to the other at almost any rung'.[26] There was a persistent tension between these two differing ideas of 'parity of esteem', the tripartite ideal and the bipartite alternative, from the 1920s onwards.

A keen debate also developed at this time over whether it was really possible to foster parity of esteem between alternative forms of secondary school, and on the kinds of reforms and conditions that might help to bring this about. The recommendations of the Hadow Report of 1926, on the education of the adolescent, stimulated argument about the likely effects of encouraging new kinds of post-primary school alongside the existing secondary schools. It was suggested that the upgrading of central and senior schools might help to 'remove the stigma of social inferiority which appeared to attach in some areas to the central as opposed to the secondary school', while at the same time 'retaining the central (or modern) school as an alternative to the secondary school in areas where it seemed to be a type of school best suited to the needs of the particular area'.[27] Even so, it was already recognized that other steps would be necessary in order to remove this 'stigma'. The newer schools would need to be provided with conditions akin to those enjoyed by the grammar schools in relation to such aspects as fees, attendance, age limits, religious instruction, and teacher salaries. The reasons for this, according to one official, were partly social, partly educational, 'partly financial and partly political'.[28]

Major practical and political difficulties were also becoming clear by the end of the 1920s. Cyril Norwood, as chairman of the Secondary Schools Examinations Council, warned in 1928 of the likely consequences of the spread of secondary education to a 'veritable flood of new material' which would be 'not of the best intellectual ability'.[29] Norwood proposed that the dangers that he regarded as inherent in this situation might be forestalled through the creation of a different examination for modern school pupils. However, it was quickly realised that such a device would confirm the modern school as an 'inferior option to the Secondary School', and would 'play into the hands of those who regard the Central School with suspicion'.[30] It would therefore tend to promote hierarchy rather than parity of esteem. On the other hand, the *Times Educational Supplement* voiced concern that 'instead of finding its own aims, the central school may tend to duplicate the secondary school'.[31]

Such issues again came sharply into focus during the 1930s, as the Spens committee prepared its report on secondary education for the Board of

Education. Members of the Spens committee were anxious to consider how to secure 'equality of conditions in post-primary schools of different types', and a sub-committee was established towards this end.[32] However, this had already become a highly contentious objective. R. H. Tawney, a leading campaigner on behalf of secondary education for all and a member of the Hadow committee in the 1920s, felt that the Board of Education would itself resist such a development partly for reasons of cost, such as the implications for teachers' salaries, but also because of 'the real issue which won't be stated – principle'.[33] He insisted, in spite of this, that the introduction to the Report should reflect the weight of evidence from local education authorities and others 'in favour of equality for all kinds of post-primary education'.[34]

Such pressures resulted in the Spens Report, eventually published at the end of 1938, making a strong endorsement of the ideal of parity of esteem between different types of post-primary schools. The introduction to the Report duly emphasized that 'everything possible should be done to secure parity of status for Grammar Schools, Technical High Schools, and Modern Schools'.[35] Chapter nine, entitled 'Administrative problems', dealt at some length with the implications of this view. It argued against the general adoption of multilateral schools, but suggested that what it called the 'multilateral idea' should 'permeate' the system of secondary education.[36] Existing barriers between different types of secondary school were, it insisted, 'the legacies of an age which had a different educational and social outlook from our own'.[37] On the other hand, it conceded that it would be necessary to reduce the differences in the regulations and conditions under which each of these kinds of schools operated. It made several specific recommendations with this end in view. In particular, teachers' salary scales should be reviewed and revised, the provision of school buildings given equal treatment, payment of fees abolished in all state secondary schools 'as soon as the national finances render it possible',[38] the minimum school leaving-age raised to the same general level in all schools, and a new Code of Regulations developed for secondary schools to include modern schools, grammar schools and technical high schools.

Even before the publication of the Spens Report, however, strong doubts were being raised as to whether such reforms would be effective in their declared aim of achieving parity of esteem. One official at the Board of Education, R. S. (later Sir Robert) Wood, was especially sceptical, and circulated a detailed rebuttal of such hopes. Wood pointed out that although the Spens proposals would 'eliminate to some extent the inferiority complex about an education confined to a so-called Elementary School, for all children alike would attend a Secondary School of one type or another', there might still develop 'a feeling that special advantage attached to the Grammar or High School and a consequent demand for an unreasonable expansion of this type of provision'. Moreover, he added, 'it may be urged that any scheme such as that outlined above is nothing more than an elaborate attempt to spoof the public mind, and by giving a new wrapper and a new name persuade them to accept the cheaper article as the higher class goods'.[39] Wood concluded that the likely proposals of the Spens committee would do little to remedy the 'disparity of prestige' between the existing secondary schools and new types of secondary schools.[40]

Members of the Norwood committee in the early 1940s also saw through this 'spoof of the public mind'. In its deliberations the pointed question was raised: 'Can a school with a leaving age of 16 ever have parity of esteem with one with a leaving age of 18? Is it all a game of "Let's pretend"?'[41] The committee decided that use of the phrase 'parity of esteem' tended to create 'confusion of thought', and that therefore 'the Report should not give any encouragement to the use of the phrase but should rather expose it as meaningless'.[42]

Experience of 'secondary education for all' following the introduction of the Education Act of 1944 soon confounded the hopes expressed in the Spens Report, and confirmed the doubts of the sceptics. It was observed that 'a deep sense of disappointment' followed the realization that 'the number of secondary school places available – in the sense that the word "secondary" has hitherto been understood – is really no more than when the Act passed into law'.[43] Many of the schools officially elevated to secondary status under the Act were recognized to be what Wood had described as the 'cheaper article' rather than the 'higher class goods'. In these circumstances, the idea of parity of esteem between different types of school was exposed as a pious and unrealistic hope. As was noted in 1947, 'entities so different in their social and cultural origins' could not gain parity of esteem simply through 'administrative action', but would need 'profound changes in prevailing social attitude and habits' in order for this to take place.[44]

Alternative roads?

The idea of parity of esteem between different types of secondary school was thoroughly discredited by the experience of the tripartite system in the late 1940s and 1950s. The weaknesses and contradictions in the notion seemed readily apparent by the mid-1950s, when Dr Olive Banks's shrewd and well-balanced study of 'parity and prestige in English secondary education' could emphasize the extent to which orthodox opinion had turned against it. Banks noted that 'While the schools can be granted "parity of conditions", the essential corollary, "parity of esteem", as the Ministry itself realizes, depends less on the action of educational administrators, than on changes in accepted social values.'[45] Banks added the appropriate moral: 'Parents are not likely to accord equal favour to all three types of secondary education while the grammar schools – enjoying in any case the reflected glory of their former esteem – still provide the chief avenue within the State system of education, to occupations of the highest social and economic standing.' For this reason, she predicted, 'The secondary grammar schools will, no doubt, continue to attract not only the more ambitious of the working classes, but all those middle-class parents for whom the independent schools are out of reach.'[46] Such perceptions helped to create increasingly broad support for the main alternative policy of establishing multilateral or comprehensive schools open to all abilities and aptitudes.

On the other hand, as parity of esteem between different types of schools came to appear increasingly chimerical, the bipartite notion of parity noted by Lord Eustace Percy attracted a great deal of attention in the 1950s. This came about especially as the Conservative government, and Sir David Eccles as Minister of Education, sought to increase the prestige of the further education sector. In 1955, Eccles appointed a new National Council responsible for making awards to successful technological students in technical colleges, to be chaired by Lord Hives, chairman of Rolls-Royce. This was developed with the aim of helping to fashion what Eccles described as 'a broad road to the top of the technical tree alternative to the normal university route'.[47] One of his leading civil servants, Anthony Part, also stressed the need to build up the prestige of further education, hitherto 'overshadowed' by the schools, and pointed out the key implication of this policy: 'Basic to all this is an effort on our part to get enough of the top 10 per cent of each age group to go into the technical colleges. We have got to get away from the idea that the cleverest 4 per cent (or whatever it is) go to universities *whatever their future career*.[48] In other words, the technical or vocational course needed to become as attractive to successful pupils as were the academic courses of the grammar schools and the universities.

It was, of course, highly significant that this endeavour seemed to entail attempting to 'liberalize' courses in further education, that is, by imitating the most entrenched and prestigious form of curriculum that was already available.[49] Familiar tripartite distinctions were certainly not forsaken in this process. The White Paper *Technical Education*, published in February 1956, emphasized the distinct categories of technologists, technicians, and craftsmen. Technologists would possess the qualifications and experience required for membership of a professional institution, would have studied the 'fundamental principles' of their chosen technology and would be able to 'initiate' practical developments. Such a person would also be 'expected to accept a high degree of responsibility and in many cases to push forward the boundaries of knowledge in his own particular field'.[50] Technicians would be qualified by specialist technical education and practical training 'to work under the general direction of a technologist'.[51] Meanwhile, craftsmen constituted the 'skilled labour' of manufacturing industry who would need increasingly to be able to appreciate 'not only the how but also the why of the work they do'.[52] There was in these distinctions a clear hierarchical overtone.

At the same time, while the prestige of technical colleges was to be increased, there was no mistaking the continued élite status of the universities. In a private note to the Prime Minister at the time of the launch of this White Paper, for example, Eccles suggested that while the universities produced 'the officers of the regular army of scientists and technologists', the technical colleges should train 'the much larger numbers of additional technologists and technicians needed to back up the regular army'.[53] In such a scenario, the idea of the 'alternative route' commanding parity of esteem with that of the grammar schools and universities appears unlikely.

A further attempt to define a coherent technical or vocational pathway that would develop on equal terms with the academic route was made in the late 1950s, through an official inquiry into the education of boys and girls of between fifteen and eighteen years of age. This inquiry, undertaken by the Central Advisory Council for Education and chaired by Geoffrey Crowther, the deputy chairman of the Economist Newspaper Ltd, again defined the relevant issues in largely tripartite terms. It was agreed that there were three general groups of boys and girls, each of which should be examined separately. Group A was to study 'boys and girls preparing for careers in which they expect to reach professional or equivalent status (i.e. a status determined partly by education, partly by social prestige, partly by responsibility of work and partly by pay'). These would include engineers, architects, doctors, teachers, accountants, solicitors, clergymen, officers in the armed forces, and business executives. Group B was concerned with those pupils 'whose careers demand some formal education beyond the age of 15 but whose probable "ceiling" is below professional status'. Such careers would include 'the whole range of clerical duties and most of those industrial occupations which would normally be classified as skilled'. Lastly, Group C would deal with 'that part of the population which enters occupations that make no demand for education beyond the age of 15, except for slight works training'.[54] These categories conformed to the familiar tripartite typology of grammar, technical, and modern. The inquiry spent much of its time attempting to define the distinctive characteristics of 'Group B', and in developing a notion of an alternative route of comparable stature to that of 'Group A'.

Chapter 35 of the Crowther Report, published at the end of 1959, succeeded in formulating such a notion under the title of the 'Alternative Road'. This involved a 'practical approach' to education, explicitly distinct from 'the academic tradition which inspires and is embodied in our grammar schools and universities'.[55] It would not be narrowly technical, but neither would it be 'academic in the old conventional sense',[56] although it would make 'progressively exacting intellectual demands'.[57] The Report suggested that by developing full-time practical courses of such a kind for able pupils of 16 to 18, the word 'practical' could be both clarified and rehabilitated, so that this approach might achieve comparable stature to the outlook that had 'traditionally dominated European education'.[58]

In spite of these aspirations, on the other hand, the terminology of the Crowther Report itself tended to betray a preference for what it called the 'type of mind which is readily attuned to abstract thinking and can comprehend the meaning of a generalisation'.[59] This ability was portrayed in a positive way whereas other types of mind were described negatively or in terms of their limitations: 'But there are other minds which cannot grasp the general except by way of the particular, which cannot understand what is meant by the rule until they have observed the examples. Some minds are analytical; others can only build up.'[60] It would remain difficult to attain parity of esteem between these two alternative routes, approaches, or 'types of mind' while such preconceptions continued to shape the ideas of even the most sympathetic reformers.

These efforts, like those on behalf of parity of esteem between different types of school, were highly elusive and disappointing in their results. By the 1960s, both notions of parity of esteem appeared thoroughly discredited. Even so, some general sympathy for Crowther's ideals did remain at this time; even if they were naïve and unrealistic, they were at least optimistic and appealing to liberal thinkers. By contrast, parity of esteem between types of secondary school was discredited in a political sense, because it had come to seem transparently cynical and based on conservative vested interests, as a failed device to forestall the more widespread development of comprehensive schools.

Parity rehabilitated

It might be expected that as a result of these experiences, we could write off the career of 'parity of esteem' as a salutary lesson of the differences between policy and practice, the social and political associations of educational change, and the problems involved in reform. This is not the case, however, because in the 1980s and 1990s ideals of parity of esteem were resurrected or rehabilitated as a central part of the Conservative government's new cycle of educational reforms.

First to be revived was the bipartite notion of the 'liberal' and the 'vocational' attaining equal esteem or value. In the White Paper *Education And Training for the 21st Century*, published in 1991, the Prime Minister, John Major, declared in the foreword: 'With the introduction of a new Advanced Diploma, we will end the artificial divide between academic and vocational qualifications, so that young people can pursue the kind of education that best suits their needs.'[61] In other words, distinctions between the academic and the vocational that had remained deeply entrenched for the past century were based on an 'artificial divide' and could be eradicated through the introduction of a new qualification. The White Paper supported the launch of a system of National Vocational Qualifications (NVQs), which it claimed would help to develop 'a modern system of academic and vocational qualifications which are equally valued'.[62] In chapter four, entitled 'Equal Status for Academic and Vocational Education', it insisted that young people 'should not be limited by out-of-date distinctions between qualifications or institutions'. It was for this reason, it continued, that 'The Government wants to remove the remaining barriers to equal status between the so-called academic and vocational routes.' In general, it concluded, 'We want academic and vocational qualifications to be held in equal esteem.'[63]

Second, the idea of parity of esteem between different types of secondary school was vividly reflected in the White Paper *Choice and Diversity*, published in 1992. This looked forward eagerly to the achievement of the Government's educational policies: 'There will be a rich array of schools and colleges, all teaching the National Curriculum and playing to their strengths, allowing parents to choose the schools best suited to their children's needs, and all enjoying parity of esteem.'[64] Indeed, it announced, the Government was committed not only to 'parity of esteem between academic, technological and creative skills', but also to 'parity of esteem between different schools', which it would rely on to ensure that 'tiers of schools' would not develop within the maintained system.[65] Although it attempted to distance itself in more general terms from the tripartite policies of the 1940s, and emphasized the potential significance of the National Curriculum, the White Paper of 1992 effectively revived a similar ideal of 'parity of esteem' to that which had been tested and failed fifty years before.

Moreover, the Dearing Review of the National Curriculum and its assessment sharpened this comparison still further by 'slimming down' the

National Curriculum, and proposing the development of 'three broad educational pathways'. The 'craft' or 'occupational' pathway would equip young people with particular skills and with knowledge directly related to a craft or occupation through NVQs. The 'vocational' pathway, 'a midway path between the academic and occupational', would lead to General National Vocational Qualifications (GNVQs). The 'academic' pathway would lead to A and AS levels.[66] At the same time, it insisted, 'The Government is right to state that the alternative pathways must be of equal quality, leading to parity of esteem.'[67]

There are several factors that help to explain this fresh eruption of what had appeared to be an extinct volcano. In political terms, it met the need to justify high expectations of all schools, at least for the immediate future, while at the same time encouraging differentiation and specialization. As in the 1940s, however, it remains doubtful that 'parity of esteem' can overcome the historical and cultural differences between different forms of education that have been so pervasive.

Parity of esteem in the 1990s might also be explained in relation to its use as an administrative device, a convenient method of divorcing education policy from wider social and historical problems. In this sense a 'technical fix' of deep-seated dilemmas is attempting to draw a line as it were beneath the failures of past generations, and celebrating the creative power of technocratic rationality. The approach is essentially ahistorical, ignoring as irrelevant the failures of similar attempts in the past. Its gaze is fixed firmly on the future, towards what are assumed to be the new needs of education and society in the twenty-first century, in the hope and expectation that the realities of education in the twentieth century will no longer apply.

Overall, the rebirth of parity of esteem in the 1990s represents a classic example of the triumph of hope over experience, perhaps once again to form a prelude to disappointment and alienation. It exemplifies Gosden's view that contemporary educational policies tend to 'reinvent the wheel', and also emphasizes the importance of understanding the social history of the policies involved. 'Parity of esteem' was always a largely hollow goal, unconnected to the history and culture of English education, and lacking an adequate theoretical justification for its success. There is little evidence that these shortcomings have been repaired since the 1940s. The issues involved are likely to remain important for the foreseeable future. The resilience of tripartism, the unresolved tensions between different ideals, and attempts to encourage 'parity' among them are all endemic and familiar features of English education. It seems especially important, in attempting to address them, first to recognize their historical and cultural characteristics. The twenty-first century, no less than the nineteenth and the twentieth, is likely still to bear witness to the power of three.

References

I am grateful to the Leverhulme Trust for its support for the research project 'Education and the working class: history, theory, policy and practice' (F.185.V); also to members of the Institute of Historical Research history of education seminar in London, 13 January 1994, for their many helpful comments on an earlier version of this paper.

1 Peter Gosden, 'National policy and the rehabilitation of the practical: the context', in D. Layton (ed), *The Alternative Road: The Rehabilitation Of The Practical* (Leeds, University of Leeds, 1984), pp. 7-8.

2 See Gary McCulloch, *Educational Reconstruction: The 1944 Education Act And The 21st Century* (London, Woburn Press, 1994), esp. Chs. 3-4.

3 See especially Stephen Ball, *Politics And Policy Making In Education: Explorations In Policy Sociology* (London, Routledge, 1991); R. Bowe and S. Ball, *Reforming Education And Changing Schools: Case Studies In Policy Sociology* (London, Routledge, 1992); and, *British Journal of Educational Studies*, 42/1 (1994), special issue on education policy studies.

4 Roy Lowe (ed), *The Changing Secondary School* (London, Falmer, 1989); Brian Simon, *What Future For Education?* (London, Lawrence and Wishart, 1992); Ivor Goodson. 'On curriculum form: notes towards a theory of curriculum', *Sociology Of Education*, 65/1 (1992), pp. 66-75.

5 Board of Education, *Curriculum And Examinations In Secondary Schools* (Norwood Report) (London, HMSO, 1943), p. 2.

6 Ibid.

7 Ibid.

8 Ibid., p. 4.

9 Ibid., p. 7.

10 Ibid., p. 4.

11 Ibid., p. 3.

12 Ibid., p. 4.

13 Public Schools Commission, *Report* (Clarendon Report, 1864), I, 56 (Parliamentary Papers, 1864, p. 20). See also Rupert Wilkinson, *The Prefects: British Leadership And The Public School Tradition* (London, Oxford University Press, 1964).

14 See Gary McCulloch, *Philosophers And Kings: Education For Leadership In Modern England* (Cambridge, Cambridge University Press, 1991).

15 For general accounts of this tradition, see Gary McCulloch, *The Secondary Technical School: A Usable Past?* (London, Falmer, 1989), esp. Ch. 3; Michael Sanderson, *The Missing Stratum: Technical School Education In England 1900-1990s* (London, Athlone, 1994), and Harold Silver, 'The liberal and the vocational', in his *Education As History* (London, Methuen, 1983), pp. 153-72.

16 See Gary McCulloch and Liz Sobell, 'Towards a social history of the secondary schools', *History Of Education*, 23/3 (1994), pp 275-86.

17 See especially Brian Simon's four-volume history of English education, 'Studies in the History of Education'; also e.g. A. Rattansi and D. Reeder (eds), *Rethinking Radical Education: Essays In Honour Of Brian Simon* (London, Lawrence and

Wishart, 1992); and Richard Aldrich, 'The real Simon pure: Brian Simon's four-volume history of education in England', *History Of Education Quarterly*, 34/1 (1994), pp. 73-80.

18 See Richard Crossman, *Plato Today* (London, Allen and Unwin, 1937); and John Dancy, 'Technology in a liberal education', *Advancement Of Science*, October 1965, pp. 379-87.

19 Sir Richard Livingstone, *On Education* (Cambridge, Cambridge University Press, 1956); R. C. Lodge, *Plato's Theory Of Education* (New York, Russell and Russell, 1947); Eric James, *Education And Leadership* (London, Harrap, 1951).

20 D.R. Hardman, memo to Minister of Education, 19 March 1946 (Ministry of Education papers, Public Record Office, Kew, ED.136/788).

21 Norwood Report (1943), p. 24.

22 Board of Education, *Educational Reconstruction* (London, HMSO, 1943), paragraph 2.

23 See Gary McCulloch, *Technical Fix? City Technology Colleges* (Leeds, University of Leeds, 1994) for further discussion of this.

24 NB e.g. Ivor Goodson, *The Making Of Curriculum: Collected Essays* (London, Falmer, 1988), esp. Ch. 8.

25 See e.g. Stewart Ranson, 'Towards a tertiary tripartism: new codes of social control and the 17+', in P. Broadfoot (ed), *Selection, Certification And Control: Social Issues In Educational Assessment* (London, Falmer, 1984), pp. 225-44.

26 Eustace Percy, *Some Memories* (London, Eyre and Spottiswoode, 1958), p. 101.

27 'Modern schools' – discussion on Wednesday 25 May [1927?] (Board of Education papers, Public Record Office, Kew, ED.24/1264).

28 Note to Sir E. Phipps (by Mr Watkins?), 1 June 1927 (Board of Education papers, ED.24/1264).

29 C. Norwood, 'The School Certificate' (n.d.; January 1928?) (Board of Education papers, ED.12/255).

30 W. R. Richardson, note, 26 March 1928 (Board of Education papers, ED.12/255).

31 *Times Educational Supplement*, 27 October 1928, report, 'Examinations for central schools'.

32 M.F. Young (secretary to Spens Committee) to Lady Simon, 26 February 1936. (Lady Simon papers, Manchester Central Library, M14/2/2/3. I am grateful to Mr Roger Simon for permission to consult and quote from these papers.)

33 R. H. Tawney to Lady Simon, 26 February 1936 (Lady Simon papers, M14/2/2/4).

34 R. H. Tawney to Lady Simon, 2 January 1937 (Lady Simon papers, M14/2/2/4).

35 Board of Education, *Secondary Education With Special Reference To Grammar Schools And Technical High Schools* (Spens Report) (London, HMSO, 1938), p. xxxv.

36 Ibid., p. 292.

37 Ibid., p. 293.

38 Ibid., p. 378.

39 R. S. Wood, memo, 30 July 1937 (Board of Education papers, ED.10/273).

40 R. S. Wood, further note (n.d.; 1937) (Board of Education papers, ED.10/273).

41 Norwood Committee, 'Detailed agenda for meetings', January 1942, IIv (Incorporated Association of Assistant Masters (IAAM) papers, Institute of Education, London, E1/1/file 3).

42 3rd meeting of Norwood committee, 5-7 January 1942, minute 4 (IAAM papers, E1/1/file 3).

43 Central Advisory Council draft Report *School And Life*, Ch. 1, 'The contrast between theory and practice', 10 May 1946 (Ministry of Education papers, ED.146/13).

44 CAC memo (n.d.; 1947?), 'Current criticisms of the proposed triad of secondary school types' (Ministry of Education papers, ED.146/13).

45 Olive Banks, *Parity and Prestige In English Secondary Education: A Study in Educational Sociology* (London, RKP, 1955), p. 7.

46 Ibid.

47 Sir David Eccles to Dr W. Jackson, 11 October 1955 (Jackson papers, Imperial College London, D3).

48 A. A. Part, note, 6 December 1955 (Ministry of Education papers, ED.46/1001).

49 See also Harold Silver, 'Intentions and outcomes: vocationalism in further education', in his *Education, Change and the Policy Process* (London, Falmer, 1990), pp. 100-146, for further details of this tendency.

50 Ministry of Education, *Technical Education* (London, HMSO, 1956), p. 2.

51 Ibid.

52 Ibid.

53 Sir David Eccles, note to Prime Minister, 27 February 1956 (Ministry of Education papers, ED.46/1002).

54 CAC memo, 'Suggested approach to the Council's work for 1956', 12 April 1956 (by David Ayerst, HMI) (Raybould papers, Museum of the History of Education, University of Leeds).

55 Ministry of Education, *15 To 18* (Crowther Report) (London, HMSO, 1959), p. 391.

56 Ibid., p. 394.

57 Ibid., p. 397.

58 Ibid., p. 391. See also McCulloch, *The Secondary Technical School*, esp. Ch. 7.

59 Crowther Report, p. 394.

60 Ibid.

61 Department of Education and Science, *Education And Training For The 21st Century* (vol. 1, 1991), foreword.

62 Ibid., p. 16.

63 Ibid., p. 24.

64 Department for Education, *Choice And Diversity: A New Framework For Schools* (London, HMSO, 1992), p. 64.

65 Ibid., p. 10.

66 Sir Ron Dearing, *The National Curriculum And Its Assessment: Final Report* (London, School Curriculum and Assessment Authority, 1994), p. 19.

67 Ibid., p. 24.

Reporting Academics:
A memoir of
The Times Higher Education Supplement

PETER SCOTT

A *Festschrift* is a collection of essays to honour a colleague and celebrate his scholarship. It is a personal tribute. So perhaps a personal memoir, which attempts to combine telling a story with more reflective analysis, is not out of place in such a collection. The story is that of *The Times Higher Education Supplement (The THES)* first published in October 1971 just when the Robbins-induced expansion of the universities was running out of steam – and into trouble – and the force of the polytechnic alternative had yet to be recognized. I was associated with *The THES* from the start; indeed, before the start because I left my previous job as a reporter on *The Times* in the summer of 1971 to help Brian MacArthur, *The THES*'s first Editor, plan the yet-to-be-published newspaper. For its first two formative years I was deputy editor. Two years later, in May 1976, after a spell as a Harkness Fellow in the United States and a leader-writer on *The Times*, I succeeded Brian as Editor. For the next 16 years my life was ruled by the rhythms of a weekly newspaper – one-and-a-half million words of leaders to write, 25,000 page proofs to check, more than 800 weekly editorial conferences to chair, not to mention bi-annual outings to AUT councils on middle-England campuses, an annual trip to the seaside to savour the Natfhe conference and quinquennial congresses of the European rectors or Commonwealth universities – Vancouver, Perth, Athens – and Birmingham!

During the two decades I was associated with *The THES*, minus time-out in Berkeley, the industry, of which this new higher education weekly formed such a small part, was transformed. It was born into a world labelled 'Fleet Street' – clanking Linotype machines, print union chapels, gentlemen-managers, distant proprietors, an environment which had changed little since Rothermere 'invented' the mass-circulation press in the 1890s. Indeed, because *The THES* was an off-shoot of *The Times* and its self-important traditions (Delane as a Victorian power-broker, Russell in the Crimea, Dawson of Appeasement infamy), echoes of an older, more enclosed and more aristocratic world of (curiously misnamed) 'public men' had not entirely faded. It was a world to which the universities still clung in 1971. So, by fortunate accident, there was a congruence between *Times* values and academic values; for both the 1980s were to be a time of rude awakening. When I left *The THES* to come to Leeds in the summer of 1992, an industrial revolution had taken place in newspapers. Hot metal had been superseded by flickering computer screens; the NGA and SOGAT vanquished by Rupert Murdoch; 'Fleet Street' with its artisanal values and anarchic practice succeeded by 'information superhighways'. All this is part of the story.

The analysis is of the impact *The THES* had on the development of higher education during these two decades, a period which saw a decisive re-shaping of the system. In 1971 there were only 176,000 students in 45 universities; the grass had barely grown on the greenfields campuses of the new universities so recently building sites; and the polytechnics were still in the process of being formed from a rag-bag of colleges of technology, art and design and commerce. But what the system, if there was a system, lacked in size and coherence it made up for in self-confidence. The state was kept firmly at arm's length by that benign buffer, the University Grants Committee – or so it appeared at the time. The universities continued to enjoy the best of all possible worlds, public patronage and institutional autonomy. The academic climate too was set fair. Despite the election of a Conservative Government a year earlier the provincialism and Philistinism of post-war England was being sloughed off. If science and engineering languished, social science crackled. An indigenous intelligentsia began, for the first time, to emerge. Its home bases were this expanding higher education system – and, intriguingly in the light of the twin themes of this essay, the media. The early 1970s, in retrospect, were both an Indian summer and a Brave New World. Only the more cynical, or more far-sighted, mentioned the souring of public enthusiasm produced by the, comparatively mild, outbreaks of student revolt at Essex, the London School of Economics and mimicked almost everywhere.

Two decades later higher education, like the newspaper industry, has been transformed. Almost three-quarters of a million students in more than 90 universities. The polytechnics very much alive in spirit, although dead in name. The UGC forgotten, but not perhaps forgiven for the 1981 cuts which so neatly bisected this period. A new iron age of acronymic oppression as HEFCE and SHEFC allocate MASNs and conduct QA and RA. The 'donnish dominion', to borrow A. H. Halsey's suggestive phrase, abolished. Yet contradictions abound; the nascent intelligentsia curbed, so a pervasive sense of academic closure, but subjects and people admitted to higher education until recently categorically excluded, so a breath – a gale – of social exposure; a Government of wretched and shrunken values, but the agent of, or accomplice in, an irreversible transition from élite universities to mass higher education.

To claim that *The THES* had any significant impact on such a profound transformation which even Secretaries of State struggled to comprehend, let alone control, is plainly naïve, hubristic. Yet the fates of this small – and, in the early years, struggling – newspaper and of the universities, polytechnics and other colleges were bound up together. Editorially *The THES* chronicled, and commented on, the events, episodes, trends week-in week-out. The cumulative effect of its reports and analysis cannot have been entirely negligible. It told a 'story', **the** 'story' perhaps because there were few rival storytellers. Commercially *The THES* lived off higher education. The 'cuts' it reported translated into fewer readers, fewer job vacancies, a less attractive market-place for advertisers; conversely the expansion of student numbers, the maturation and eventual promotion of the polytechnics, the development of a volatile research culture with its high-velocity jobs and, most recently, the re-configuration of further education were good news.

But there was perhaps a deeper synergy, a more significant alignment of experience. *The THES* was caught up in the decline and fall of the old print industry; its climacteric came in 1978 when it together with *The Times* ceased publication for almost a year. The 'shut-down' acquired an almost mythological resonance in the company and among my former colleagues, a line drawn in history between 'before' and 'after'. Higher education, or at any rate the universities, passed through a similar revolution – or was it a counter-revolution? Its, their, before-and-after moment came in 1981. The 'cuts', like the 'shut-down', marked off innocence from experience.

The company

When *The THES* was first published in 1971 the company, Times Newspapers, a subsidiary of the Canada-based Thomson Organisation, was only four years old. It had been created by an amalgamation between the former Times Publishing Company, the Astor family company which had owned *The Times* since the 1920s, and *The Sunday Times* element within the former Kemsley Newspapers empire acquired by Roy, later Lord, Thomson in the late 1950s. It was not a happy association; rather the relationship between the two main titles resembled a Fleet Street version of higher education's own binary policy.

At Blackfriars *The Times* tradition was austerely honoured by an old guard which barely tolerated the Thomson-appointed Editor, William (now Lord) Rees-Mogg, who had come from the rival *Sunday Times*. Its members recalled the paternalism of the Astors, staff outings to Hever Castle in charabancs etched in the folk, if no longer, actual memory; leading articles in the 'Thunderer' which guided the thoughts of the political establishment; advertisements rather than news on the front page. The circulation-boosting strategies pursued since Thomson had bought the paper in 1967 seemed a betrayal of this long tradition. Shortly after *The THES* had been established, a near-revolt by this old guard, named after the pub 'The White Swan' in which the plot was hatched, forced Rees-Mogg to adopt a more conservative or respectable, policy. This tension between populism/profitability, the former generally unconvincing and the latter never securely achieved, and respectability, irrevocably dwindling, has shaped the fortunes of *The Times* ever since – the initial dash for growth followed by retrenchment, even stagnation, from the mid-1970s until the end of the Thomson regime; and a continuing pattern of stop-go through the Murdoch era.

The character of *The Sunday Times* in Gray's Inn Road on the eastern fringe of Bloomsbury was very different. It had been shaped by two inspired Editors. First, Sir Denis Hamilton, who after 1967 became editor-in-chief and chairman of Times Newspapers, had intuitively grasped the changing tastes of post-war newspaper readers, less snobbish and more sophisticated, qualities encouraged and endorsed by the advance of education. It was Hamilton who pioneered newspaper serialization of memoirs and biographies, his chosen instrument for the elevation of the middle-brow. Harold Evans, his successor, brilliantly developed the formula, combining a very Sixties preoccupation with 'style' (the first colour magazine) with a commitment to 'investigative' reporting (thalidomide and all that). The trouble with Times Newspapers' own peculiar version of the binary policy was that, while *The Times* believed it was best, it was the financial strength, the personnel and, above all, the values of *The Sunday Times* which dominated the company. This was confirmed in the mid-1970s when *The Times* was moved to Gray's Inn Road, tearing up roots almost two centuries old and leaving New Printing House Square to be occupied by an American bank.

In retrospect the move to Gray's Inn Road was a great mistake because the fissure between the rival cultures of *The Times* and *The Sunday Times* ran from top to bottom of Times Newspapers – from leader-writers' corridors through the news and composing rooms to the press hall. *The Times*'s printers shared fully in the paper's tradition. Even in the 1970s it was possible to imagine them, or their fathers, making up pages with leading articles by Geoffrey Dawson advocating appeasement or E. H. Carr supporting Beveridge. There was no tug of loyalty between newspaper and trade union. Industrial relations were good. But the printers on *The Sunday Times*, like all Sunday paper printers, were casualized. They came in once a week for a long lucrative shift. (Sometimes they didn't come in but were paid anyway!) Industrial relations were weekly war. The move to Gray's Inn Road entrenched this antagonistic industrial culture – with disastrous, indeed terminal, results for Times Newspapers.

For *The THES* this corporate schizophrenia posed an awkward dilemma. It, like its elder siblings *The Times Literary Supplement* and *The Times Educational Supplement*, came from *The Times* side of this shot-gun family. Its origins and orientation were reinforced by the 'core' readership, university dons regarded as natural *Times* readers (to such an extent, in fact, that some people at *The Times* argued the new paper was likely to damage its parent's interests). Many of *The THES*'s characteristics, too, could be attributed to the 'respectable' values it inherited – the emphasis on weighty leaders and high policy, the avoidance of flashy design, the attempt to provide comprehensive newspaper-of-record coverage. Yet it was a new publication; and there was no doubt that *The Sunday Times* offered a far more dynamic and modern model of journalism. Also its potential readership extended far beyond its donnish *Times* core to embrace lecturers in new universities, polytechnics and colleges much closer to the contemporary outlook of *The Sunday Times* and, among daily newspapers, *The Guardian*.

The decision to publish *The THES* was essentially reactive and defensive. It was not a strategic initiative to exploit the Robbins and Crosland-induced expansion which was creating not only a larger but also a distinct market in higher education. Brian MacArthur, the deputy features editor at *The Times* (and formerly the earliest *doyen* of the education correspondents) who was to become *The THES*'s first editor, and Stuart Maclure, editor of *The TES*, had already made the case for a higher education weekly on the lines of *The TES*. But the decisive impetus came from outside. In 1970-71 two attempts had been made to establish publications aimed at an academic audience. The first, provisionally titled *Faculty*, was planned by a magazine company, recently acquired by a Fleet Street newcomer Rupert Murdoch; the second *New Academic*, of which a pilot issue appeared, by Macmillan who, as publishers of *Nature*, were perhaps more sensitive to the coming sea-change in higher education. Times Newspapers, through their ownership of the highly profitable *TES*, saw education as their territory. The company was not prepared to take any risks with trespassers. *Faculty* withered of its accord, but Macmillans were bought off.

Although editorially *The THES* was an immediate *succès d'estime* under Brian MacArthur, in the company's eyes it was a marginal enterprise. A newspaper of 24–28 tabloid pages produced by five journalists in the attic of an old building with a creaky lift at the back door of New Printing House Square did not represent a significant investment. Even the fearsome Fleet Street print unions had not felt it was important enough to argue over, and as a result had got a poor deal. In its first few years *The THES* was essentially seen as an offshoot of *The TES*, a marginal-costs operation. This was reflected in the status of its editors. Although both Brian and I were formally accountable to Sir Denis Hamilton as editor-in-chief, it was made clear that on a day-to-day basis our line manager and mentor was to be Stuart Maclure. The fact that, when Brian left to become news editor of *The Times* in 1976, I was appointed editor at the age of 28 was a further indication of how peripheral *The THES* was in Times Newspapers.

In a wider sense all three Supplements were peripheral. *The TLS*, of course, possessed an insouciant donnish prestige. After all, Virginia Woolf, T. S. Eliot and almost every significant figure in twentieth-century literature, bar F. R. Leavis, had been among its (anonymous) contributors. *The TES*, despite a tardy conversion to mainstream opinion on comprehensive education, dominated the market-place for teachers' jobs and, as a result, was among the company's fattest cash-cows. But both, along with the new *THES*, were subordinated, organizationally, to *The Times*. Under the Thomson Organisation the marketing director of Times Newspapers was responsible for the three Supplements. The first was Derek Jewell who moonlighted as *The Sunday Times*'s jazz critic. His chief love was Duke Ellington not marketing; his Christmas cards were printed with his own poetical tribute to the Duke. Others were Don Cruikshank who went on to work for Richard Branson and manage the National Health Service in Scotland and Michael Mander, corporate man through-and-through, who delegated much of his responsibility for the Supplements to his deputy Colin Pettet.

This was not such a strange arrangement as may appear. In terms of production, finance, personnel, circulation and all other major respects the Supplements were effectively integrated into *The Times* operation. For example, *The THES* was just another job for the day shift in the composing room, along with early features pages or special reports on Hong Kong. Because of this management accounts, and management meetings, concentrated on volume measures – circulation and advertising share – rather than on profit/loss figures which depended entirely on the (arbitrary) apportionment of costs across the company. No attempt was made to run the Supplements, individually or collectively, as a separate business. In these circumstances the choice of the marketing director made sense. I rarely saw Duke Hussey, the managing director, except on social occasions. To his youngest and most junior editor he seemed avuncular and aristocratic. Unmistakable in his metal gait (he had lost a leg at Anzio), married to a Lady-in-Waiting to the Queen, and later to become chairman of the BBC governors, he was a distant figure who was able to spend little time on the peripheral concerns of the Supplements.

Another reason for the arm's-length relationship between the Supplements and the company was that the Thomson Organisation operated a strict division of power between editors and managers. This was rigorously respected. I can remember several occasions when complainants (including a choleric Paul Johnson who had written a column in the *Daily Mail* about 'slum universities' to which I responded in a *THES* leader deliberately phrased in intemperate Johnsonian language!) were politely rebuffed by Duke Hussey, and their letters forwarded without comment to me. In one sense the Supplements editors had even greater freedom than the editors of *The Times* and *The Sunday Times*. Although free as editors William Rees-Mogg and Harold Evans were directors of Times Newspapers and consequently implicated in company policies. In contrast the Supplements editors counted as middle-managers without significant corporate responsibilities. But, as editors, they answered not to the relevant main board director but to Denis Hamilton – and in his capacity as editor-in-chief not company chairman. Sir Denis was not a man who put you at your ease; his penetrating stare and prolonged silences were legendary. Yet he had been a great editor who believed with equal passion in editorial quality and independence. From our first interview he made it clear both that *The THES* was **my** responsibility, and that it was a **heavy** responsibility.

In the 1970s two things changed. The first, and less significant, was that the Supplements ceased to be so peripheral within Times Newspapers. *The TLS*, challenged by the growth of high-quality literary journalism in the Sunday papers and other weeklies (and perhaps spurred on by the example of *The New York Review of Books)*, underwent overdue modernization. The most dramatic reform was the naming of reviewers. But the overall effect was to slough off the inward, amateur dilettantism with which *The TLS* had become associated. The success of *The TES* in attracting more advertising meant that its profitability became an important company asset (I remember Duke Hussey telling me in, I think, 1980 that *The Sunday Times* and *The TES* were there to make profits; they were, in Bagehotian terms, the company's 'efficient' component. *The Times, The TLS* and *The THES* just had to break even; they were its 'dignified' component). *The TES*'s success also embroiled it in the industrial relations difficulties which were about to engulf the company. More advertising meant more pages, which meant that the production of the Supplements could no longer be regarded as a marginal operation filling in time on the day shift.

The THES, as it too grew in size, had a similar effect. Its creation had also made the Supplements a more coherent bloc of titles. As an educational paper its affinity to *The TES* was obvious, but through its articles and book reviews new connections were established with the literary-intellectual world of *The TLS*. In retrospect this seems to be just another example of the coming-together of mass education and (élite) intellectual culture, the outcome of which has yet to be resolved. In more practical and immediate terms *The THES* raised the profile of the Supplements within Times Newspapers. By the end of the 1970s a quarter of the members of *The Times* National Union of Journalists chapel (office branch) worked for the Supplements. The Supplements came out from the shadow of their parent. They ceased to be, even in the loosest and most symbolic sense, 'supplements' of *The Times.* Suggestively they came to be known more and more by their abbreviated acronyms rather than by their full titles. They were now a powerful grouping within the company in their own right.

The second change was the crisis that engulfed Times Newspapers, which in turn was part of a larger drama, the decline and fall of Fleet Street. Ostensibly a battle between unions and employers, this crisis had wider ramifications. At stake too was the privileged status of national newspapers (and of their journalists and editors) which arguably was an anachronism within an industry, which in its corporate structure was now global rather than 'national' and was being transformed by the revolution in media technologies. The company's original approach was consensual and corporatist; a so-called 'Programme for Action' was agreed with the print union general secretaries under which new computer-based technology would be introduced with minimum modification of existing working practices. *The THES* was to be the guinea-pig and go 'live' first. Drinks in the boardroom, to which the Supplements editors were invited, were arranged to celebrate the deal.

It is doubtful whether, in the light of the radical potential of new technology and the entrenched power of the print unions, a gradualist approach had any chance of success. But in any case 'Programme for Action' was rejected by the Fleet Street chapels. The company then embarked on a policy of confrontation. Each chapel was presented with a new agreement which committed its members to operating new technology. If they did not sign by December 1, 1978, all their members would be dismissed. Few chapels agreed, not even *The Times* NUJ chapel, which Sir Denis and William Rees-Mogg regarded as an incomprehensible act, disloyal and self-destructive. (I disagreed with the ultimatum and publicly said so, and was magisterially, and ominously, rebuked by Rees-Mogg.) The reasons for the journalists' refusal to sign were complex. Trade union solidarity and syndicalist sentiment played their part, for which the younger journalists on *The THES* and *The TES* were especially blamed by the company. But so too did discontent with the Thomson management, nostalgia for the old ways of *The Times* and a lack of affection, even respect, for Rees-Mogg. The long-term effect was to alienate the journalists from the Thomson management, which was compounded two years later by a brief strike when the company refused to honour an arbitration award. The short-term effect of the chapels' refusal to sign new agreements was that publication of all the company's titles was suspended for 11 months.

It was a time of great excitement. There were frequent and emotional chapel meetings, one in particular I remember was addressed by Rees-Mogg who was urging the journalists to support the company, only to be dramatically interrupted by news that a secret attempt to print *The Times* at a Frankfurt plant had been violently disrupted by a mass demonstration of German print workers. It was not a time of hardship. The journalists were not dismissed on the casuistical grounds that the chapel had in fact signed a new agreement – to make a new agreement at a later date! So full-pay journalists politicked in pubs while print workers picketed. This led to divisions, and suspicions, within the work-force which were exploited by a new owner, Rupert Murdoch, five years later when the journalists, after much Pontius-Pilate hand-wringing, agreed to move to his new (non print-union) plant in Wapping. It was also a sad time. Not only were friendships of long-standing destroyed, but *The Times* tradition, externally haughty and internally feudal but worthy for all that, was also a casualty.

The shut-down eventually ended in November 1979, on terms which favoured the unions and bred in them a fatal over-confidence. The titles reappeared. *The Sunday Times* and *The TES* were little affected by the interruption; they were too big and too complex for rivals to mimic. *The THES* too escaped without damage; the higher education market was still not seen as sufficiently attractive by potential interlopers. But *The TLS* now faced an influential rival in the shape of *The London Review of Books*. *The Times* was broken-backed, the Astor 'Top People Take The Times' mould broken and the Thomson-inspired 'Overtake the Daily Telegraph' alternative discredited. The will of the management too was broken; they had no strategy except to hold on grimly. The commitment of the parent company dwindled; instead of being a jewel in the crown Times Newspapers had become a by-word for unruly industrial relations. It came as no surprise when it was announced in 1981 that the company was up for sale.

Both William Rees-Mogg and Harold Evans struggled to organize editorial buy-outs, the latter with a better expectation of success than the former. *The Times* journalists organized a semi-co-operative. (I have my share certificate still, less valuable even than Imperial Chinese Bonds I suspect.) The three Supplements editors attended discreet meetings in City offices. We were surprised by the uncritical enthusiasm of the money men for investing in our titles. A friend in finance promised me three-quarters of a million in a weekend telephone call. What they liked, of course, was *The TES*'s cash flow. In fact there was never much chance of Thomson selling the company in bits and pieces and the unions, worried about jobs and pay-offs, supported a single sale. But the choice of Rupert Murdoch, whose *Sun* was just getting into its awful stride, as the favoured bidder caught many people by surprise – including myself.

On the Monday, as usual, Laurie Taylor had sent in his weekly column for the back page of *The THES*. It was a pastiche of what the paper would be like if Murdoch (then considered a remote, even ridiculous, purchaser) bought Times Newspapers – and was written inevitably in the style of *The Sun*. By Wednesday morning I knew this was no joke. Should I still run the column? I did. Next week, when the Supplements editors were introduced to Murdoch by Denis Hamilton, Laurie's column was not mentioned. For once I was grateful for *The THES*'s low profile. Murdoch was hardly likely to read higher education's 'trade paper' (a description which usually made me cringe), although I suspected that Sir Denis would have read the column and no doubt regarded my decision as another example of un-editorish recklessness.

Something else which Murdoch said at this first meeting stuck in my mind. He said that the only free editor was the editor of a profitable newspaper. This I accepted as a challenge. *The THES* had been profitable by the accounting conventions that prevailed up to the 'shut-down'. But after publication was resumed the rules were changed. *The THES* began to 'lose' large sums of money. In the last months of the Thomson regime there had been talk of radical economies, even closure, which I had tried to combat by drumming up support among vice-chancellors and other members of the academic establishment. I can still recall inviting Sir Edward Parkes, then the chairman of the University Grants Committee, to lunch in one of the Gray's Inn Road dining-rooms. Sir Denis who joined us for a drink beforehand was conspicuously reluctant to leave us alone. He was worried that I was organizing an unauthorised 'Save *The THES*' campaign. He was right.

Rupert Murdoch's reputation was not such as to make him the natural owner of a national institution which is how, despite the battering it had suffered in the previous 20 years, *The Times* still saw itself. Much attention was paid to reinforcing the role of the national (i.e. independent) directors when it became clear that Mrs Thatcher's Government had no intention of referring the Murdoch bid to the Monopolies and Mergers Commission, despite the profitability of *The Sunday Times*. However the national directors, who included Hugh Trevor-Roper (Lord Dacre) of subsequent *Hitler Diaries* fame, were not responsible for the three Supplements and could offer them no protection from a rampaging Murdoch. Instead the three editors approached Christopher Price, the Labour MP who was chairman of the House of Commons Select Committee for Education, Science and the Arts (and later Principal of the Leeds Metropolitan University) to ask for his help. Christopher decided that, because of their (arguable) educational and cultural significance, his committee would be entitled to invite Murdoch to meet them and to write a report – which, in extreme circumstances in the future, might offer some protection. Murdoch was duly invited and, coached by Sir Denis who disapproved of our manoeuvre, offered appropriate (but unspecific) assurances. The report was published. I have it still – in the same drawer as my share certificate for JOTT (Journalists of *The Times*).

News International was in most ways an improvement on the demoralised Thomson management – from the point of view of the Supplements. The fate of the main titles was more sombre; *The Times* has had four editors since Murdoch bought the papers (Harold Evans sacked, Charles Douglas-Home died, Simon Jenkins sidelined and Peter Stothard still in post when this was written) and *The Sunday Times* tradition of Hamilton and Evans was gutted by Andrew Neil, the quintessential Murdoch editor, friend of Thatcher, de-regulation and privatization and foe of liberal cant (especially in the BBC). But, although I am still surprised, and even appalled, by my own conclusion, Murdoch was good news for the Supplements. First, responsibilities were clarified. News International was a black-and-white world. Either I was free to decide or it was decided for me. Nothing in between. The Thomson world, in contrast, had been full of greys. As *The THES* was the smallest and youngest of the company's titles I was left alone most of the time. Its editorial line was my sole responsibility, although I was under no illusion about the wide gap between my own personal and the company's values. At election times ex-colleagues, usually from the safety of *The Independent* or *The Guardian,* loved to stir things up by pointing out that *The THES* was the only Murdoch title to tell people to vote Labour (which it didn't, but only because academics don't like to be told!).

Secondly, the new owners persuaded the print unions to agree to contract printing of the Supplements. Typically the transition was abrupt. In the middle of the weekly production cycle work was shifted lock-stock-and-barrel from the Gray's Inn Road composing room to a jobbing printer in a Clerkenwell back-street. The papers were printed first in Northampton and later in Derby. This change had two advantages. In the short run, the Supplements escaped from the high-cost environment of Fleet Street which was smothering even the highly profitable *TES*. It also meant that, for the first time, an accurate profit-and-loss account became possible. Crippling overheads disappeared. The threat to the future of *The THES,* which had been real in the dog days of the Thomson regime, was removed. In the longer run, contracting-out meant that the Supplements largely avoided the bitter struggle which broke out when production of *The Times* and *The Sunday Times* was shifted to Murdoch's new non-union plant at Wapping. The Clerkenwell typesetters and Northampton printers, both union plants, continued to work (almost) normally. There had never been much solidarity between Fleet Street chapels and other print workers.

Thirdly, Murdoch created a more sensible management structure for the Supplements, as a fortuitous by-product of a larger reorganization. His new managing director was Gerald Long, former chief executive of Reuters (and a 'foodie' who filled most *The Times*'s op-ed page one day with an article denouncing a restaurant for its miserable selection of French country cheeses – fewer than 20! – and allegedly provoked the company's butler Paul to resign after a heated argument about whether to serve redcurrant jelly or mint sauce with lamb). Shortly after his appointment Long sent a one-sentence memo round Gray's Inn Road – 'Use of the term marketing is forthwith discontinued'. Under the Thomson regime the marketing department had acted rather like a corporate *Gosplan*, which is why Murdoch abolished it. It had also been directly responsible for the Supplements. New arrangements therefore had to be made. Long appointed as Publisher, a new post, Ian Trafford, former managing director of *The Economist*. At first I was unhappy; the appointment of a Publisher seemed to compromise my freedom as editor. But Ian proved himself a subtle corporate politician and able defender of the Supplements. A good luncher he never bothered the three editors much, although he grumbled about *The TLS*'s donnish disdain of the profit motive, and he kept Wapping happy, surviving bi-annual encounters with Murdoch over budgets.

When Ian retired the arm's-length system he had constructed began to break down – at very much the same time as the arm's-length UGC system which had protected the universities for so long from the over-attention of the State. He was briefly succeeded by Barry Winkleman, who combined being publisher of the Supplements with his existing job as head of Times Books. The Supplements were then established as a separate company, Times Supplements Ltd. But this change of status was nominal. All News Group companies had – and have – only one boss, Rupert Murdoch himself. I only met him four or five times, once when the Queen visited Gray's Inn Road to celebrate the bi-centenary of *The Times* during the miners' strike. But these brief encounters left me in no doubt about Murdoch's intuitive charisma, based on an extraordinary ability to grasp detail while thinking, and acting, strategically. I can still recall being closely questioned by Richard Searby, an Australian lawyer who was then Murdoch's right-hand man, about *The TLS*. Across the lunch table Murdoch listened intently saying nothing. I have no doubt the merits, or otherwise, of *The THES* were similarly discussed – in my absence.

The chairman of the Times Supplements was Sir Edward Pickering, vice-chairman of Times Newspapers and a distinguished editor of the *Daily Express* in the 1950s. At first Dennis Styles, the former advertising director of the Supplements and the man above all responsible for building up *The TES*'s massive advertising volumes, became (briefly) managing director. But, lacking Ian's guile, he was quickly replaced by Michael Hoy, the

Australian managing editor of *The Times,* who became executive vice-chairman of Times Supplements. Michael was a Murdoch man – or so it seemed to us when he arrived, although I came to like (although never to agree with) him. He was hyper-active, summoning editors to breakfast meetings and poring over design briefs. Dennis Styles was forced into early retirement. Some of his closest colleagues on the commercial side of the company, including Christopher Lorne, *The THES*'s first advertising manager, were sacked, after being left to twist in the wind for a few weeks.

But Michael Hoy was not content to stick to the business side of the papers. Any idea of a separation of powers between editors and managers would have struck him as ridiculous. He was determined to leave his personal mark on all three Supplements. The editor of *The TLS,* Jeremy Treglown, was sacked and replaced by Ferdinand Mount. Stuart Maclure had recently retired as editor of *The TES* after more than 20 years and been succeeded by his former deputy Patricia Rowan. Both papers were radically redesigned. This left *The THES.* Michael was determined to do something, but what? My dogged line was 'if it ain't broken, don't try to fix it', which drove Michael to distraction. In our weekly management meetings he passed over the paper's rising circulation and profit figures in sulky silence. I took all the credit, of course, as I would have had to take all the blame, although it should really have gone to the Baker boom in student numbers. Our eventual battleground was over Michael's plan to redesign *The THES* and, in particular, to change its name to *The Higher.* On the first he won; the second was a draw, which created prolonged confusion among the readers who were left unsure about what to call it. Soon after Michael left in the autumn of 1991 to 'fix' the *South China Morning Post* in Hong Kong. When I last heard he had moved on to *The Age* in Melbourne.

Shortly afterwards I too left to come to Leeds. My colleagues were convinced it was because of Michael Hoy. That was only partly true. Sixteen years are long enough to be an editor. I had seen off five editors of *The Times,* three of *The Sunday Times* and two each of *The TES* and *TLS.* My luck could not last for ever. Nor was there any prospect of returning to *The Times;* in any case writing articles or leaders for someone else would have been difficult after writing so many of my own. Finally, and decisively, few people are fortunate enough to have a chance to pursue a second career although I suppose my years at *The THES* had turned me into a kind of academic already. But my tussle with Michael did force me to recognize how much the newspaper industry had changed. Pre-Fordist, Fordist and post-Fordist phases seemed to have been compressed into a couple of decades. When I became editor the memory of journalism as a craft still lingered; while I was editor newspapers passed through an iron age which the old 'Fleet Street' did not survive; when I left the global highways of the mass media beckoned. The role of editor too radically changed. When I began the editor was a leader, more especially a leader-writer, but the feel was collegial. Then the editor had to become a manager, and was caught up in the turbulent them-and-us politics of industrial transformation and confrontation. Now the editor's primary responsibility is the skilful packaging of the media-product. It was time to go.

The newspaper

I became editor of *The THES* in May 1976. The news that Brian MacArthur was leaving to become news editor of *The Times* had leaked out two months or so earlier. I was never asked to apply for the job. It was simply assumed that I would be a candidate on the basis of having been deputy editor from 1971-73. One day I was taken to lunch by Stuart Maclure for what I took to be an interview. We talked mainly about leaders, I recall. However, the process of choosing a new editor was not straightforward. The mid-1970s was a period when workers' participation was, briefly, popular. Two national newspaper editors, Peter Preston at *The Guardian* and Donald Trelford at *The Observer,* had recently been appointed by a quasi-syndicalist process. *The Times* NUJ chapel now proposed that *The THES*'s journalists should be consulted – not, I suspect, because it was very interested in who became editor of *The THES* but to establish a precedent which could be used when the editorship of *The Times* became vacant. The company, of course, refused but the chapel went ahead regardless. Four people who were thought to be candidates, including myself, were invited to meet the staff under the neutral chairmanship of Clifford Longley, a former NUJ father-of-the-chapel (chairman of the office branch) and also *The Times*'s religious affairs correspondent. The idea was that the *THES* journalists would place the candidates into one of two categories, acceptable or not-acceptable, and communicate the outcome via Clifford to Sir Denis.

I remember very little about the 'interview'. It was polite and undemanding. Next day I went to Leeds to write a piece about the local elections. That evening when I returned to the Queen's Hotel there was an urgent message to call Jake Ecclestone, the current FOC and now deputy general secretary of the NUJ. He told me that an item would appear in *The Guardian* diary the next day about *The THES* editorship which would say, among gossip about the other contenders, that I was seen by the staff as the 'company candidate'. The item duly appeared. But what could have been a damaging episode was turned to my advantage. The following day *The Guardian* published a letter signed by every *THES* journalist denying the story – or, rather, its implication that I was unacceptable to them. The fortunate, and fortuitous, result was that I was labelled both the management's preferred candidate **and** a candidate who was acceptable to the workers (and have *The Guardian* cuttings to prove it!). The following Thursday I was interviewed by Sir Denis, although the interview mainly consisted of long pauses in which he scrutinised me carefully. Next day I was summoned to his office, told I had got the job and ordered to start straightaway (I think Sir Denis, unnerved by the chapel's manoeuvring, feared he might have a revolt on his hands). Needless to say, journalists' participation in the appointment of editors did not catch on. I was the first – and, I am sure, the last – Times Newspapers editor to be appointed in this way.

When I became editor *The THES* was well established. It had already recruited some distinguished journalists – Peter Hennessy, now professor of contemporary history at Queen Mary and Westfield College, who single-handedly invented Whitehall reporting at *The Times* and *The Independent* after he left *The THES;* Michael Binyon, later *The Times*'s Moscow and Washington correspondent; Roger Grinyer, now head of information at the Higher Education Funding Council for England; and David Hencke, who later established *The Guardian*'s highly successful style of investigative reporting. The political essayist Christopher Hitchens too, had begun his career as a *THES* trainee, although it was a brief and unhappy encounter. I remember Derek Jewell telling me that he would not forget I came in at 'the top'. As the paper was less than four years old, this was a high compliment to the first editor, Brian MacArthur. The trading account was healthy, even showing a modest profit (although five years later 'revised' figures indicated that *The THES* had lost money through the 1970s).

Its reputation was high, particularly among two groups. One was the vice-chancellors who Brian had assiduously lunched and dined. He practically lived in L'Escargot in Greek Street. When I had been deputy editor, I dreaded his return from lunch because so often he had agreed to publish another article from a vice-chancellor, registrar or similar dignitary. At one stage there were so many semi-commissioned articles in the files it would have taken more than a year to publish them all. One afternoon Brian and I had to sit down and go through them. After a few seconds' scrutiny they were pronounced hits or misses. Authors of the latter received letters apologizing for our 'sloppy behaviour'! The vice-chancellor tendency was pronounced in the early *THES*. Eric Ashby, the former vice-chancellor of Cambridge, and Charles Carter, then vice-chancellor of Lancaster, were among its first regular columnists (so was Robert Jackson, then an All Souls-based *Times* leader-writer, who was to return to haunt higher education more than a decade later). By the time I became editor this strategy of targeting the academic establishment had been remarkably successful. Many vice-chancellors had been weaned off their traditional allegiance to *The Times*.

The second group was the new polytechnics. The relationship between *The THES* and the polytechnics was symbiotic from the start. We both needed each other; *The THES* because its success depended on the creation of a higher education 'market' which extended beyond its university heartland, and the polytechnics because a pre-condition of their successful development was unchallenged incorporation in higher education (and ultimately detachment from the world of local authority education, although few people, myself not excepted, recognized this in the 1970s). This was clear from the very first issue. Two pages were devoted to a profile, written by me, of the then City of London Polytechnic (now London Guildhall University). Over the next two years as deputy editor I travelled up and down Britain, from Plymouth to Aberdeen (Robert Gordon Institute of Technology), writing polytechnic profiles, while Brian lunched vice-chancellors! The targeting of the polytechnics worked too. Early readership research indicated polytechnic lecturers were more likely to read *The THES* than university lecturers.

It sounds cynical, an unholy alliance between *The THES* in search of new readers and more job advertisements and the polytechnics whoring after academic respectability ('academic drift' became the standard phrase). In fact the synergy between higher education's new newspaper and higher education's new institutions was both more positive and subtle. It was one small but suggestive aspect of a wider evolution of the higher education system. The academic establishment's shuffling switch of allegiance from *The Times*, the top-people's newspaper, to *The THES*, arguably a 'trade paper', was evidence of a fundamental shift in its outlook – from automatic membership of the great-and-good to a more professional (and sectional?) orientation; and from regarding universities as above, and apart from, the rest of education to identification with the wider world, not only of education but of the whole welfare state. The growth of the polytechnics, in turn, hastened this shift from an élite, enclosed, self-referential view of higher education to a more popular, open, outer-directed view.

The early identification of these two groups, vice-chancellors and other members of the university leadership class and the polytechnics, with *The THES* was a significant strand in the paper's history. However uncomfortable the thought, *The THES* clearly thrived on the growth of managerialism in higher education. Managers were natural readers; they also placed the advertisements. Their business was 'higher education'. They confronted an increasingly complex policy world, as the trickle of occasional notes of guidance from the UGC (or, in the case of the polytechnics, the minutes of the further education sub-committee) were

succeeded by a flood of circulars and consultation documents from the
UGC and the National Advisory Body respectively and later the funding
councils which replaced the UGC and NAB. *The THES* was a primary
source of intelligence about this world, whether high-minded comment or
low-life gossip.

For almost two decades *The THES* held a pivotal, but solitary, position.
Old-style *Times* university reporting declined in the early 1970s, just when
The THES was getting under way. This was not a coincidence, in a double
sense. First, as has already been explained university leaders gradually
ceased to identify so strongly with the good-and-great, while polytechnic
leaders never aspired to such high status. As a result *The Times,* in its
capacity as the house journal of the politico-administrative élite, became
less interested in universities. Secondly, Times Newspapers' corporate (and
commercial) interest in the academic world was displaced from *The Times*
to *The THES*. At very much the same time the education correspondents,
with no more student revolts to report, turned to other topics in the early
1970s. Even when *The Guardian* began to publish its Tuesday 'Education'
section, most of its articles were about schools (although, significantly, most
of the advertising came from higher education).

Paradoxically, therefore, the short-term effect of *The THES* was probably
to discourage rather than stimulate an interest in university affairs by other
newspapers. However its medium and long-term effect was to establish a
body of high-quality journalism which provided a solid foundation on
which wider media interest could be relaunched when higher education
again became a 'story' in the later 1980s (partly because a mass system was
clearly emerging, endorsed by the Government; but partly because *THES*
émigrés staffed the education desk of the newly established *Independent*).

The link with the second group, the polytechnics, was equally suggestive.
If *The THES* had been established a decade earlier, almost certainly
'university' would have appeared in its title. It was the Robbins Report
which had first introduced the category 'higher education' to a wider
audience, as a description of a set, or system, of institutions rather than
simply a stage of education. Previously the effective categories had been
'universities', 'teacher training colleges' and 'advanced further education'.
Even when *The THES* was first published the use of 'higher education' in
its contemporary sense was not yet fully accepted. It was still a neologism,
a semi-bureaucratic category. I recall on an early visit to a university being
told by the vice-chancellor that he regarded *The THES* as something 'for
the registry'. Although naturally offended I understood what he meant.
Science and scholarship, research and teaching belonged to the
'university'; 'higher education' merely denoted the administrative context
within which these activities took place. Only in Times Newspapers, which

already published *The Times **Educational** Supplement,* did it seem natural to include the label 'higher education' in the title of the new paper.

The THES, therefore, was the medium through which the idea of higher education, as a system of institutions which, despite their division into separate sectors, nevertheless had much in common, became familiar. Almost regardless of what *The THES* said about polytechnics, its existence symbolized (and realized week-in week-out) the essential unity of higher education. As a result it became a powerful tool in the polytechnics' re-orientation, away from the fragmented world of further and technical education towards the more open environment of higher education. They were embraced within a new discourse, in a precise rather than pretentious sense, represented by *The THES.* The same is happening to further education in the 1990s. Having been removed from local authority control and established as incorporated bodies, FE colleges are searching for new identities. The growing prominence of FE in *The THES,* therefore, is no accident. It is a rerun of what happened two decades earlier with the polytechnics. The only difference is that this time language is not on their side. The category of 'higher education' helped the polytechnics; it hinders the FE colleges.

The polytechnics were not the only allies of the early *THES.* The relationship with the Open University and adult education was equally close, for similar reasons. All 'marginal' groups and institutions liked the new paper, not simply because its attention seemed to confer status but because it represented an enlargement of what could be legitimately described as 'higher education'. In broader terms *The THES* also helped to establish an identity of interest between the greatly expanded number of teachers and research workers, often less hierarchical by temperament and more left-leaning, within the new and expanded universities of the 1960s, and polytechnic lecturers who increasingly shared many of their characteristics. Both groups, in a sense, stood against the dons. They read *The Guardian,* unlike the dons who had read *The Times* (or, later, *The Independent*). But they also read *The THES,* which perhaps made a more sharply focused contribution to the formation of this new academic class.

The THES was among the very first trans-binary institutions, anticipating the abandonment of the binary system by more than 20 years. It is hardly surprising that it was well supported by the polytechnics. It was where they could rub shoulders with Oxford and Cambridge, and where their staff could mix with the FRSs and FBAs. By and large this support was reciprocated. *The THES* probably had a 'house' bias, instinctively preferring polytechnics to universities, the National Association of Teachers in Further and Higher Education to the Association of University Teachers, the NAB to the UGC. But the bias went deeper. Both editorial

F

and commercial logic demanded that *The THES* support an ever-expanding system. Sympathy with 'marginal' institutions on the advancing frontier of the system was a structural requirement. But these were almost invariably the least intellectual institutions in the system. This was a dialectic which dogged my entire editorship. On the one hand I was determined to transform *The THES* into an ideas paper which would carry weight in the heartland of higher education; a long drawn-out reply to the vice-chancellor who had relegated it to the registry. On the other hand not only was I personally committed to building a wider system I had to recognize that, as with the development of managerialism, *The THES* thrived on the advance towards mass higher education.

The phrase 'trade paper' I particularly hated. To me the phrase suggested a practice of journalism which was both amateur, because of inadequate expertise and resources, and uncritical, because the relevant 'trade', higher education in *The THES*'s case, was the source of both rationale and legitimacy. 'Magazine' was not much better in my view. It implied two equally undesirable qualities. The first was the lack of a professional division of labour between reporters, sub-editors and other types of journalist. Instead magazine journalists did a bit of everything – not very well. The second was the absence of any tradition of reporting. Magazines trade in secondary journalism, like much of TV and radio. Newspapers, on the other hand, produce primary journalism. Reporters are researchers, they find new things out. I saw *The THES* as neither a 'trade paper' nor a magazine but as a proper newspaper, for a number of reasons.

First, it had sufficient resources. When it was established it had five journalists. When I left the total had grown to 19. Its journalists did not have to sit in the office rewriting press releases or conducting interviews by phone. Instead they could go out and about to report the news. *The THES*'s capacity to produce primary journalism owed much to its origins within *The Times* stable. Times Newspapers, as the name suggests, were newspaper publishers. *The THES*, therefore, was conceived of as a pocket-sized national newspaper. This was reflected in salaries, expenses, staffing levels. It would have been resourced much less generously if it had been established by a magazine publisher. Secondly, *The THES* could never have traded in secondary journalism. To an even greater extent than national newspapers, which can always rely on news agencies, it had to find all its own news. There were no alternative sources. Thirdly, *The THES*'s potential readers were, and are, demanding. Many had been weaned off *The Times;* most still read *The Guardian* or later *The Independent;* they expected the journalism in *The THES* to be of an equal, national newspaper, standard.

I never had any doubt about the primacy of news, although my own instincts, and skills, as a journalist were those of the leader or feature writer rather than the reporter. Nor did I have much doubt that news, for *The THES*, meant primarily news about policy-making. It was not simply that the leadership class, whether yesterday's donnish vice-chancellors or today's senior management teams, were core readers; it was also that an understanding of, and so involvement in, policy-making should not be a monopoly of this leadership class. As the system expanded and institutions became more complex policy-making was bound to be diffused. It could no longer be regarded as an activity confined to the Athenaeum, of little interest to the bulk of the academic profession. There was a second reason for believing that policy-making should have pride of place. Although tabloid-sized *The THES* had to be a quality rather than a popular paper, in the terms of that dichotomy which distinguishes the press in Britain. So its priorities were unavoidably those of its broad-sheet peers-policy not people. Occasionally I regretted the surfeit of acronyms and lack of people in *THES* stories which were the result.

The primacy of policy was brought home to me within two weeks of becoming editor. On Friday evening I had just arrived in Buxton to attend Natfhe's annual conference, in company with David Hencke, the author of a story in that morning's edition reporting that six – or was it 10? – more colleges of education were soon to be closed by the then Department of Education and Science. The Secretary of State, Fred Mulley, was due to address the conference the following day. David's leak was not calculated to make his reception warmer. Shortly after arriving David and I were sitting in the hotel bar. Suddenly I became aware of an anxious Clive Booth, then Mr Mulley's private secretary and now vice-chancellor of Oxford Brookes University (whom I had got to know when we were both Harkness Fellows in Berkeley), bearing down on me, followed by an angry Secretary of State. In the next few moments I learnt several valuable lessons – about the key role played by *The THES* as an intermediary between policy-makers and the system, about the sensitivity of ministers, about the accountability of editors, and about professional solidarity.

Most newspapers have a mix of general reporters and specialist correspondents. *The THES* in effect had no general reporters. Everyone was a specialist, although only two had titles – the science correspondent (successively Alan Cane, now at the *Financial Times,* Robin McKie, *The Observer*'s science correspondent, Jon Turney, now a research fellow at University College London, and Martin Ince, *The THES*'s current deputy editor) and the Scottish correspondent later editor (Olga Wojtas who single-handedly established *The THES*'s reputation north of the Border). There were two reasons for this. First, unlike a general paper *The THES* had almost no diary of fixed events – whether the local magistrates' court or Parliament. Journalists had to go out and get stories; the stories did not come to them. So informal contacts, which had to be nourished by trust that in turn demanded continuity of personnel and demonstrable expertise, were indispensable to news-gathering. Secondly, many *THES* stories were complex, even arcane. There would no point sending a general reporter to cover a story about the UGC's research selectivity exercise or the NAB's latest funding methodology, armed only with random cuttings to read in the taxi.

During my editorship several of my colleagues demonstrated a professionalism as reporters which, privately, I was not sure I could ever have matched. Ngaio Crequer knew what the UGC was up to before the chairman. John O'Leary understood public expenditure better than anyone in the Department of Education and Science.

They both moved on to become, respectively, education editors of *The Independent* and *The Times*. Their styles were very different. Ngaio never doubted that the most important thing in the world was to find out what the UGC would decide next week – and write about it first in *The* THES. Most of her contacts, including the then chairman Sir Peter Swinnerton Dyer and successive CVCP chairmen, succumbed to her forceful commitment. They were harassed on the phone and in various London restaurants until they did. John's approach was more cerebral. His success depended on complete mastery of his brief. His contacts in Government and quango-land realized he three-quarters knew the story already and that he would get it right. There were others too. What David Jobbins did not know about the politics of the AUT and Natfhe was not worth knowing. Karen Mac Gregor, a superb professional who returned to South Africa after the fall of apartheid, took over John's responsibility for Whitehall-watching. It would be easy to extend the list – and perhaps unfair not to do so.

The result of this emphasis on specialization (and sub-specialization) was a string of 'scoops' – the botched Government take-over of the polytechnics which led to the creation of the NAB, the Jarratt Report and so on. It also helped to establish a climate of trust. The timing of the formal announcement of the UGC's 1981 cuts fell badly for *The THES*. Our final deadline was – is – Wednesday and the paper goes on sale on Friday. As a result Thursdays, when the UGC planned to make its announcement, are a bit of a black hole in terms of news. There was a risk that *The THES* would be a week late with the biggest higher education story of the decade. I had to persuade the then chairman, Sir Edward Parkes, not normally a man at ease with journalists, to give *The THES* a private preview of the committee's controversial allocations. I recall sitting in his office early on Wednesday morning (I had to catch the first shuttle from Edinburgh where I had been attending a Leverhulme seminar on access). We talked for a while in general terms. Then he said: 'I expect you want to know the winners and losers' and reached into a drawer in his desk. If he had not trusted me, and *The THES,* he would never have contemplated releasing such sensitive information early.

Occasionally I felt the relationship was too close, leading to what could almost be described as 'insider trading'. Like all newspapers *The THES* was used by politicians and civil servants. The best example was shortly after I became editor and the AUT's 'Rectify the Anomaly' campaign was in full cry. (Increases in university teachers' salaries had been restricted by the Government's policy on pay restraint in the public sector in 1975/76, although schoolteachers had been treated as a special case. The AUT campaigned under the memorable 'Rectify the Anomaly' banner.) One morning a colleague and I were invited to a briefing at the DES where we were told that the Government intended to meet (most of) the claim. I am not sure that the vice-chancellors in their capacity of employers had yet been told. But an AUT council was due and ministers were anxious to end the dispute. Later, when the Conservatives came to power, the cosy relationship between the DES and the left-leaning *THES* cooled. As a journalist I was rather glad. However the relationship persisted in a more low-key but still worrying way. Because *THES* journalists became so expert in their fields, sometimes policy-makers accepted their version of what was really happening – which we then reported as the thoughts of the policy-makers. At lunch with senior civil servants I was sometimes unsure who was being interviewed. I remember being asked by Kenneth Clarke shortly after he became Secretary of State who the good vice-chancellors were. I mentioned Graeme Davies who had just been elected chairman of the CVCP. Mr Clarke noted his name on a napkin. A few weeks later Professor Davies was appointed chief executive of the UFC (and later HEFCE). I often wondered about the link.

The THES's preoccupation with policy was not expressed only through reporting. We also tried to make the news. The earliest and most serious example was the Leverhulme inquiry into the future of higher education, a series of two-day seminars held between 1981 and 1983. Research papers were commissioned in advance, later published by the Society for Research into Higher Education, and about 30-40 people were invited. Today they would probably be labelled 'key players' or 'stake holders'. The co-directors were Gareth Williams, professor of educational administration at the Institute of Education, and Tessa Blackstone, later Master of Birkbeck College. *The THES* was involved in a double sense. First, it was in at the start. Perhaps it was the start, because the idea of the inquiry grew out of a lunch meeting I organized in the Times Newspapers boardroom to discuss the feasibility of establishing a higher education 'think tank'. Secondly, we published an extensive two-page report of each seminar, with a leader thrown in. It was at these seminars, and through the reports of them in *The THES*, that many of the issues which came to dominate higher education policy later in the decade were first considered. The Leverhulme inquiry also acted as an informal staff college; a good proportion of the leadership class in British higher education was involved in one or more of its seminars.

Another example of *The THES* shaping the policy agenda was the decision in the mid-1980s to publish rankings of departments; we called these rankings 'peer reviews' because they were based on questionnaires sent to all heads of department in the relevant subjects. They were asked to list in order the best five departments, in terms of research and teaching. It was a controversial initiative. At times I felt as if I was in acrimonious correspondence with half the professors in British universities. The initial view seemed to be that our questions were impertinent, an invasion of academic privacy. However, the 'winners' quickly ceased to complain. The general view mellowed. In no time *THES* rankings were being guiltily quoted in prospectuses. My original intention had been to expose those silent hierarchies on which the UGC and other bodies relied so heavily in making funding allocations. 'Informed prejudice' was the complacent (and oxymoronic) phrase employed to justify this mode of operation. Looking back I suppose these 'peer reviews' opened a Pandora's box. Not only did they reflect the rising tide of consumerism, they also anticipated (and perhaps helped to sanction) the quality assurance/audit/assessment apparatus which has now become such a burden to universities.

Occasionally *The THES*'s policy interventions grew out of efforts to market the paper. In 1989, as a result of a chance meeting with John Fielden (then of KPMG Peat Marwick) on a northbound train from King's Cross, I agreed to co-sponsor an award for the best annual report by an institution of higher education. The first winner was the University of Liverpool. The award was presented by the Secretary of State Kenneth Baker at a grand lunch at the Savoy. Both *The THES* and KPMG had their own, easily identifiable, agendas. Neither perhaps was fulfilled. Yet the award sent a powerful signal to the system, which was reinforced by the Secretary of State's endorsement through his presence. It symbolized (again, perhaps, sanctioned) the idea of corporate culture, which just a few years earlier would have been entirely unfamiliar and profoundly uncongenial to higher education, and also the marketing means to promote this culture.

The final way in which *The THES* demonstrated its commitment to the making of higher education policy was through leaders. I have an old-fashioned love of leaders, partly because I self-indulgently liked writing them, partly because leaders represent one of a dwindling number of outlets for literary and rhetorical English in the age of the sound-bite, and partly because leaders directly express the ideas, and values, which indirectly shape a newspaper's selection of and approach to news, its choice of articles to publish and books to review, indeed everything about it. Leader-writing, therefore, is an exercise in coming clean. But in the context of policy-making leaders have a more precise function. Unlike news stories, which claim to report facts, leaders can only ask questions, express aspirations, offer interpretations. The former cannot easily be argued with; they can only be taken or (more probably) left; the latter provide the elements for a dialogue, a conversation. News is closed, end-stopped; leaders are open, provisional, fluid. Very much like policy-making, where unintended outcomes are often more important than planned results, where incoherence and inconsistency of goals are routine, where deep-set tradition encounters volatile ambition.

As editor I wrote all but a handful of the leaders. Usually there were two, one of about 1200 words and the other of 500 or so. At the Monday afternoon editorial conference we discussed leaders, as well as news, articles and reviews. If I am honest, I suppose I told my colleagues what I was planning to write although I listened to their views. I felt settling the 'line' was my personal responsibility because it set the tone and, over time, established the ethos of the paper. The primary role of the editor, in my view, is to exercise intellectual leadership rather than to impose managerial control over talented professional colleagues. I think most of them preferred it that way round. In any case I always saw leaders as opening up issues, not offering pat answers, as reflective rather than authoritative. Occasionally, as a result, *The THES* may have seemed to have supported contradictory, or not easily reconciled, positions endorsing the opening-up of higher education while being firmly committed to the preservation of a liberal university tradition; espousing equal opportunities and social justice while insisting on the central importance of a high intellectual culture, despite the danger of donnish reaction; supporting the aspirations of the polytechnics, even anticipating the creation of a unified system, while arguing to keep the role of local authorities in higher education.

Leaders were also important in realizing my second objective for *The THES*, for it to be taken seriously as a journal of ideas. I saw leaders as a bridge between the front half of the paper, devoted to news (generally of higher education policy) and the back half, made up of articles and book reviews. This division, tension perhaps, is a recurring feature of newspapers. In the case of Kingsley Martin's *New Statesman* it verged on schizophrenia, with the front half dedicated to leftist politics and the back half to an élitist aesthetic agenda. (John Gross, who was editor of *The TLS* when I took over *The THES,* had been literary editor of the *New Statesman,* although he was very far from being a man of the left.) My grand ambition was to create a paper which addressed higher education not only as a political but also as an intellectual system, and to relate one to the other. I wanted it to be read as avidly by the dons as by the managers. Some progress was made towards achieving this goal. Successive readership surveys showed the gap narrowing between the two groups, and book reviews in *The THES,* although never as grand as those in *The TLS,* became equally influential. Most leaders, of course, were concerned with policy issues. They were rooted in news. However they attempted to place policy in a wider interpretative, occasionally even an intellectual, context. So the case for the repatriation of the Scottish universities would be discussed not simply in political, administrative and funding terms, or even in the context of their continuing links to the wider research community, but also in terms of Scotland's distinctive intellectual culture and the role played by the universities in sustaining it. Every summer the connection between policy and ideas was made explicit in a series of so-called 'summer leaders', in effect a four-part essay of 10,000 or so words. Its origins were severely practical. Leaders shared the back page with Laurie Taylor, whose column with its gallery of characters, Professor Lapping, Maureen and so on, was certainly the most famous feature of *The THES*. Laurie could not be expected to write a column 52 weeks a year. He needed a holiday. So more space was available. August was a quiet policy month. If there was a season for reflection, surely it was high summer, the depths of the long vacation.

My original plan had been to travel round universities and colleges like a latter-day Cobbett in an attempt to capture, and then report, the 'mood' of higher education. I remember visiting St Andrews University and Ealing College of Higher Education (now Thames Valley University) in the summer of 1981 with this is mind. But it came out differently; I was certainly no Cobbett and perhaps higher education was not a sufficiently dramatic landscape. Instead the result was a discursive essay, which turned out to be a form and style of writing well suited to my ambition to contextualize policy and, at the same time, concretise ideas. It allowed for greater development of themes than would ever have been possible in a single leader; it encouraged a mood of reflection and curbed the temptation to editorialize. But the essay-form was much more fluid and open, and invigorating, than, say, the journal article or the contributed chapter. Argument could roam freely unencumbered by methodology and bibliography. Over the next eleven years I certainly ranged widely and often self-indulgently – knowledge, culture and the universities one year;

the ebb and flow of modern thought (with a sideways glance at the exceptionalism of the English) the next; Matthew Arnold on the centenary of his death; mass higher education (at the moment of its birth perhaps?).

However leaders were not the only, and certainly not the most important, medium through which I tried to realize by ambition to turn *The THES* into a journal of ideas. The paper had always had a strong book review section, ably edited in turn by Philippa Ingram (now on the op-ed page of *The Times*), Brian Morton (who resigned to take up a free-lance career and now frequently heard in the wee sma' hours reviewing jazz on Radio 3) and Peter Aspden (who moved on to the *Financial Times*). The first and the last also doubled up as deputy editor. One of my first decisions as editor had been to abolish the post of full-time deputy editor. My conscious reason was that such a post could not be justified on a small paper like *The THES* and it was better to deploy the maximum number of journalists at the sharp end, as reporters. Subconsciously, perhaps I wanted to avoid an alternative focus of loyalty – or maybe I was an early convert to flat management hierarchies!

The original intention had been that the books pages should concentrate on reviews of books about higher education, whether memoirs of vice-chancellors or the proceedings of the latest international conference. But already when I became editor this narrow formula had been abandoned and *The THES* had begun to review academic books across all disciplines. The reasons were both commercial and editorial. The economics of advertising demanded that reviews be grouped into 'special numbers' so that publishers could be persuaded to advertise their new titles in these specialised fields. So there was sustained pressure to devise more and more 'special numbers' – history, philosophy, management, women's studies. Paradoxically this commercially-inspired segregation of titles produced a broadening of the remit of *The THES's* books pages. At the same time it had become clear that many, perhaps most, potential readers were much more interested in their own disciplines than in higher education policy. They were historians, engineers, physicists first and university (and, less surely, polytechnic) teachers second. As a result they had to be appealed to through their disciplinary loyalties – which meant principally through the books pages.

Over the years an illuminating contrast developed between *The THES* and its more celebrated stable-mate *The TLS*. The new wave of publishers came to prefer the former and even eminent scholars did not disdain to be *THES* reviewers. The reasons, I suspect, had less to do with the absolute merits of the two papers than with a wider shift in the character of the British intelligentsia. *The TLS*, although most of its readers were academics (many, it seemed, in the American Midwest), continued to address them, no longer perhaps as members of a cultural-literary estate, 'men of letters', but still as if they belonged to a broadly defined intellectual class. *The THES* addressed its readers, many of them the same or similar people, in their professional capacities as teachers and researchers. As a result *The TLS*, despite (or, perhaps, because of) its donnishness, remained true to an older rhetorical tradition, while *The THES* developed a more focused and more functional intellectual style. The intelligentsia moved out of the salons, clubs and publishing houses and into the expanding higher education system.

Consequently in my efforts to turn *The THES* into a journal of ideas I was swimming with the tide of social and cultural change. Midway through my editorship I attempted to give greater emphasis, and coherence, to the ideas part of the paper by creating a new section labelled 'Perspective' which brought together articles and book reviews. In terms of design and type they were treated alike, and unlike the news pages. (For those absorbed by such detail, headings in 'Perspective' were in Times Roman capitals and small capitals while headings on the news pages were in Times Bold upper and lower case.) The effect was perhaps to establish a rather sharper demarcation than I had originally had in mind. A positive bias against publishing articles and book reviews about higher education policy developed, with the unintended result that a pen-happy vice-chancellor was more likely to be published by *The Guardian* than *The THES*. But at any rate the stigma of being a mere 'trade paper' was sloughed off.

My own, no doubt utopian, hope was that by emphasizing the ideas element within the *THES* formula the policy-makers, who continued to be its core readers, would be encouraged to develop a broader vision of their responsibilities and to see the development of higher education as a task which demanded intellectual imagination as well as managerial skill. At the same time I hoped that the academics who concentrated on the back half of the paper would come to recognise that donnish isolation was not a realistic option, that they must take policy seriously. In any event I never had any doubt that any paper devoted to higher education, a realm of reflection, had to take ideas seriously. And, of course, trying to establish *The THES* as a journal of ideas was great fun. Some of my most satisfying, perhaps self-indulgent, experiences were not as editor but as a writer of profiles of the intellectual great-and-good – Karl Popper hidden in the Home Counties so far removed from Vienna between the wars and Thomas Kuhn in MIT, Fernand Braudel at the Maison des Sciences de l'Homme in Paris and George Steiner in mid-flight between Cambridge and Geneva, Friedrich von Hayek at a London club and E. P. Thompson in his study looking out over the water meadows to Worcester cathedral. The reading required to conduct such interviews and to write them up into profiles was a rigorous, but joyous, form of continuing education. Perhaps it was right that the editor of *The THES* should himself have had to be a life-long student.

My third objective was to make *The THES* more international. Again editorial and commercial objectives were entwined. I was aware that *The THES* had few international rivals. The nearest equivalent was *The Chronicle of Higher Education* in the United States. *Le Monde* published a monthly supplement *Campus*. In Australia *The Australian*, another Murdoch paper, published a weekly section devoted to higher education. But there was not much else. However it was not easy to unlock *The THES*'s international potential. While rhetorically universities celebrate their internationalism, in practice modern higher education systems are deeply embedded in national practice. The stories which appeared on the front-page of *The THES* were likely either to involve the intricacies of national policy making, expressed in the obscure language of acronymic quangos, or else 'rows' in institutions ('Principal resigns after vote of no confidence', that kind of thing). Neither was likely to mean much to a professor in Berkeley or a lecturer in Adelaide.

My answer to this dilemma was, first, to make sure that there was always a foreign story on the front page and, secondly, to increase by 50 per cent (from two pages to three) the space devoted to foreign news. Earlier the company had been persuaded to pay for a full-time staff correspondent in the United States, shared with *The TES*. This post was filled first by Michael Binyon, followed by Clive Cookson (now at the *FT*), David Walker (now at the BBC) and Peter David (now at *The Economist*). It represented a substantial investment, well over $60,000 a year, which could not be sustained in the cost-cutting final days of the Thomson regime. The internationalization of *The THES*, however, was not confined to news. While much of policy is determined by specifically national circumstances, most ideas are international in their scope. In the back half of the paper the number of foreign contributors and reviewers, mainly from the United States and Australia, was increased. I also decided that some of the paper's regular columnists should come from outside Britain. Steven Muller, president of Johns Hopkins, Timothy Healy, president of Georgetown, and Sheldon Rothblatt from Berkeley successively offered a transatlantic perspective, while Wolf Lepenies, rector of Berlin's Wissenschaftskolleg, provided a (continental) European view.

Certainly in terms of advertising and arguably in terms of sales the overseas market was important for *The THES*. Many (old and new) Commonwealth universities continued to advertise their academic vacancies in the paper and, as older ties were loosened and new associations formed, jobs in other European universities also came to be advertised on a larger scale. In the early 1980s when it seemed that the expansion of British higher education was grinding to a depressing halt 'abroad' was also seen as a source of new readers. Both considerations, the need to keep existing overseas advertisers sweet and to attract new advertisers and the hope that the overseas circulation could be significantly increased, emphasized the importance of marketing the paper outside Britain. The strategy was geared round major conferences, in particular the congresses of the Association of Commonwealth Universities (Vancouver, Birmingham and Perth during my time as editor) and of the Conference of European Rectors (Athens and Durham). The key was to establish a strong *THES* 'presence'. Copies of the paper containing a special feature on the relevant congress were distributed to all delegates. So too were gifts, sometimes rather naff like a leatherbound 'personal organiser' at Perth in 1988, sometimes more tasteful like a print by the Royal Academician Tom Phillips at Athens. And, of course, the event was reported in the most solemn terms.

The most adventurous example of overseas marketing was in Chicago in 1978. The idea was to contribute a British element to the annual extravaganza of the Association of American Higher Education. It was envisaged almost as a 'launch' of *The THES* in the United States. I agreed to find and fly over two speakers, who in the event were Shirley Williams, then the Secretary of State for Education and Science, and Richard Hoggart, in transit from Unesco to Goldsmiths. The DES decided it would be inappropriate for the Secretary of State to fly to Chicago at Lord Thomson's expense, which saved *The THES* one fare. But the department was jittery about allowing the Secretary of State out without civil servant minders. I was summoned and asked, in effect, to act as an unofficial private secretary with instructions to have her speech transcribed and sent to London for 'corrections' before its release to the press. Not a request likely to be received favourably by the journalist. I ignored it, with the endorsement of Mrs Williams.

Further complications arose. Burnham negotiations were at a delicate stage. Premature return to London loomed. The programme of the AAHE was rearranged to produce a plenary spot. The British consul-general became involved. But that is another story, more appropriate for a *Fawlty Towers* script perhaps than a memoir of *The THES*. It is enough to say that Mrs Williams gave her address not once but twice, to general acclaim (sadly for Richard Hoggart the daughter of the author of *Testament of Youth* was better known in Chicago than the author of *The Uses of Literacy*). Whether *The THES* gained more than reflected prestige will never be known. Later that year the paper was shut down along with all Times Newspapers titles in the first grand confrontation with the print unions.

America was a powerful attraction in a much more serious, and personal, sense. My own higher education, at Oxford, and personal academic inclinations, which were (and probably are) élitist rather than populist, had not persuaded me of the need to go beyond the ambitious but nevertheless limited expansion envisaged in the Robbins report. The benefits of that expansion, of course, I could not deny. I was the child of Robbins. Yet, throughout my editorship I supported a much more radical extension of the higher education 'franchise'. Part of the reason was the world I discovered travelling round Britain writing profiles of the emergent polytechnics as deputy editor during the early 1970s. But a much more important reason was the insight I gained, and inspiration I received, after I ceased to be deputy editor and went as a Harkness fellow to the University of California at Berkeley in the summer of 1973.

When I became editor three years later I was a changed person. I suppose I had seen the future and it worked. In Berkeley I learnt that excellence and opportunity could co-exist, stripping away the sub-Leavisite assumptions I had acquired in Oxford (and which are still deeply twisted into English culture). California not only had the world's best universities, as I have believed ever since in a spirit of displaced patriotism; it also had a higher education system which embodied near-universal entitlement. The community colleges of San Francisco, Marin, Alameda and Contra Costs counties influenced me as much as, probably more than, the polytechnics of middle England I had visited two or three years before. I was already a believer in mass higher education when I became editor of *The THES*, a decade or more before it became fashionable, or even feasible for someone brought up entirely within the English academic tradition.

My guide and mentor was Clark Kerr, who had been president of the University of California during the turbulent 1960s. Since his dismissal had been engineered by Governor Reagan, he had been chairman of the Carnegie Commission on Higher Education. From his office on Shattuck Avenue he was a kind of president-across-the-water. And it was in this office that I was based. It was the happiest of accidents. I was actually attached to the Graduate School of Public Policy and my formal academic patron was Martin Trow. But there was no room for me in the school's cramped building. So I ended up on Shattuck Avenue. (The Carnegie Commission shared the eighth floor with the local, very taciturn, bureau of the FBI.) The great-and-good of American higher education flowed through Clark's office. During my 18 months in Berkeley I met, and had lunch, with most of them. It was a stratospheric initiation – and an experience which shaped my responses, intellectual and political, at *The THES*.

Of these ambitions the first, making *The THES* a key player in the policy game, was certainly achieved. But I suspect that only a small part of the credit must go to myself as editor, or to my colleagues who so ably reported the development of a mass system. Certainly we told the 'story' week-in week-out, and until recently it was the only available version, and I proselytized for my own vision of higher education, liberal and humane **and** open and mass. But the main reason was the explosion of policy-making. *The THES* was just there, in the right place at the right time. Higher education is now permeated by policy. The acts of the Department for Education, the funding councils and the many other national agencies penetrate into every crevice of institutions. It was not like that two decades ago. Teaching and research were autonomous, even private, worlds little affected by politics and policy. I am less certain about the fate of my second ambition, my favourite, to try to make *The THES* an agent of intellectual culture, binding together (in Martin Trow's suggestive terminology) the 'public' and 'private worlds' of higher education, policy and ideas. Perhaps the best that can be hoped for here is a constant reiteration of the attempt.

The success of my third ambition, to make *The THES* more international, is also difficult to assess. The paper gave more space to higher education outside Britain. It certainly became better known. But whether it truly grasped the globalization of teaching and, especially, research, higher education's own 'information superhighways', is less certain. Or, as with policy, its internationalization may simply have reflected this larger re-configuration. But, in any case, these were grand, even grandiose, ambitions. Newspapers are perhaps better judged in more down-to-earth terms. Their success depends on the 'fit' between their values and interests and the routines of their readers. Familiarity is the key. So it was – is – with *The THES*. Newspapers influence through the inarticulate rhythms generated by familiarity, banality even, not through grandly engineered persuasion.

Concluding reflections

To attempt to assess the influence or achievements of *The THES* is almost impossible for me. My personal engagement was – is – too intense. It is for others to judge with the dispassionate wisdom of hindsight, just as it was for the readers and advertisers to judge week-in, week-out contemporaneously. This has been a personal memoir with elements of analysis lightly attached. However, perhaps two limited statements are acceptable by way of conclusion. First, *The THES* survived. There were several occasions before I became editor and while I was editor when its survival seemed far from assured. It was threatened from within by the corporate turbulence within Times Newspapers, which itself was an aspect of the decline and fall of Fleet Street. It was threatened from without by the stagnation of British higher education in the late 1970s and the cuts of the 1980s. There were times, most especially between 1981 and 1985, when it seemed that a depressed and perhaps dwindling market could not support *The THES*'s editorial ambitions. Published on the cusp of the Robbins age, too late perhaps to take full advantage of an earlier age of optimism, the paper appeared condemned to atrophy, and perhaps to die before a new wave of expansion arrived.

Secondly, the evolution of *The THES*, in however trivial a way, was part of the ebb and flow of British higher education. And that more-flow-than-ebb is a grand story, pregnant with social opportunities and intellectual possibilities. It has shaped modern Britain far more powerfully than is generally acknowledged. If Britain in the last decade of the twentieth century is more open, less class-bound, wealthier, more cultured, much of the credit must go higher education. The Robbins expansion, the establishment of the (first) new universities, the development of the polytechnics and, most recently, the turbulent growth of the past decade – these have been decisive events in creating a new Britain, as important as the retreat from empire, entry into Europe or the rise and fall of the welfare state. It is a story that has yet to be told. Perhaps in its enormity it seems banal. Perhaps it is too close to home. Some day though it will be told, not as an internal history of higher education but as part of a larger account of the transformation of British society or, even more ambitiously, of the modern world. This memoir is merely an extended and anticipatory footnote.

A NOTE ON SOURCES
The primary source, of course, is my own memory of the events I have described. However memory is fallible and selective and I have checked many of the facts and shared many of my impressions with other participants. Of course, the interpretations I offer are my own. I have also consulted the archives of Times Newspapers now in Wapping. Material about The THES *has only been patchily preserved – as I know because when I ceased to be editor I handed over a fairly random collection of papers and files. Finally I have consulted relevant published works, notably Harold Evans' memoirs of his editorship of* The Times *and the official history of* The Times. *However in these, and other books,* The THES *makes only fleeting appearances.*

From local governance to LEA and from LEA to local governance:
a study of the
management and
government of schools in
England from
1839 to 1994

PAUL SHARP AND JOHN DUNFORD

The purpose of the Committee of the Privy Council on Education, set up in 1839 with James Kay-Shuttleworth as its first secretary, was to administer the grants for schools made by Parliament. The Committee immediately made it a condition of aiding schools that they should be open to inspection. Inspectors were instructed that they should generally announce their visits 'to the parochial clergyman, or other minister of religion, connected with the school, or to the chairman or secretary of the school committee, and proceed to examine the school in their presence'.[1] It soon became apparent to the Committee of Council that in many instances the arrangements for school committees and management were unsatisfactory. The Secretary to the Diocesan Board of the Deanery of Bristol was told:

> The provisions for school management in the trust deed comprised every form of negligent or discordant arrangement. Often there was no management clause; in which case the government of the school devolved on the individual trustees and their heirs, who might be non-resident, minors, lunatics or otherwise incapable. When a management clause was inserted, there was seldom any provision for the supply of vacancies or re-election, nor any qualifications for the office of managers.
>
> Consequently, in the great majority of these schools, the seeds were sown of future parochial disputes or litigation; of uncontested usurpation; of alienation of the trust property to other public uses; or of an absorption of the property into the estate of the proprietor. Time and opportunity alone were wanting to ripen this harvest of discord, confusion or plunder.[2]

From 1845 the Committee of Council began to negotiate with the Church of England about suitable 'management clauses'.[3] Although this matter remained a bone of contention with some elements in the Church for many years, in 1847 it was agreed that each school receiving grant should adopt one of four approved management classes.[4] Later, very similar provisions were applied to the other denominations. According to Kay-Shuttleworth's biographer, the aim was 'to give due place to the three groups of interests in every school: the subscribers, the religious or educational Society with which the school was connected and the Committee of Council as the distributor of national funds.'[5]

The arrangements for school management committees varied according to the size of population and the perceived wealth and intelligence of the inhabitants of the district to be served.[6] The table[7] opposite summarizes these arrangements.

These provisions ensured that not only the clergy but also, as far as was possible, the laity who were property owners and subscribers were involved in school management. As Richard Johnson has emphasized,[8] school

Districts where schools should adopt	Description of district	Those eligible for membership of Anglican school management committees
Clause A	Populous districts of towns in which the intelligent and wealthy inhabitants are numerous.	Clergy, church wardens, local Anglican property owners who subscribed at least twenty shillings per annum to the school.
Clause B	Towns and villages in which the well-educated and wealthy classes may be less numerous, and rural parishes having not less than 500 inhabitants, with at least three or more resident gentlemen, or intelligent yeomen, manufacturers or tradesmen	Clergy, local Anglican property owners who subscribed at least twenty shillings per annum to the school.
Clause C	Very small rural parishes in which the resident inhabitants are all illiterate and indifferent to the education of the poor, and in which the clergyman has, by his exertions and sacrifices, given proofs of his zeal for the education of his parishioners.	The clergyman normally acted as sole manager unless and until the bishop decided it was expedient to set up a management committee with membership as in B.
Clause D	Rural parishes containing fewer than 500 inhabitants, and in all school districts in which, from poverty and ignorance, the number of subscribers is limited to very few individuals, and great difficulty is experienced in providing a succession of school managers.	Clergy, individually named persons who were Anglicans and who on death, incapacity, or resignation were replaced by election by the remaining members of the Committee.

managers were required to be from the comfortably off and respectable levels of Victorian society and from classes above those from which both the elementary teachers and their pupils came.

Perhaps the most demanding task for managers in the mid-nineteenth century was to raise subscriptions for their schools continually and without respite. Management committees controlled the selection, appointment and dismissal of teachers and the use of premises and funds. From time to time managers visited their schools during working hours and superintended activities of various kinds. Such matters were not normally regulated by formal requirements, but included supervision of registers, meeting inspectors, ordering educational equipment and organizing treats for pupils.[9]

The Revised Code of 1862 restructured the payments from public funds to elementary education and consolidated them into one annual grant made on the attendance of scholars and their individual results in nationally prescribed tests. Direct payments to teachers and pupil teachers were abolished, and 'teachers were no longer, in any sense whatever, servants of the State.'[10] Grant earned was paid directly to the managers 'who were left to make what terms they pleased with the teachers as to service and salaries, provided the requirements of the Code were complied with'.[11] Robert Lowe, the architect of the Revised Code, speaking in the Commons claimed that 'it gave the managers almost entire freedom', but he added more ominously, '[it] made the interest of the school identical with the interest of the public, tested thoroughly the work done and gave Parliament a complete control over the education grant'.[12] In many ways the tensions inherent in these statements illustrate the paradoxes in the government of elementary education in the third quarter of the nineteenth century. In theory, school managers were given discretion and choice, but in practice they operated within a highly circumscribed national or even nationalized system. Central government normally, and probably inevitably, exercised a tight rein over its budget for education, but, in addition, through the Code controlled in some considerable detail the elementary school curriculum and assessment procedures. Central regulations were also in force for many other aspects of schools' activities. In reality, there was comparatively little scope for individual school managing bodies to experiment or to deviate from the required norms. By their very nature school managing bodies operated as isolated units and as such their power base was limited. There was never any prospect of them working together either to promote their own interest or to develop elementary education. Consequently, in this period elementary education was almost entirely dependent upon central government for initiative and development. Despite the so-called 'freedom', school managing bodies were rarely in a position to be pro-active even within the confines of their own individual schools and almost never beyond them. There can be little doubt that those who devised the model for controlling education in the 1860s assumed that school managers were there primarily to implement the educational and financial requirements of central government.

The importance of the Education Act of 1870 in the evolution of school managing bodies has probably been underestimated. Having said this, it must be stressed that this Act was intended 'to fill the gaps' in provisions for schooling. It was passed to supplement and not to supersede the existing voluntary system, and, indeed, in large areas of the countryside school boards were never set up because sufficient places in voluntary schools were available. The management of voluntary schools was not directly affected by the Act, and the arrangements and practices set up in this sector in the mid-nineteenth century largely persisted until 1902. It was in the large urban areas, where school boards so often became the major providers, that there was scope for change and eventually for the establishment of a new and different tradition in school management.

Under the 1870 Act, school boards, if they thought fit, could set up bodies of managers for their own schools and delegate powers to them. Such action was entirely optional and many school boards chose to ignore this provision in the legislation. The major exceptions to this were Liverpool and London which both appointed managing bodies for individual schools. Liverpool believed that its system worked well, and claimed that its school managers were drawn from a wide variety of business and professional backgrounds.[13] At the outset London had separate managing bodies for each of its schools, but, as numbers increased, found it necessary to arrange for the grouping of several schools under one body. The appointments of heads were made by managers until 1889, but later a sub-committee of the Board selected three candidates from among whom the managers made the appointment.[14] It is interesting to note that the Cross Commission strongly recommended that larger school boards should appoint local managers seeing many benefits for the schools.[15] The extent of the delegation of functions to local school managers varied considerably from board to board,[16] and Liverpool and London were at the opposite end of the spectrum from towns such as Birmingham, Manchester, Salford, Leeds, Bradford, Hull and Sheffield which ran their schools entirely and directly from central board offices. It was in such places that alternative notions and concepts of school management began to develop.

In the large towns the school boards set to work with considerable purpose. New schools were built and staff engaged. By 1880 attendance at school became compulsory for all children. The boards, with their access to rates, were soon outstripping the voluntary schools, which still had to rely on subscriptions, in terms of expenditure per child. Often boards in large towns offered higher salaries to teachers and they tended to attract the best qualified staff. Once 'the gaps were filled' some of these urban boards extended their activities beyond a limited conception of elementary education. Large higher grade schools, which were neo-secondary in nature, were established, and by the 1880s and 1890s these boards were justly proud of their achievements. Taking into account the problems which they had to overcome the progress made in education in a relatively short period was remarkable. What amounted to active, progressive local education authorities had emerged by the last quarter of the nineteenth century.

Leading local citizens from industry, business and the professions were regularly elected to the school boards in the large towns. In Leeds, for example, members of the board were of higher social status than members of the town council.[17] Such people were committed to exercising their duties and powers to the full and were interested in developing progressive educational services for their towns. They had no wish to deny themselves direct influence over their schools by delegating powers to local managing bodies. Much was made of the fact that school board members were the democratically elected representatives of the people. A school board had a popular mandate to run its schools directly and normally did so through a school management committee. Reverend Dr Henry Crosskey, chair of Birmingham School Board school management sub-committee and one of the honorary secretaries of the Central Non-conformist Committee, which wished to make school boards universal, attached immense importance to these democratic principles. He maintained that, when parents elected their representatives to school boards, they became interested and involved in their children's schools, and that in contrast the voluntary sector's system of school management failed to engage such parental interest and involvement.[18] In his view these factors had important consequences for the quality of the education provided in the different sectors. Like most free church people he had no doubts that, in general, education in board schools was superior to that in the voluntary schools. It was acknowledged that this was partly accounted for by the disparities in funding. However, Non-conformists objected strongly to the fact that parents and the public had no vote and no voice in the choice of voluntary school managers, and Crosskey agreed with W. E. Forster's principles expressed when introducing the Education Bill of 1870:

> The education of the people's children [should be managed] by the people's officers chosen in their local assemblies controlled by the people's representatives in Parliament.[19]

Some members of urban school boards which did not appoint local managing bodies believed that this was a weakness. Reverend Joseph Nunn, the Anglican chair of Manchester School Board, held this view, but was unable to persuade the Board to adopt his opinion.[20] Archdeacon Sir Lovelace Stamer [later Bishop of Shrewsbury], chair of Stoke-upon-Trent School Board, agreed with Nunn and maintained:

> I believe that for inducing heartiness and earnestness in the work there is nothing like the management of a good voluntary school, where the clergy and others who are interested in the schools are continually there and take a direct and personal interest in the whole thing. The difference I can see between the voluntary schools and the board schools is just the difference between a private firm and a limited liability company. That affects the teachers and it affects the children and everybody.[21]

There can be little doubt that it was the religious affiliations of these three which determined their attitudes to this issue.

In Birmingham, local managing bodies were not used, but local inspectors visited schools and reported regularly to the Board's school management subcommittee. When challenged as to whether the Birmingham inspectors took personal interest in the children, Crosskey replied that the inspectors dealt with scholastic progress but added how Birmingham schools were developing home/school relations.[22] He believed that greater involvement of teachers and schools with parents and their communities was much more vital to the personal development of the children than the existence of a body of local managers.

Crosskey's views exemplified those of the free churches, and Non-conformists were, of course, strongly represented on most urban school boards. Local school managing bodies were seen as the mechanisms by which the Anglicans and Roman Catholics ordered their educational affairs, and, as such, something to be avoided. In the nineteenth century denominational rivalry extended to the very apparatus of school government. In avoiding the voluntary school model, these urban school boards founded a new concept of local educational management. For the first time public elementary schools without individual managing bodies came into existence and a tradition of direct school management by elected local education authorities was established. To many, especially the free churches, this approach seemed more democratic, more modern and more likely to develop the education service than the old voluntary sector model. Soon the educational achievements of several city school boards were the sources of considerable local civic and municipal pride and seemed to point the way to the future.

The Royal Commission on Elementary Education reviewed the relative merits of the models of school management adopted by the board and voluntary sectors. Diplomatically it maintained that there were virtues in each. The board system was superior in 'that branch of administration which can be transacted outside the school . . . [and] dispersing the money of the ratepayers'. On the other hand, the voluntary sector was better at achieving 'the closest supervision of the school . . . and the most effective sympathy between managers and teachers or between managers and scholars.'[23] The Commissioners concluded that in the future progress should be looked for 'in the combination of the advantages of both systems.'[24] It is to be regretted that the Commissioners were largely ignored, for one of the major long term shortcomings of English school government has been that either one or other of these models has been emphasized and rarely, if ever, have attempts been made to combine the advantages of the two.

The recasting of the education system in 1902 mainly served to entrench further the existing contrasts in the arrangements and practices in the management of elementary schools. Although school management was not a main cause of contention in 1902, it was closely linked to the basic controversial issue – the proposal to fund voluntary schools from the rates. Because the newly created LEAs were to be made responsible for the recurrent funding of the voluntary [non-provided] schools, they were given jurisdiction over matters involving expenditure. In the whole area of secular instruction the LEA was made supreme and the managers of non-provided schools were required to carry out its directions. On the other hand, managers continued to control religious education and retained powers to appoint and dismiss teachers. From 1902 local authorities appointed one third of the membership of the managing bodies of non-provided schools, but the foundation managers remained in a clear majority.

Much has been written about the Balfour Government's measures to support the voluntary schools with rate aid and the determined opposition of the Non-conformists and the Liberals to this. However, the implications of this controversy for the role of school managing bodies has been relatively neglected. In their attempts to persuade the Non-conformists, the Liberals and the public at large that giving rate aid to the voluntary schools would not lead to undemocratic denominational control of public money, the Conservatives, led by Balfour himself, stressed that the LEA should have 'absolute control over secular training in the voluntary schools'[25] and that 'it was clearly set out in clauses 8 and 12 that the council and paymasters have control of the education committee and the education committee have control of the managers in both board and voluntary schools, so that the managers were the instruments of the representatives of the ratepayers.'[26] Balfour clearly saw it as politically essential to provide such reassurances to the electorate, but, it must be said, that the Liberals and Non-conformists remained largely unconvinced. In the longer term, however, it was much more significant that in continually emphasizing the supremacy of the LEA, the role of the managing bodies was inevitably downgraded. There is no evidence that efforts were made to explore how the advantages of both systems could be combined.

As the Conservatives had found it necessary to underline the supremacy of LEAs over the managing bodies of non-provided schools, they were hardly in a position to deal with the managing bodies of provided schools differently. Accordingly in the 1902 Act, LEAs which were boroughs or urban districts could appoint managing bodies for provided elementary schools if they thought fit but were not obliged to do so. Many took no action and, thus, in many towns and cities, the pre-1902 situation was perpetuated with the LEA's elementary education management sub-committee effectively in charge of the schools. In the counties, provided schools were required to have bodies of managers consisting of four appointed by the county council and two by the minor local authority. During the debate on the 1902 Bill, Lloyd George had suggested that county councils serving large areas would not possess the necessary local knowledge to select the best people to manage schools.[27] He proposed that in these districts school boards should be retained purely for purposes of management. Balfour rejected this, but believed that there was substance in the local knowledge argument. To meet this point the appointees from the minor local authorities were included.

Under the legislation two or more schools could be grouped together under one managing body. In some large counties considerable use was made of this provision. In the Liberal-controlled West Riding, for example, district sub-committees acted as the managers of all provided elementary schools in their areas.[28] There were 88 district sub-committees in total [in 1904 in charge of 287 provided schools] and 48 of these corresponded exactly with former single-school-board districts. The other 40 included more than one board areas and localities which had an adequate number of voluntary school places and therefore no school boards. As well as acting as school managers, the district sub-committees were channels for local interest in education, much as the school boards had been before them. In this large county authority there was certainly considerable continuity between the pre-and post-1902 practices in school management.

The tradition of direct school management by elected local education authorities and their sub-committees was certainly not destroyed by the changes of 1902. In many ways it was strengthened because the major political parties were acknowledging, even stressing, the supremacy of the

LEA over managing bodies concerning secular instruction. The managing bodies of voluntary schools still retained important powers and influence, but they had surrendered substantial independence in exchange for rate aid. As the proportion of children educated in the voluntary schools steadily declined in the twentieth century, the paramount position of the LEA became stronger and dominant in the education system.

The arrangements for the governance of secondary schools developed on rather different lines. In its 1864 report on the nine leading public schools[29] the Clarendon Commission found great diversities in the government and constitution of the schools, but attached great importance to governing bodies and their work. It set out what was later regarded as the classic statement concerning the powers of governing bodies of secondary schools and discussed in interesting detail the respective roles of governors and heads in such matters as buildings, appointments and staffing, admissions, curriculum, teaching methods and school discipline.[30] Throughout the nineteenth century, secondary schools operated independently and were not normally connected with local authorities. Towards the turn of the century some secondary schools began to accept grants from the newly created technical instruction committees of local authorities and in consequence were required to put local authority representatives on to their governing bodies. In 1895 the Bryce Commission recommended that local authorities for secondary education should be set up with rights to appoint representatives to the governing bodies of secondary schools serving local people in their areas.[31] It was also proposed that schools should be required to submit their accounts to the local authority and that heads should normally attend governors' meetings but without voting rights.

The Education Act of 1902 enabled local education authorities to set up their own secondary schools and successfully encouraged the considerable expansion of secondary education for both girls and boys over the next two decades. The question of the governance of secondary schools was not addressed in the legislation and a large element of discretion was left in the hands of individual LEAs. At this time Robert Morant was made Permanent Secretary to the Board of Education, and his views concerning the nature of a 'good' secondary schooling and how this could be achieved coloured developments for several years. In its annual regulations the Board stressed that schools should be conducted by governing bodies which should protect heads from 'unnecessary interference in matters of school administration.'[32] The control of the LEA and its relations with school staff were to be exercised through the governing body and were not to be too close or too minute. The Board, and particularly Morant, saw governing bodies as a means of ensuring some professional autonomy for heads and teachers.

In 1907 the Board's secondary regulations [Article 22] required that grant earning schools should be conducted in accordance with instruments of government which defined the constitution of the governing body and its functions. These instruments had to be approved by the Board. It was soon ascertained that many local authority secondary schools were being administered either without instruments at all or with unsatisfactory ones,[33] and at the end of 1908 the Board issued model articles of government for provided secondary schools. It was mentioned that these model articles were for guidance and were not prescriptive, but it was clear that the Board hoped to see the establishment of a governing body for each provided secondary school which guaranteed some independence from the LEA in certain areas such as appointments and staffing.

Several urban LEAs in the north and midlands were hostile from the outset to the model articles. Leeds, led by its Secretary of Education, James Graham, protested strongly and soon orchestrated a campaign against them. Leeds, which had made great strides in municipalizing its secondary schools over the last five years, argued that 'it should be left free to manage its own schools according to local needs without being tied to inelastic schemes'.[34] It believed that its Higher Education Sub-committee could deal with these matters quite adequately and successfully and accused the Board of 'ignorance of "the actual working conditions of educational administration under large LEAs"'.[35] The Board rejected this attack and denied that its proposals aimed 'to limit in any way the full right of control that is vested in the LEA; this control is, in any case, effectively secured to the Authority by its absolute power of the purse.'[36] The Board repeated its case for independent governing bodies and asked Leeds to comply with Article 22.

Although, at this point, Leeds amended the duties of its Higher Education Sub-committee to some extent, Graham made it clear that Leeds, which was now receiving support from the Association of Municipal Corporations, had no intention of meeting the Board's demands. An acrimonious meeting in London in March 1910 brought no progress,[37] with the Board still criticizing 'the concentration of power in the hands of the Higher Education Sub-committee and the consequent lack of authority of the head teachers and the governing bodies'.[38] In July the Board threatened that no grants would be paid until Leeds complied. Graham was infuriated by this, believing that the Board was trying to undermine his position as Secretary of Education. A reply went to the Board which stated that Leeds City Council 'would not provide money for schools over which they have not full and complete control' and would not do anything 'to belittle the dignity or stultify the position of the Secretary of Education.'[39] It was also alleged that the Board was exceeding its powers under the 1902 Act.[40]

After a long delay, there is evidence that in February 1911 Morant personally negotiated the Board's climb down with Graham.[41] Eventually it was admitted that Leeds had the right to manage its secondary schools in the way that it wished. Graham was jubilant and told fellow secretaries of education that they should quote the Leeds case as precedent in any disputes with the Board. Graham received replies from 45 education officers applauding the Leeds victory.[42]

These events were of considerable significance for the future of school government in England. The Board, especially Morant, had tried to force reluctant LEAs to set up relatively autonomous governing bodies for their provided secondary schools. Several urban authorities led by Leeds had resisted, and after a long battle the Board had to concede that it had no power to insist. There was certainly nothing in the 1902 Act which gave it such authority. The Board had tried to impose its conceptions of good secondary school government through complex grant regulations, but discovered that, if LEAs resisted, it could not get beyond a position of ill-tempered stalemate. The LEAs had now demonstrated beyond much doubt that they had the right to govern their secondary schools directly through their education committee structures and their education officers. In addition Graham had been successful to a large degree in presenting their dispute as a struggle for preserving local freedom from autocratic central government control. By challenging the LEA position and losing Morant had only succeeded in drawing attention to the strength of their case. In these circumstances it was not surprising that no further challenges were made for well over half a century.

The arrangements for the government and management of schools were reviewed in the Second World War during the preparations for the 1944 Education Act. There was wide agreement that there should be instruments 'providing for the constitution of the body of managers or governors'[43] for all schools. In the case of county [formerly provided] schools instruments were to be made by order of the LEA whereas the Minister was to make the orders for instruments of voluntary schools. Primary schools were to be conducted by rules of management made by their LEAs, but secondaries were to be run according to articles of government [for county schools made by the LEA and approved by the Minister and for voluntary schools made by the Minister]. Articles of government determined 'the functions to be exercised by the LEA, the body of governors and the headteacher respectively.'[44]

The provisions for primary schools were largely uncontroversial although some Labour MPs wanted to remove the distinctions between primary 'managers' and secondary 'governors' which they interpreted as differences of social status and snobbery.[45] It was also suggested in the

Commons that rules of management for primaries should be subject to ministerial approval because LEAs could easily diminish the status of managers in the rules they laid down.[46] R. A. Butler rejected this, arguing that the Minister would be put in 'a quite intolerable position'[47] if the cases of all primary schools had to be processed centrally. He added that it was unnecessary to take the ordinary governance of primary schools out of the purview of local authorities. In the 1940s there were few who disagreed with Butler about county primary schools which were still normally perceived as ex-LEA elementaries, and no real attempt was made to challenge existing practice.

The position regarding secondary schools proved much more complex and controversial. The Headmasters' Conference predicted that the independence of grammar schools [especially of heads and governors] would be threatened by rigid controls which LEAs and their Directors of Education might choose to impose. Soon a pressure group consisting of the Headmasters' Conference, the Joint Four and the Governing Bodies Associations and led by Canon Spencer Leeson, headmaster of Winchester, was putting pressure on the Board of Education concerning this issue.[48] It was alleged that county boroughs, particularly in the north of England, interfered with the freedom of provided grammar schools over a number of issues including the curriculum. It was also maintained that local party political considerations should be kept out of these schools. There can be little doubt that Spencer Leeson and his colleagues feared that the entry of the modern schools from the LEA elementary sphere to the new expanded field of secondary education could injure the existing grammar schools, their status and esteem and 'level down' their standards.[49] Butler was not sympathetic to these arguments, but he saw dangers in uniformity. He insisted that schools should be offered scope for variety and individuality. The Fleming Committee on the public schools emphasized much the same points and may have been prompted to take this line by G. G. Williams [Secondary Branch, Board of Education] who served as assessor to the Committee.[50] To ensure that LEAs did not include undue restrictions, it was proposed that they should be asked to prepare instruments and articles of government in line with a model issued by the Board. This proved acceptable and such a model was circulated by the new Ministry of Education in January 1945.[51] In Parliament there were clashes between members who criticized the close control ['the tyranny of a narrow bureaucracy'[52] one MP claimed] over the grammar schools of the northern city LEAs and others who maintained that the wishes of the democratically elected bodies had to be respected.[53] Butler himself asserted that LEAs could 'not be deprived of their influence on the schools which the children of their own citizens attend',[54] and, although Chuter Ede acknowledged that in a very few cases reform was necessary, he denied that excessive tyranny by the education office was at all common.[55] Butler, with his determination to ensure parity of esteem, was consistently adamant that all post-1944 secondary schools should be treated in the same way regarding governing bodies whatever their origins and traditions. He refused to perpetuate a situation in which grammar schools kept their governors 'while secondary modern schools were simply "run by the office"'.[56] To placate his critics Butler undertook to publish a White Paper on principles of government in secondary schools.[56] This appeared as early as May 1944, and set out some detailed guidance on the constitution, composition, size and grouping of governing bodies and on their roles and relations with other parties in respect to finance, appointment and dismissal of staff, internal organisation and curriculum and admission of pupils.

The decision to continue to permit the grouping of schools under one managing or governing body caused considerable concern amongst some MPs. From personal experience some members pointed out how difficult it was to have close and detailed knowledge of individual schools if they formed part of a large group.[58] A former Chairman of London Education Committee endorsed this view and added, 'There is a danger that if the new secondary schools are grouped in the same way as elementary schools are, the impression will go abroad that the claim we made that we are providing secondary education for all is nothing but eyewash.'[59] Butler was clearly very uneasy about grouping and expressed some sympathy for those who opposed it. He said that his discussions with LEAs, and, particularly with their directors of education who were the practitioners actually running the service, had made it clear to him that it was absolutely essential to have powers to group schools including some which would fall in the secondary sphere.[60] It was not his intention, and he did not believe it was the LEAs' intention to misuse these powers and overrun and destroy the independence of individual schools. He promised to speak further to headteachers about this issue, but warned that the provisions for grouping were widely desired.[61] The practice of grouping for purposes of school government continued in many areas and was one of the major weaknesses of the system in the post-war era. In this respect, as in others concerning school government, the legislation of 1944 served to perpetuate rather than challenge existing local practices. There was no real pressure to change the provisions for the management of elementary schools destined to become primaries after 1944 and in large measure the 1902 structures and practices were retained. In the secondary field there were more complications. The Secretary of the Association of Education Committees, Sir Percival Sharp, indicated that he did not wish to see governing bodies set up for provided secondary modern schools. It was clear that he still regarded the latter as ex-senior elementary schools which should be run by the LEAs. Sharp believed that 'it was unwise to be too logical'[62] and argued that the best plan might be to give the managing bodies of secondary moderns different powers from the governors of grammar schools. On the other hand, Butler was worried that this did not give equal treatment to the two types of schools. Chuter Ede insisted that parity of esteem must be achieved by 'levelling up' and not 'down'. In his view the HMC's position on governing bodies 'was prompted by the belief that the Headmaster could more easily manage his governing body than he could an LEA!'[63] He thought that the solution might be in grouping secondary schools under one governing body. Ultimately, the Board went for parity of esteem, and, regarding governance, put grammar schools and secondary moderns on an equal footing. In doing this Butler and Ede successfully resisted some of the claims of the grammar school lobby pointing out that it was adopting an élitist position. Sharp's similarly élitist stance was never made public and the LEAs, who were given very largely what they wanted, quietly accepted that all secondary schools would come within the same framework for governance.

During the post-war period, with the important exception of the voluntary sector, governing bodies played a relatively minor part in the development and management of schools. In many ways this was the heyday of the LEAs and the teacher unions with figures such as William Alexander of the AEC and Ronald Gould of the NUT playing particularly crucial roles in the education service. In local government, party politics were increasingly dominant with appointments to governing bodies normally made strictly on the basis of party allegiance. In some county areas LEAs were required to delegate certain administrative functions to divisional executives which meant there was less 'space' in which governing bodies could operate. For some years, therefore, governing and managing bodies continued to find themselves very much in the background without indispensable roles to perform. On the one hand, LEAs normally pursued active policies and exercised firm controls across their areas. On the other, at the level of individual schools, heads and senior staff fully expected professional autonomy in matters such as the curriculum and often readily took on important initiatives.

It was not until the 1960s that some of these assumptions and practices began to be questioned. New approaches to the government of the teacher training colleges, the new polytechnics and further education colleges were adopted.[64] From the early 1960s the Association of Teachers in Colleges and Departments of Education [ATCDE] pressed the LEAs for more staff and university representation on the governing bodies of training colleges and more autonomy for these governing bodies. As they were normally constituted as part of the local authority committee structure, they often found their aspirations for development as independent higher education institutions thwarted. In 1963 the Robbins Report recommended that the training colleges [to be renamed colleges of education] should be taken out of local authority control and their existing links with the universities further strengthened. The local authorities opposed this and, as it turned out, so did the senior civil servants at the DES. The Secretary of State made it clear that, if the colleges were to remain with the local authorities, there would have to be reform of college governing bodies.[65] He acknowledged that illiberal government of colleges was not a problem everywhere, but in some areas there were serious deficiencies to be remedied. The leaders of the local authority associations accepted this, and it was agreed that a Study Group on The Government of Colleges of Education should be set up under the chairmanship of Toby Weaver, a deputy secretary at the DES.

The local authority leaders knew that they would have to make concessions, although it is clear from evidence in the AEC files that several chief education officers [CEOs] were very unhappy about some of the likely changes. It was recognized that the governing bodies of colleges would have to be taken out of the local authority committee structure, and the Weaver Study Group proposed new legislation requiring LEAs to make instruments and articles of government [to be approved by the Secretary of State] on the lines that had operated for secondary schools since 1944. It was also agreed that there was no need for LEA representatives to be in a majority on college governing bodies nor for chairs always to be LEA people. Throughout, both the LEAs and the DES were conscious of the fact that there could not be undue differences in the arrangements for the government of colleges of education and further education colleges particularly as the Association for Teachers in Technical Institutions [ATTI] was pressing much the same points as the ATCDE had done for the colleges of education.

Without delay the Labour Government moved to implement the recommendations of the Weaver Group. This was done in the short Education [No. 2] Act, 1968, and in the same measure the opportunity was taken of bringing the arrangements for the governing bodies of further education colleges into line with those of secondary schools. Some individual LEAs, particularly the chief education officers, continued to oppose aspects of these changes, but local authority association leaders, such as William Alexander, now favoured 'a high degree of delegation of authority to governing bodies of colleges, and indeed of schools'.[66] Alexander had to move carefully, however, as he could not afford to alienate the members of his Association who were more conservative on this issue. In the end the changes in college government owed much to the interest and persistence of certain political leaders who worked hard to ensure the smooth passage of the necessary legislation through Parliament. Edward Boyle, the Conservative education spokesman was fully committed to the changes and refused to allow them to fall from the political agenda. Shirley Williams, who was the Minister of State during the crucial period, never made a secret of her enthusiasm for these reforms and, according to Alexander,[67] her considerable contribution in this area was the main achievement of her period of office.

The attention focused on the arrangements for governing colleges in the mid 1960s led directly to the position of schools being reconsidered. In its evidence to the Royal Commission on Local Government submitted in 1966 and 1967, the DES argued for fewer but larger local education authorities.[68] Sir Herbert Andrew, the Permanent Secretary at the DES, suggested that a corollary of large authorities was 'the build-up of governing bodies attached to particular schools and colleges'[69] He wanted to see more delegation to governing bodies and felt that it was the weakness of the present law that they did not have enough to do. The DES believed that the existing system of divisional administration introduced an additional and unnecessary stage and led to delays and duplication. It favoured the abolition of divisional executives and excepted districts with the local community interest being better represented by effective governing bodies.[70] The DES came out strongly against the extent to which the grouping of managers and governors was used in certain areas, and argued that 'any steps which led to each school having its own governing body composed of knowledgeable and enthusiastic people, prepared to take time and trouble over its affairs, would be of great benefit to the schools'.[71] In terms of membership, the DES acknowledged the case for parental representation and for nominations from local business [at various levels] and other institutions such as universities and colleges.[72] It wished to see continued representation for second-tier local authorities, but did not want school staff as members of governing bodies although the head should have the right to be present at all meetings. It is also interesting to note that the AEC put forward very similar ideas to these in its own submission,[73] and that the local authorities themselves were contemplating major reforms which would increase the power and influence of school governing bodies at the level of the individual institutions. A little later the National Union of Teachers [NUT] joined what was an emerging consensus concerning the reform of school governing bodies in the second half of the 1960s. It wanted to see an end to grouping and heads placed on all governing bodies.[74] Except in very small schools, it also wanted teaching staff represented. In addition, the

G

NUT favoured some form of parental representation but did not underestimate the complexity of this notion.

Thus, by the time of the Wilson Government, there was considerable agreement that school governing bodies should be vitalized and that they should play an enhanced role in the future of education service. Emphasis was placed on greater participation and on the need to involve local community interest in local schools. It is also clear that by 1970 several LEAs were interested in the possibility of appointing teachers and parents to governing bodies. The school teachers' associations, having seen the successes of the college teachers in this respect, were keen to push the case of their members. The AEC received several letters on this subject during the period 1969 to 1971. The AEC advised LEAs that there was nothing to stop them appointing parents as representative governors, but guidance from the DES on teacher governors was sought. This brought an interesting and positive response.[75] Although the model instruments of January 1945 had ruled out teacher governors and this view had prevailed for many years, a change could be brought about 'if there was a widespread desire among authorities, governors and teachers for change'. No amendment to the law was required, and changes to instruments of government, which in the case of county schools LEAs already controlled, would suffice. Sheffield and the Inner London Education Authority altered their instruments to include parent and teacher governors as early as 1971. Baron and Howell's research published in 1968 showed that only 9 counties and 11 county boroughs provided for parent governors and hardly any at all for teacher governors.[76] By 1975, with the formal framework for instruments unchanged, the situation had been transformed with 70 out of 82 LEAs surveyed providing for parent governors and 62 out of the 82 had set aside places for teachers.[77] Radical reform of governing bodies had taken place even before the Taylor Committee held its first meeting.

The Taylor Committee was set up in 1975 to review the current state of governing and managing bodies. It presented its report "A New Partnership for our Schools" in 1977. Two main issues were featured in the terms of reference originally presented to the Committee. The first was concerned with the composition of governing bodies and the second with their responsibilities.[78]

The Committee responded to the challenge by making use of the innovations which had been established in the 1944 Education Act but which, to a large extent, had never been implemented. Namely, their recommendation was for each school to have its own managing or governing body and to do away with the large scale grouping tactic adopted by many local authorities.

A further recommendation, referred to in the title of their report, was for a partnership to be formed within these individual school bodies of equal numbers of local authority representatives, parents, school staff and members of the local community. It was clearly intended that no one group should be able to dominate the others on a governing or managing body but rather that there should be a broad-based, balanced representation of 'consumers' and 'providers', all of whom should work to the needs and interests of the school.[79]

The Committee identified the responsibilities of governors as covering the appointment and dismissal of staff, the admission of pupils, certain financial matters, and the fixing of some holidays. In addition, the governing or managing body should also have responsibility for internal organization. Governors or managers should establish the aims of the school and oversee the development of the curriculum.

Reaction to the Report was mixed. Those groups which had pressed for decentralization and wider representation were, naturally, impressed, and gratified by the major recommendations. On the other hand, some teacher unions were quite strongly opposed seeing it as a threat to teachers because it gave lay people an opportunity to dictate to them on professional matters. The local education authorities were also disquieted. Neither the Labour controlled AMA nor the Conservative controlled ACC gave their full support to the report. Jack Smart speaking on behalf of the former stated that 'Whilst there were some challenging suggestions in the report these should not obscure the unique position of the democratically elected LEA. Responsibility for education must rest with the LEA elected by the whole community'.[80]

Despite such opposition, the Taylor Report was widely respected for its integrity, its common-sense approach and its innovative and challenging stance. However, the view of a four-way, equally balanced composition of governing and managing bodies proved too much for the Government to accept. The objections of the local education authorities held sway, prompting Shirley Williams as Secretary of State, in an Education Bill of 1978, to reject the idea of the equal grouping of governors in favour of giving LEA representatives up to half the total number of places on each governing or managing body. Furthermore, she decided against adopting the Report's recommendations concerning the redefinition of the powers of governors and managers, deeming that the time was not yet right for such legislation. The bill fell at the general election of 1979 and never became law.

Notwithstanding this rejection, the Report still represented a major landmark in the process of change towards the significant reforms of the 1980s because it acted as a vehicle to promote the principles embedded in the 1944 Education Act, in terms of school government. The fact that its main proposals were considered, at the time, to be too radical proved to be nothing more than a temporary setback. Rather, it was the case that the proposals were not before their time, but that local and central government were reluctant to share their power.

A change of government, following the general election of 1979, did help to promote some of the Taylor Report's recommendations, but in no more than a modest way. In fact, Baron suggests that, in some ways, the Education Act of 1980 represented a further retreat from the proposals, because all that was now required of LEAs was for them to provide places for a minimum of two parents and one or two teachers on governing bodies and to fill the remaining places as they chose. In effect, this provided the opportunity, which many took, for LEAs to retain a majority of their own nominees, as there was no limit to the size of governing bodies.[81]

In other ways, however, the Government, through the 1980 Education Act, acknowledged the good sense of the Taylor Committee, primary school managers became governors in line with their secondary colleagues and parents were given more rights in stating a preference of school for their children. Schools were required to provide specific and detailed information for parents and members of the wider community and minutes of governing body meetings were to be made available to interested parties. These relatively small changes marked the beginning of a period of much more radical reform.

This began in 1984 and was led by Sir Keith Joseph, the Secretary of State for Education, who issued a Green Paper entitled, 'Parental Influence at School'. The proposals in it were clearly aimed at strengthening the hand of the 'consumer' element of the educational process, namely the parents, for Sir Keith wanted parent governors to have an absolute majority on the governing bodies of all county and controlled schools. Furthermore he wanted increased powers for them, thus, in effect, seeking to diminish the power of the local education authorities.[82]

The Green Paper created a huge response with some four hundred and seventy written responses being received. Only thirty-three of them supported the major aim of putting parent governors in the driving seat. Not surprisingly, the organization representing LEAs and teachers attacked the proposals as did, more surprisingly, a number of organized parental groups and the National Association of Governors and Managers.[83]

However, the main contribution of the Green Paper lay in the fact that it stimulated discussion sufficiently to highlight certain unpopular measures within the Government's overall plan for school governance. The Government listened to the hostile views and took account of them. As a result, when the White Paper, entitled 'Better Schools' [1985], was issued, the idea of putting parents in the overall majority on a governing body, was dropped. Instead, the proposals were more closely matched to those of the Taylor Report. The number of parent governors was to be increased but no group was to predominate over the others. The groups were LEA representatives, teachers, the headteacher [if he or she chose to be a governor] and co-opted governors. Governors, it was proposed, would be appointed for a period of four years.[84]

The proposals of the Green Paper concerning governors' powers and responsibilities for curriculum, discipline, appointment and dismissal of staff, finance and annual reports to and meetings with parents were all carried forward into the White Paper.

The chief architects of the White Paper were keen to point out that the intended legislation would, for the first time ever, clearly outline the composition and functions of school governing bodies. It would, at the same time, remove certain barriers which previously, they reckoned, had prevented governing bodies from realizing their full potential. For example, insufficient account being taken of parents' interest in their children's education; the practice of certain local authorities appointing an absolute majority of their representatives; the lack of clear direction for governors of their powers and functions.

Most of the proposals lodged in the 1985 White Paper were translated into law in the 1986 Education [No. 2] Act which, itself, embraced the most far-reaching measures for governing schools yet seen. The composition of governing bodies was revised in line with the terms of the White Paper which meant that, for county schools the number of parent governors matched the number of LEA representative governors and varied, according to the size of school, between two and five in each group; that there was to be one or two teacher governors depending on whether the school had more or less than three hundred pupils; that the headteacher would be a governor, unless he or she chose not to be; and that the co-opted governors would represent the largest single group, being one larger than the parent and LEA groups. Thus parents and the local and business community, through the group of co-opted governors, were given much more potential power and influence than under the terms of the 1980 Education Act.

The other main provision of the Act was to extend the powers of governors over the curriculum and conduct of the school by a considerable degree. For example, governors of county schools were called upon to state the aims of the schools' secular curriculum and to prepare and maintain written statements concerning their curriculum policy. The Act also made it the governors' duty to consider the local education authority's curriculum policy, except for sex education, and to decide whether or not it was necessary to modify the policy in relation to their school. In drawing up their written statements, governors were to take account of the views expressed by the local community, including the police. In the case of sex education, the governors had to decide whether or not it should be included in the curriculum of the school and had to prepare a written statement of the content and organization of such sex education or of their reasons if it was decided not to include it in the curriculum.

Under the terms of the 1986 Act, governors were charged with the responsibility of directing the conduct of the school. The discipline of the school was to be determined by the headteacher providing he or she acted 'in accordance with any written statement of general principles provided for him by the governing body' and paid regard 'to any guidance that they may offer in relation to particular matters'. Only the headteacher might exclude a pupil but in so doing had to inform the LEA and governing body, giving reasons for it if the period of exclusion exceeded five days in any term. Parents also had to be informed of the details and of their right to make representations to the governing body and the LEA.

On the subject of finance, the LEA had a duty, under the Act, to furnish the governors with a financial statement, annually, in order to allow them 'to judge whether expenditure in relation to their school represents economic, efficient and effective use of resources'. The governors also had responsibility over an annual sum of money, given to them by the LEA to spend on books, equipment and stationery. This was quickly overtaken by the local management of schools provisions in the Education Reform Act 1988.

Sections 30 and 31 of the Act required the governors of county schools to prepare a brief annual written report containing 'a summary of the steps taken by the governing body in the discharge of their functions during the period since their last report' and to hold an annual parents' meeting to discuss this report. In the report, information had to be included about the composition of the governing body; the financial position of the school, showing how the governors had apportioned the school's budget; any examination and assessment results; the governors' efforts to strengthen links with community, including the police.

The annual meeting was to be held not less than two weeks after the distribution of the report to all parents of registered pupils at the school. If the number of parents present equalled or was greater than one fifth of the number of pupils registered at the school, the meeting could pass resolutions which had to be considered by the governors, the headteacher or the LEA, whichever was most appropriate. Written comments resulting from such considerations were to be included in the next annual report.

The appointment and dismissal of staff was under the control of the LEA, under the terms of the Act. However, in appointing a headteacher, there had to be a number of governors equal to, or in excess of, the number of LEA representatives on the selection panel. In appointing other staff, the governors had full responsibility. In cases of staff dismissal, the LEA had to consult the headteacher and governing body. Both governors and headteacher had the power to suspend a member of staff but they were required to reinstate if directed to do so by the LEA. Some of these provisions have since been revised in subsequent legislation.

The Secretary of State for Education, Kenneth Baker, claimed that the Education [No. 2] Act, 1986 would encourage parents, teachers, local education authorities, governors and the local community to work effectively together in providing the best education for our children. On the other hand others noted the intricacies and, in a number of provisions, the obscurities written into the Act, suggesting that . . .

> Litigious parents [and] governors who fancy themselves as barrack-room lawyers, heads who are jealous of their prerogatives . . . will be tempted to rush to their solicitors every time one protagonist or another fails to observe the letter of this complicated and for much of its length, unnecessary law.[85]

This has not happened and the amount of educational litigation is still negligible. However, scarcely had governors begun their attempt to assimilate the complexities of this new law, than they were immersed into another, yet more demanding piece of legislation in the form of the Education Reform Act, 1988.

Once more, governors were at the centre of change, for this Act further increased their powers and duties at the expense of the local education authorities, which found their functions diminished. There was also an emphasis on centralizing policy thus providing the Secretary of State with considerable powers.

Although the composition of governing bodies remained unchanged from that set out under the 1986 Act, there were very significant changes concerning the curriculum, financing of schools, open enrolment and the appointment and dismissal of staff, which affected the responsibilities of governors. It was now their duty, along with that of the LEA and headteacher, to ensure that the National Curriculum was fully implemented in their school and that the legal requirements for religious education were effected. The curriculum policy statements, which governors were required to produce as a result of the 1986 Act, had to be compatible with the National Curriculum and were required to be systematically reviewed.

Wide-ranging financial responsibilities were delegated to governors initially for schools with more than two hundred pupils on roll, but later to all schools. Under these terms, governors had to manage a budget which included headings for all staff salaries, certain building expenses, energy costs, capitation expenditure and other costs for examinations, furniture, fittings, telephone charges and so on.

This responsibility was an onerous one, for a governing body which signally failed to discharge its duties could be brought to account. Moreover, where there was 'substantial or persistent failure' to manage funds 'in a satisfactory manner', the LEA was empowered to withdraw a governing body's delegated powers, under Section 37 of the Act.

Although there was an obvious element of risk involved in managing a budget, there were also intended to be advantages for governors involved. They had considerable choice over how the overall budget was to be spent and through the process of virement, could transfer monies from one cost heading to another, thus providing further opportunity for decision-making and prioritizing. In practice, much depended on the size of the budget given to each governing body annually. Even though the formula used to decide the budget allocation was pupil-driven, [at least eighty per cent of it must be based on pupil numbers] certain funds could be kept by LEAs 'at the centre'. Some LEAs have been criticized by their headteachers and governors for failing to release a sufficient proportion of these centrally held funds, thereby placing schools under severe pressure because of inadequate budgets.

In view of the fact that so much of a school's budget was dependent on the number of pupils on roll, the sections of the Education Reform Act which have extended the principle of open enrolment have taken on a particular significance for governing bodies. Open enrolment, as well as aiming to increase the choices open to parents, sought to encourage competition between schools, in an attempt to improve their quality; it also tried to develop the economical use of school accommodation through the closure of schools which failed to attract pupils. Such aims had particular consequences for school governors. In no circumstances could they afford to be complacent; to do so might put their school at risk of closure.

The 1988 Education Reform Act also gave governors and/or parents the right to choose whether to remain under the control of the LEA or to become a grant maintained school. This right was reinforced in the 1993 Education Act. Governors now have a duty to discuss once a year whether they wish to ballot parents on whether the school should apply for grant-maintained status – if they decide to ballot the parents, or if a petition signed by at least twenty per cent of the parents is presented to the governors requesting a ballot, then this must be carried out within ten weeks of the resolution being passed, or the request received.

The composition of the governing body of a grant maintained school is laid down in the 1993 Education Act. The first or foundation governors have to be in a majority and must include at least two parents. The rest of the governing body comprises five elected parents, one or two teachers and the headteacher. The governing body of a grant maintained school is a corporate body responsible with the head for the running of the school. The LEA still retains certain powers on such matters as special educational needs and home to school transport. In other areas the DFE acts as a surrogate LEA concerning itself with such issues as parental complaints over the delivery of the National Curriculum or admission procedures. The Secretary of State has the right to appoint [and has actually appointed] additional governors. The governing body receives its finance from the Funding Agency for Schools [created 1 April 1994].

The last fifteen years have witnessed a tremendous transfer of power from democratically elected LEAs to the governing bodies of all schools. Increasingly England has moved from a 'national system of education locally administered' to a state system of education locally governed. Whilst the term 'state schools' is still *de jure* incorrect, it is actually the situation and of course grant maintained schools and city technology colleges are indeed 'state schools' in almost every sense. One of the results of this is that there are considerable concerns, not only amongst the opponents of the reforms, about the public accountability of non-elected governing bodies. For reasons other than misdemeanours, the only governors who can be removed during their term of office are LEA representatives and foundation governors of both aided and grant maintained schools. Whilst others may well have to put themselves forward for re-election or re-co-option at the end of four years, the eligibility regulations mean that very few are likely to be able to stand for several terms of office. Indeed it is even possible for a parent to serve three-quarters of his/her term of office without a child in the school. Scott wrote 'governing bodies are to be given greater discretion to manage the resources available to schools without reference to the wishes of the LEAs . . . LEAs will no longer be able to limit pupil intakes to secure an even distribution of places across their schools. These measures certainly encourage, indeed oblige, schools to take responsibility for their own management. But they also undermine efforts to make them more accountable.'[86] From January 1994 all governing bodies became corporate bodies and this has paved the way for the return of the system of over a century ago in which there were two tiers – a central government department and individual school governing bodies with little or nothing in between. Has the wheel indeed turned the full circle? The implications of this for the education service – both in terms of accountability and development – need to be considered very carefully in the next few years.

References

1 *Minutes of the Committee of Council on Education*, 1839/40, p. 22. Instructions for inspectors, 4 January 1840.

2 Ibid, 1847/8, Volume 1, p. lxxv, Kay-Shuttleworth to Revd. G. N. Barrow, Secretary to the Diocesan Board of the Deanery of Bristol, 7 October 1847.

3 Ibid.

4 Ibid., 1848/9, pp. 1-9, Minutes respecting the management clauses of school deeds, 28 June 1847.

5 F. Smith, *The Life and Work of Sir James Kay-Shuttleworth* [1923], p. 187.

6 *Minutes of the Committee of Council on Education*, 1848/9, p. 4

7 Ibid.

8 R. Johnson, 'Educational Policy and Social Control in early Victorian England' in *Past and Present*, No. 49, [November 1970], pp. 96-119.

9 P. Gordon, *The Victorian School Manager.* [1974], pp. 25-29.

10 Code of Regulations for Day Schools 1896/97, [*School Board Chronicle* edition, 1897], p. xxxiv.

11 Ibid.

12 Robert Lowe, House of Commons, 13 February 1862, quoted in *Royal Commission on the Elementary Education Acts*, Report, [1888], p. 17.

13 P. H. J. H. Gosden, *The Development of Educational Administration in England and Wales*, [1966], p. 136.

14 Ibid., p. 137.

15 *Royal Commission on the Elementary Education Acts*, Report, [1888], p. 69.

16 P. Gordon, op. cit., Chapter 4, 'The Operation of Local Management under the School Boards', pp. 136-172, provides several examples.

17 *Royal Commission on the Elementary Education Acts*, op. cit., Evidence, W. Lee, Q37,645

18 Ibid., Evidence, H. W. Crosskey, Qq41,053-4 and 41,076-7.

19 Ibid., Q41,414.

20 Ibid., Evidence, J. Nunn, Q37,075.

21 Ibid., Evidence, Sir L. Stamer, Q24,236.

22 Ibid., Evidence, H. W. Crosskey, Qq 31,243-6.

23 Ibid., Report, p. 69.

24 Ibid.

25 *Hansard, House of Commons*, Volume cxl, col. 376, A. J. Balfour, 16 July 1902.

26 *The Manchester Guardian*, 20 October 1902, statement by A. J. Balfour.

27 *Hansard, House of Commons*, op. cit., col. 377, D. Lloyd-George, 16 July 1902.

28 P. H. J. H. Gosden and P. R. Sharp, *The Development of an Education Service: The West Riding 1889-1974.* [1978], p. 22.

29 Eton, Winchester, Westminster, Charterhouse, St Paul's, Merchant Taylors', Rugby, Shrewsbury, Harrow.

30 *Clarendon Commission*, Report on the Revenues and Management of Certain Colleges and Schools, [1864], Volume 1, pp. 4-7.

31 *Bryce Commission*, Report on Secondary Education, [1895], Volume 1, pp. 298-9.

32 Board of Education, *Secondary Regulations*, [1904/5], Prefatory Memorandum.

33 Board of Education, *Report 1908/9*, p. 127.

34 L. Connell, 'Administration of Secondary Schools: Leeds v. Board of Education, 1905-11', in *Journal of Educational Administration and History*, Volume V. No. 2 [July 1973], p. 27. Connell is quoting the Leeds Higher Education Sub-committee memorandum on model articles of government, January 1909.

35 Ibid.

36 Board of Education, *Report 1908/9*, p. 128.

37 W. R. Meyer, 'James Graham versus the Board of Education, in *History of Education Society Bulletin*, No. 51 [Spring 1993], pp. 22-3.

38 Connell, op. cit., p. 28.

39 Meyer, op. cit., p. 23.

40 Connell, op. cit., p. 28.

41 Meyer, op. cit., p. 23

42 Connell, op. cit., p. 30.

43 Education Act, 1944, Section 17[i].

44 Ibid., Section 17 [3] [b].

45 *Hansard, House of Commons*, Volume 397, cols. 2241-7, 9 March 1944.

46 Ibid., col. 2249.

47 Ibid., col. 2251, R. A. Butler.

48 Public Record Office, Ed 136/224, President's meeting with Secondary School Associations, 18 December 1942.

49 Ibid., Spencer Leeson to Butler, 4 March and 29 April 1943.

50 This is suggested by R. N. Heaton who was a senior civil servant in the Board at this time in DES, *A New Partnership for our Schools*, [1977], p. 161.

51 Ministry of Education, Administrative Memorandum No. 25, [26 January 1945].

52 *Hansard, House of Commons*, Volume 397, col. 2266, 9 March 1944.

53 Ibid.

54 Ibid., col. 2275.

55 Ibid., col. 2323.

56 P. Gosden, *The Development of Educational Administration in England and Wales*, [1966] p. 206.

57 Board of Education, *Principles of Government in Maintained Secondary Schools*, [1944].

58 *Hansard, House of Commons*, Volume 397, cols. 2325-7, 9 March 1944.

59 Ibid., col. 2328.

60 Ibid., col. 2329.

61 Ibid., cols. 2330-1.

62 Public Record Office, Ed 136/378, Note of Meeting Board of Education and Association of Education Committees, 11 August 1943.

63 Ibid.

64 For a more detailed account of these developments, see P. R. Sharp, *The Creation of the Local Authority Sector of Higher Education*, [1987], pp. 17-36 and pp. 56-67.

65 Association of Education Committee [AEC], File A1133, DES note of meeting with representatives of local authority associations, 30 November 1964.

66 AEC, File A713, Alexander to Harding, 25 March 1969.

67 *Education*, 31 October 1969.

68 Royal Commission on Local Government, Volume Memoranda of DES dated October 1966, December 1966 and June 1967.

69 Ibid., Evidence of Sir Herbert Andrew, Qq 493-502.

70 Ibid., DES memorandum, October 1966.

71 Ibid.

72 Ibid., DES memorandum, June 1967.

73 Ibid., Memorandum of AEC dated November 1966.

74 NUT, *Into the 1970s*, April 1969.

75 AEC, File A1135, Harte to Alexander, 31 December 1970.

76 G. Baron and D. A. Howell, *School Management and Government*, Research Studies 6, for Royal Commission on Local Government, 1968.

77 DES, *A New Partnership for our Schools*, [1977], p. 10.

78 Ibid., p. 1.

79 Ibid., p. 104.

80 *Times Educational Supplement*, 23 September 1977.

81 G. Baron, *The Politics of School Government* [1981] p. 98.

82 DES, *Parental Influence at School*, [1984], pp. 3-11.

83 *Education*, 16 November 1984.

84 DES, *Better Schools*, [1985], pp. 63-66.

85 *Times Educational Supplement*, 24 October 1986.

86 P. Scott, 'Accountability, responsiveness and responsibility', in R. Glatter [editor], *Educational Institutions and their Environments: Managing the Boundaries*, [1989], p.12.

Illiteracy in provincial maritime districts and among seamen in early and mid-nineteenth-century England

W. B. STEPHENS

Over the past quarter century much research has been undertaken into historical aspects of literacy in Britain, especially England. The main thrust of this work has been in analysis of the ability to write (and by inference to read) at a modest level. Research has involved assessing the numbers and proportions of people in possession of these basic skills and analysing the characteristics of such persons (and of those who remained illiterate) geographically and over time. This has embraced classification of literates and illiterates by socio-economic groups, analysis of the typology of communities and localities containing varying proportions of literates, and attempts to explain the differences between geographical areas and types of community.[1] As a consequence, we now have for England reasonably firm evidence of the proportions of the adult population as a whole attaining literacy at a basic level over the period from the sixteenth century to the introduction of compulsory education from 1870. In addition we have evidence of the nature of differences, as far as basic literacy is concerned, between various types of community and between one part of the country and another, as well as between social and economic groups.[2]

This work has been based largely on statistical calculations mainly derived from evidence of the ability of adults (from 1754 brides and grooms on marriage) to sign their names. The arguments for accepting signature evidence as a measure of basic literacy are well known and not confined to the study of literacy in Britain.[3] They will not be reiterated here, but it may be noted that generally it has been felt that ability to sign one's name probably indicated ability to read, perhaps reasonably well. Until the mid-nineteenth century a child began to learn to read before beginning writing, and not *pari passu*. Not until a certain standard was reached in reading did writing commence. Many children, therefore, left school before the writing stage was reached. Because reading was a skill easier to learn than writing, because it was more expensive to keep a child at school long enough to learn to write than to read only, and because for many people reading was a skill more likely to be useful than writing, almost certainly more people could read than could sign their names – though to varying degrees. In an age when, in general, working people rarely needed to sign their names and where little if any stigma attached to making a mark, there would have been, it has been argued, little point in learning as a social accomplishment to write one's name and nothing else. Even if a proportion of those able to sign their names could possibly do little more, there is no evidence to suggest that the proportion varied erratically – and the main value of signature statistics is not as a provision of an absolute measure, but rather as a means of comparison chronologically and geographically.

Although much energy has been expended in the comparison of the extent of illiteracy in different types of community and different types of area, however, no attention has, as far as I am aware, been given to the position of maritime areas as such. There is, of course, some difficulty in an island like Britain in seeking to demonstrate any distinctive characteristics of maritime areas as opposed to inland ones – for more than half the English counties had a sea coast and a few more communicated with the sea (like the West Riding of Yorkshire through Goole and other river ports). Yet as far as levels of signature-literacy are concerned, counties with coastlines do seem generally to have had more literate spouses than do inland counties.

This can be demonstrated by examining proportions of spouses making marks on marriage (that is indicating inability to sign their names) as recorded in statistics published in the annual reports of the Registrar General of Births, Deaths and Marriages (which embraced every marriage in England and Wales from 1839 into the twentieth century). Over the six years 1839–45 the counties registering the lowest proportions of marriage markers were Cumberland (where only 26 per cent of spouses were unable to sign their names), Northumberland (28 per cent), Westmorland (28 per cent) and the East and North Ridings of Yorkshire (30 and 32 per cent respectively) – all maritime counties. The counties of the southern seaboard (except Dorset and Cornwall) were also demonstrably superior to most other counties: only 34 per cent of spouses in extra-metropolitan Kent made marks in those years, and 35 per cent in Sussex, Hampshire and Devon. Another maritime county, Gloucester, had 36 per cent, while London (not, of course, a county) recorded 18 per cent, lower than any county. Only two inland counties – little Rutland with 33 per cent and extra-metropolitan Middlesex with 34 per cent – could compare with these levels.[4] The levels recorded for the other inland counties bear out the difference between illiteracy levels in inland and maritime counties: see Table 1.

Nevertheless there remains a number of maritime counties (listed in Table 2) not so far mentioned where the proportions of marriage marks were not noticeably lower than those of many inland counties. Indeed these figures are sufficient to indicate that any impression of obvious educational superiority of maritime counties over inland ones is superficial. The comparative illiteracy levels of most English counties are in fact more readily explicable on grounds other than the possession of a coastline. Moreover, all seaboard counties (except perhaps Cornwall) contained large inland areas. In many, too, large proportions of the population were connected more with agriculture, industry and mining than with the sea. I have argued elsewhere that varying levels of illiteracy

Table 1

Percentages of spouses making marks on marriage in inland counties, 1839–45

Rutland	33
Middlesex (extra-metropolitan)	34
Surrey	37
Derbyshire	40
Oxfordshire	40
Warwickshire	40
Cambridgeshire	41
Herefordshire	41
Leicestershire	42
Berkshire	43
Nottinghamshire	44
Northamptonshire	45
Shropshire	48
Buckinghamshire	49
Wiltshire	49
Huntingdonshire	50
W. R. Yorkshire	51
Staffordshire	52
Worcestershire	53
Hertfordshire	54
Bedfordshire	58

Source: Annual Reports of the Registrar-General of Births, Deaths and Marriages.

Table 2

Percentages of spouses making marks on marriage in certain maritime counties, 1839–45

Durham	37
Dorset	39
Lincolnshire	39
Somerset	43
Cornwall	46
Norfolk	47
Cheshire	49
Suffolk	49
Essex	50
Lancashire	53
Monmouthshire	58

Source: Annual Reports of the Registrar-General of Births, Deaths and Marriages.

in the different parts of England can be explained largely in terms of the
extent and nature of industry, the type of farming carried on, population
density and movement, and characteristics like child employment,
parental and employer attitudes towards education, and the extent of the
involvement of the clergy and other middle-class folk in the provision and
encouragement of working-class schooling. Thus the low levels of marks in
the counties of the far north of England are more likely to stem from a
comfortable farming population, busy market towns, and a tradition of
schooling among a population of independent pastoral farmers, than from
the fact that the sea lapped their coasts.[5] Similarly, Lancashire's high levels
of marks are attributable, among other factors, to concentrations of
population in mushrooming industrial towns and mining villages and to
widespread use of child labour, rather than to its ports. The signature-
literacy records of other counties can be similarly explained.[6]

Analysis of the illiteracy rates of counties with above 2 per cent of men
engaged at the time of the 1851 census in 'sea navigation' occupations, as
calculated by Thomas A. Welton in 1860[7] and set out in Table 3, serves to
illustrate only that even in those counties the vast proportion of men (90
per cent and more) were not engaged in such occupations. The
proportions of grooms belonging to the sea navigation trades cannot have
been large enough to have affected materially the county proportions of

Table 3

*Counties with over 2 per cent of adult males in
sea navigation occupation, 1851*

County	% in sea occupations	% Male marriage marks, 1839–45
Durham	10.8	25
Northumberland	6.9	19
E. R. Yorkshire	5.9	20
Hampshire	4.7	31
Cumberland	4.6	16
Kent (extra-metropolitan)	4.2	29
Lancashire	4.0	39
Cornwall	3.9	36
Devon	3.6	28
Dorset	3.4	34
N. R. Yorkshire	2.5	23
Gloucestershire	2.3	29
Norfolk	2.3	44

Sources: Thomas A. Welton, *Statistical Papers on the Census of 1851* (1860); *Annual Reports
of the Registrar-General of Births, Deaths and Marriages*. Royal Navy and Marine personnel
not included.

marriage signers and markers. Thus, to take a single example from the Table, the percentages of illiterate grooms in Gloucestershire and Norfolk varied by 15 percentage points, though the proportion of men in sea navigation trades was the same in each of those two counties. It is quite clear that counties are not suitable units for our purpose. More appropriate are the subdivisions of counties (census registration districts) for which the Registrar-General also provided marriage signature statistics and for which the percentages of men in sea navigation occupations are available in the census – giving an indication of parts of counties which were more genuinely 'maritime' in nature.

In England as a whole (Wales is not covered here) there were some 550 census registration districts in 1851. The Appendix presents an analysis of the marriage mark statistics for 1856 for each of the 84 of those census districts which (by Welton's calculations) had at the census of 1851 at least 3 per cent of adult males in occupations connected with sea navigation – together with a breakdown of the numbers in the various trades embraced in that category. They were seamen, pilots, dock labourers (who included also 'others connected with sea navigation'), shipwrights (who included also 'shipbuilders' and 'others engaged in fitting ships'), and hemp manufacturers (who included ropemakers, sailcloth manufacturers, and 'other workers in hemp'). In addition the Appendix indicates for each district the percentage of the total population at day school in 1851, together with an indication of the illiteracy statistics for 1856 for the counties to which the districts belonged (or, in the case of the metropolitan districts, the illiteracy rate for London).

Of the Appendix it may be noted here that the information given relates to each whole district and not merely to the town which may have given the district its name. Scarborough district, for instance, included a large rural area as well as the port after which it was named. (But not all districts bore the names of important ports within them — Deal and Sandwich, for example, were in the district of Eastry.) Two inland registration districts are strictly eligible for inclusion in the Appendix – Abingdon and Yeovil – but this is due entirely to the fact that high proportions of workers in hemp manufacture lived there; they have therefore been excluded. Royal Naval personnel and Marines, concentrated in only a few districts, are not included in the Appendix, though something is said about them towards the end of this chapter. And although nine metropolitan districts appear in the Appendix (Poplar down to Greenwich) they have not been included in the calculations and discussions which now follows. The peculiar demographic structure of these heavily populated London districts and its relation to educational factors require more investigation than can be attempted in a short essay and merit a separate study.[8]

Analysis of the data in the Appendix reveals some interesting facts. These are presented in Table 4.

This demonstrates that in 1856 about two-thirds of the 75 provincial maritime districts listed in the Appendix registered levels of marriage marks (both for grooms and brides) at or beneath the average level of the counties to which they belonged. Additionally, over 70 per cent of the districts had lower percentages of marks than did England and Wales as a whole. Moreover, if the 75 are divided to distinguish those with over 10 per cent in sea navigation occupations from those with 3 to 10 per cent (as they are in Table 4), it is clear that the tendency for districts with higher proportions of men in maritime occupations to record lower levels of marriage marks is greatly increased.

All this may seem to lead to the conclusion that the greater the concentration of men concerned with such trades, the more likelihood there was of lower levels of illiteracy in the district to which they belonged. Care, however, is needed to avoid drawing conclusions from statistical data

Table 4

Illiteracy levels in the seventy-five provincial census districts listed in the Appendix, 1856
(compared with county and national levels)

Number of districts	Number and % ( ) of districts in which % of marks was equal to or less than the level of their own county		Number and % ( ) of districts in which % of marks was equal to or less than the national level	
	Grooms	Brides	Grooms	Brides
75 (a)	52 (69)	50 (67)	54 (72)	57 (76)
21 (b)	16 (76)	17 (81)	18 (86)	17 (81)
54 (c)	36 (67)	33 (61)	36 (67)	40 (74)

(a) All the 75 provincial districts in the Appendix. The nine London districts (Poplar down to Greenwich) are excluded.

(b) Those of the 75 districts with over 10% in sea navigation occupations, 1851.

(c) Those of the 75 districts with 3–10% in sea navigation occupations, 1851.

Sources: As for the Appendix.

which are not merited. The statistics presented in the Tables above and the Appendix are matters of fact, but, as so often with exercises in historical quantification, they do not answer the really significant questions. Thus while there appears to be a connexion between comparatively large numbers of men in sea navigation occupations and low illiteracy levels, the figures do not demonstrate any causal relationship, nor if there were one explain why this should have been so. The co-existence of such factors is, however, unlikely to be merely accidental. Since in the vast majority of districts the largest group listed in 'sea navigation' occupations was that of seamen (see Appendix), an easy step would be to assume that the existence of seamen bridegrooms enhanced the incidence of literacy in their districts. But these data in themselves are insufficient to support such a conclusion and this hypothesis requires more evidence before acceptance. It is explored further later in this study.

Of course, where only 3–10 per cent of the male population were in sea navigation trades (54 districts; see Table 4), it is improbable that the small proportion of grooms likely to derive from this group could have affected materially the illiteracy levels of their districts. After all, 90 per cent and more of the male population followed other occupations. It might, however, seem more likely that in districts where 17 per cent and over were in sea navigation jobs bridegrooms among them could have been sufficiently numerous to affect the incidence of illiteracy to some extent. But investigation does not bear out such a hypothesis. There were nine such districts (leaving aside the Scilly Isles): Falmouth, Poole and Stockton (each with 17 per cent of adult males in sea navigation occupations), Tynemouth and Hull (with 18 per cent each), Liverpool and Yarmouth (20 per cent each), South Shields (30 per cent), and Sunderland (31 per cent). If, however, the male illiteracy rates for 1856 are examined (see Appendix) it will be seen that, though all but Yarmouth had lower illiteracy rates than the national level for grooms (or in the case of Poole rates equal to that figure), many of the other maritime districts with smaller proportions of men in sea navigation occupations had a lower percentage of illiterate grooms than did these nine districts.

Thus, while the data in Table 4 may suggest that where over 10 per cent of men were in sea navigation occupations literacy rates tended to be better, it would appear that where proportions of such men became higher than 1 in 6 (17 per cent) of the adult male population no such relationship is discernible. An explanation of this apparent anomaly is not offered here, and, indeed, can be determined only by extensive research at the local level. But it may be hazarded that it probably lies not so much in the likely incidence of illiteracy in seamen, dock labourers, hempmakers and the like, as in the general social and economic structure, and in the educational composition of the population of particular port towns. All recent investigations into the literacy levels of occupational groups in the nineteenth century suggest a hierarchy – with those in the professional classes, distributive trades, skilled craftsmen and so on (and in that order) much less often illiterate than were farm labourers, general labourers, factory workers, miners and those engaged in the domestic textile trades.[9] This would suggest that dock labourers and hempmakers would be more likely to be illiterate than those in many other occupations found in port towns. As for Welton's 'shipwrights' (embracing also shipbuilders and 'others engaged in fitting ships') (see Appendix) they undoubtedly included not only highly-skilled men likely to have been literate (and discussed later), but many – perhaps a majority – engaged in labouring and other work in shipyards for whom literacy was not a necessity. It seems probable, therefore, that in districts where dock labourers, hemp manufacturers and the like and labourers in shipyards were numerous (as seems to have been the case in such districts as Stockton, Hull, South Shields, Sunderland, Liverpool, West Derby and Medway) they would have tended to affect the incidence of literacy adversely. Indeed, of Liverpool in 1841 it was noted that 'besides seamen, there are vast numbers of others employed about the docks and warehouses whose opportunities of education have been scanty'.[10] The case of seamen is discussed below.

But these are not the only occupational groups likely to be relevant to our purpose. Research by historians of literacy has shown that over the period from the eighteenth century onwards, and probably before that, the highest levels of signature-literacy were to be found in market towns which were generally superior in that respect to both rural areas and to the industrial towns and large towns generally.[11] The explanation generally proposed for this is that market centres were places where literacy skills were needed by many as a function of their economic life. And such towns, being also old centres of population, tended to be better provided with schooling than, for instance, were the newer factory towns or those burgeoning cities where rising populations swamped existing educational facilities. It could be argued, and is here, that seaports, which from a demographic point of view often tended to make up a high proportion of the population of maritime census districts, were themselves mart towns of a specialized kind. Ports were inevitably places where much buying and selling went on, and where warehousing, ship loading and unloading, transfer of goods to and from land transport, the planning of ships' voyages, the victualling and crewing of vessels, and the arranging of the purchase and sale of cargoes in other ports, and so on, required correspondence, form filling and record keeping of various kinds – all embracing transactions for which literate people would be needed. There would be port and government officials and their staffs (customs and excise officers, coastguards, harbourmasters, and the like), merchants, agents, shipowners, chandlers, victuallers, lawyers, bankers, and so on, often with their clerks – for all of whom literacy would be a functional asset and often a necessity.

The socio-economic composition of such places may explain, too, why the incidence of illiteracy among brides also tended to be lower in maritime districts than in census districts generally (see Table 4): a fact which cannot be attributed to employment in seafaring jobs. Wives and daughters of professional men, officials and merchants were much more likely to be literate than those of hempmakers and dock labourers. Also the existence of positions in middle-class families for domestic servants may, too, have promoted female literacy, since, as I have surmised elsewhere, female domestics were more often literate than women engaged in industry or agriculture.[12] The educational position of women in seaports, however, requires further investigation.

The parallel between market towns generally and ports may be extended to the state of schooling in the 75 provincial maritime districts. The last column on the right in the Appendix shows that the proportion of population actually at school on census day 1851 was equal to or higher than the national level (10 per cent) in 59 of these districts. Of the 16 maritime districts with less than 10 per cent of population at school, 11 had 9 per cent. Of the 21 districts with over 10 per cent of their populations in sea navigation occupations in 1851 only two fell below the national level for proportions at school – the districts of Liverpool and King's Lynn – and each of these had 9 per cent. On the other hand, 82 of the districts in England with fewer than 3 per cent of the population in sea navigation occupations had less than 9 per cent of their populations at school.[13]

Extensive research into the occupations of those individual grooms[14] who signed their names and of those who made a mark (ascertainable from the marriage records of port towns, where they have survived) would be necessary to assess just how far the general occupational structure of ports promoted the incidence of signature-literacy found in many maritime districts, and the extent to which the presence of those in various kinds of sea navigation occupations affected those levels. Such a task would be daunting and it has not been feasible to undertake it here, though some fresh evidence is given below, particularly for mariners.

David Alexander has noted that the extensive body of contemporary literature about sea-going in the nineteenth century 'does not provide a very clear portrait of . . . (mariners') education and the social and economic circumstances of their families',[15] while Simon Ville has remarked that 'the level of literacy among seamen remains a mystery due to lack of evidence'.[16]

The 'mystery' may remain but the 'lack of evidence' is an exaggeration: the signatures or marks of seamen who married appear in the marriage registers (like those of other grooms), crew agreements (which in certain circumstances sailors signed or marked) exist in quantities in the Public Record Office, county record offices and at the Memorial University of Newfoundland,[17] records of shipowners and shipping companies could well divulge useful information, and, despite Alexander's caveat, the huge literature of memoirs written by British mariners in the nineteenth century is unlikely to be bereft of useful data and its very existence points to a relatively high level of literacy in some seafarers.

Yet, aside from Ville's own brief note on the subject for the late eighteenth and early nineteenth centuries, and incidental information on English sailors serving in Canadian vessels in the later nineteenth century provided by Alexander,[18] virtually nothing on the basic literacy of British mariners has to my knowledge appeared in print.[19] Ville's sample of the wage receipts of 1,218 merchant seamen (not including masters) in thirteen vessels in London over the years 1788–1815[20] suggests that 45 per cent of sailors where probably illiterate. This overall proportion, however, disguised considerable variations within crews. While something like 60 per cent of those designated 'seamen' were illiterate, of 85 mates all but four (5 per cent) signed their names, of 105 carpenters only 24 (23 per cent) made marks and of 129 cooks 70 (52 per cent). These figures may be contrasted with the likely national illiteracy rate among the more restricted age-group of men on marriage (1785–1814) of 39 per cent, a proportion which embraced rates ranging from 65 per cent illiteracy for labourers and servants to 18 per cent for yeoman and farmers and 5 per cent for officials and the like.[21]

All this suggests that ordinary seamen were less often illiterate than were labourers and that ships' officers were as likely as officials on land to be literate, with sailors with some specific skills approaching comparability with yeomen and farmers. An unpublished analysis of parish register evidence for Gainsborough (Lincs.) for the ninety years 1754–1844 provides a similar picture, with the illiteracy rates for mariner grooms consistently above those for tradesmen but equally consistently some 15 percentage points below those for labourers.[22]

The topic of nautical education (as opposed to the study of basic literacy among seamen) has not been ignored by historians, but cannot be pursued in any detail here.[23] The advantages of a degree of education in ships' officers is obvious. That a comparatively high standard of education was possessed by some masters and other merchant officers is hardly surprising considering the growth in the number of naval and other academies from the eighteenth century which provided young men seeking to enter the merchant marine as well as the Royal Navy with instruction in navigation and other subjects relating to the sea.[24] On the other hand many merchant navy officers would not, of course, have had the benefit of such formal instruction and the degree of education needed by a master would undoubtedly vary: the captain of a large vessel trading overseas would usually require to be literate, numerate and knowledgeable of nautical subjects, while the needs of a skipper of a local fishing boat or the master of a collier would be considerably less.[25]

Voluntary examinations of competency for masters and mates of foreign-going British merchant ships were introduced in 1845. An Act of 1850 made the system compulsory and another of 1854 extended it to officers of home-trade passenger vessels.[26] To obtain their Board of Trade certificates masters and mates were required, among other things, to 'write a legible hand, and understand the first five rules of arithmetic'.[27] Certification was not, however, needed of the skippers and second hands of fishing vessels until the early 1880s (that is outside the chronological scope of this chapter),[28] while masters and mates of home-trade cargo ships (which were permitted not only to carry on coastal trade but also to visit continental ports between the Elbe and Brest) did not require certificates until a century later (1980).[29]

The generosity of Dr R. S. Schofield in providing me with copies of statistical analysis forms derived from the marriage registers of forty-four parishes containing record of marriages of mariners over the years 1754–1844 (representing all the parishes recording sailors' marriages found in the random sample of registers from 274 parishes on which he based his seminal study of marriage signature evidence)[30] has enabled me to add further information. The calculations derived from these data are presented in Table 5.

They suggest that the illiteracy rates for marrying sailors (excluding fishermen) in the forty-four parishes (32, 36 and 26 per cent for the periods 1754–84, 1785–1814, and 1815–44) compare very favourably with rates for grooms generally over Schofield's 274 parishes. These latter ranged between 38 and 41 per cent over the years 1754–1814, falling to about 33 per cent by 1840.[31] Even if ships' officers in the sample (who were nearly all signature-literate) are excluded from the percentages, sailors appear as being less often illiterate than the overall cohort of grooms, even though that included those of all social classes. Certainly further support is given to the likelihood that the ordinary sailor was less likely to be illiterate than were many other working men.[32]

Further evidence of such a hypothesis for years later in the century may be derived from Board of Trade Agreements and Accounts of Crews (henceforth called crew lists), documents which crew members were

Table 5

*Percentages of sailors making marks on marriage in
forty-four parishes, 1754–1844*

Designation in register	1754–1784 No.	%	1785–1814 No.	%	1815–1844 No.	%
Mariner, seaman, sailor	209	33	410	39	580	27
Master mariner, captain, mate, ship's officer	7	0	41	0	34	6
	216	32	451	36	614	26
Fisherman, oyster dredger	10	80	5	80	136	30

Source: Derived from data in marriage register analysis forms (Cambridge Group for the Study of Population and Social Structure), kindly lent by Dr R. S. Schofield. The parishes from which the data were derived are: *Cambridgeshire:* Barnwell. *Cheshire:* St Mary's, Chester. *Cornwall:* Budock; Sithney; *Devon:* St Paul's, Exeter; Plymstock; Wembury; Widecombe; Bishopsteignton. *Dorset:* Allington; Bradford Abbas; Turnworth. *Durham:* Whitburn. *Essex:* Bradwell-on-Sea; East Donyland; North Benfleet; Little Bentley. *Hampshire*: Avington; Worting; Brighstone. *Kent:* Faversham; Frindsbury; Whitstable. *Lancashire:* Caton; Overton; Pennington; Walton, Liverpool. *Lincolnshire:* Messingham. *London:* St Antholin and St John the Baptist. *Norfolk:* Clenchwarton; Cley next the Sea; Holme next the Sea. *Northumberland:* Earsdon. *Somerset:* Dunster; Haselbury Plucknett. *Suffolk:* Hopton; St Mary's, Ipswich; Woodbridge: All Saints, Iden. *Surrey:* Camberwell. *Yorkshire, E.R.:* North Frodingham; Sproatley; Ebberston. *Yorkshire, W.R.:* Rotherham. Entries for 44 Royal Navy officers in these records have not been included in the above figures. All but one signed.

required to sign or mark when joining a ship for a voyage. These give a clue as to the possible proportions of literate and illiterate British seamen. Though ships were registered in specific ports, however, their crews did not necessarily originate in those places nor probably in many cases (particularly in the case of larger vessels) live there permanently. Indeed the crew lists (which record the birthplaces or countries of origin of each individual) demonstrate that sailors in a single ship could often come from a wide variety of places throughout Britain and overseas (though foreign seamen have been excluded from all my calculations). The conclusions drawn from samples of crew lists described below, thus provide general data on British mariners rather than evidence specific to the seamen of any particular port.

In a sample of crew lists for 32 British vessels in the coastal and overseas trade for 1860–1, 26 per cent of sailors (excluding masters) made marks,[33] while a survey of such records for Canadian ships in the years 1865–9 shows 30 per cent of British crew members (none of them masters) as illiterate.[34] Analysis of a sample of 97 crew lists for Devon-registered ships in 1863 (henceforth referred to as 1863 Sample A), containing some 750 signatures or marks made by British sailors (all for foreign voyages), is presented in Table 6. The overall proportion of illiterate crew members shown in the Table (20 per cent) compares very favourably with the national level for grooms of 24 per cent in 1863.[35] An even lower illiteracy rate of 17 per cent is revealed by another study of 186 crew lists for foreign-going Devon ships in 1863 (henceforth referred to as 1863 Sample B), confined to able and ordinary seamen and boys born in Cornwall, Devon, Somerset and Dorset (343 subjects).[36]

More pertinently (since the marriage age of grooms at that time fell predominantly in the late 20s), the proportion of illiterate sailors aged 26–30 in 1863 Sample A (20 per cent excluding masters, 18 per cent with them) is lower than the national level for grooms as a whole (24 per cent), and therefore even lower than the likely level among working men generally. A similar age-analysis for 1863 Sample B shows men (seamen only) aged 26–30 with an illiteracy rate of 24.5 per cent – about the national level for grooms of all classes.[37]

The possibility of some bias in the apparently rather low incidence of illiteracy in mariners revealed by the crew lists must, however, be admitted. Since seamen in the merchant marine were more often faced than were most working men with the need to sign their names or make a mark, they may have been more likely to have learned to sign and nothing else.[38] If so, comparison of sailors' illiteracy rates derived from wage receipts and crew lists with general levels calculated from marriage signatures may underestimate somewhat the relative levels of illiteracy in mariners. On the other hand, most of the signatures examined in the 1863 Sample A of crew lists do not give the impression of having been written by men who found management of the pen difficult, and the existence of non-signers of one in five (Table 6) indicates no universal feeling of obligation to learn signing solely for the purpose of signing the crew agreement. The impression remains that the evidence outlined above indicates that sailors as a group were probably somewhat less often illiterate than was the general run of working men in England.

One must not, of course, exaggerate the level of literacy indicated by the ability to sign one's name, nor suggest that illiteracy among seamen was

Table 6

Percentages of marks in a sample of crew agreements, 1863 (a)

Ages	% excluding masters	% including masters
11–15	36	36
16–20	19	19
21–25	30	28
26–30	20	18
31–35	20	13
36–40	32	19
41–45	16	13
46–50	17	12
over 50	55	30
All	22	20

(a) This is the sample referred to in the text as 1863 Sample A.

Source: Devon Record Office, Exeter, Collection of Board of Trade Crew Agreements and Accounts. This sample comprises some 750 signatures or marks by British sailors in the 97 agreements for all Devon-registered ships with names beginning with the letters A, B and C leaving Devon ports for foreign ports in 1863 contained in the DRO collection (itself a *c.*10 per cent sample of agreements for Devon ships for the period *c.* 1862–1914 originally held by the Board of Trade).
Foreign seamen have been omitted from the above calculations as have a few illegible entries. For some ships there was more than one agreement in the year, so that, although ships often took on new men at each voyage, some men have been counted more than once.

uncommon. The crew list samples are biased towards those serving in foreign-going vessels: it appears that the incidence of illiteracy was probably greater among fishermen and those engaged in the coastal cargo trade. The crew list samples do not include fishing vessels and what little evidence is available from parish registers[39] indicates that fishermen were less likely to be literate than were other sailors. Skippers and second hands of fishing vessels were not required to sit Board of Trade examinations for certification until the 1880s[40] and common sense suggests that literacy in crews of local fishing craft, even among skippers, would not have been as functionally necessary as in many trading vessels.

Masters and mates of colliers, other coastal craft and cargo vessels trading across Channel, too, were less likely to be educated than the officers of deep-sea foreign-going craft. Indeed, it has already been noted that they did not require certification until the twentieth century. And ordinary crew members of such vessels were less often likely to be literate than were their officers. In the sample of crew lists for 1860–1, analysed generally above, 29 per cent of those (excluding masters) in coastal craft made marks as opposed to 24 per cent of those in foreign-going ships.

It is thus not surprising that contemporary literary evidence of illiteracy among seamen in port towns is fairly easy to find. For instance, of 614 sailors admitted to the Marine School at Liverpool in 1815, 'many', it was reported, 'did not know their alphabet . . . others had almost entirely forgotten the instruction received in early life',[41] while a generation later in the same port, it was noted that 'numbers are sent to sea without any education at all beyond reading and writing (if so much)'.[42] Again, in a letter of 1853, the Superintendent of Merchant Marine Pensioners at Sunderland (where there were concentrations of coastal coal vessels) alleged that 'the illiterate state of British sailors is lamentable . . . the majority of seamen cannot write their name'. He remarked, too, that he had two illiterate former masters on his pension list.[43] The evidence of the crew lists and parish registers cited above, however, points to the exaggerated nature of the claim that the generality of sailors could not at that time sign their own names, and the superintendent's experience was evidently somewhat outdated being with elderly and former rather than with serving sailors. The comment on his letter made by the Revd. D. J. Stewart, HM Inspector of Schools for the northern counties at the time, that 'the ignorace which sailors have, even of their own profession, is too well known to require any discussion' seems to have referred to instruction in navigation rather than to the mere ability to write.[44]

Nevertheless the quality of school education in the towns of Sunderland and Shields, which saw huge increases in population, 1841–51, was at a very low level in the 1850s, reflecting not only, it was said, a poverty-stricken seafaring community but a large industrial population.[45] It is likely that the literacy rate of sailors did bear some relationship to their place of birth or upbringing and the cultural ethos and educational opportunities available there. The illiteracy rate of 26 per cent for British sailors in the crew list sample for 1860–1 embraces 24 per cent for Scots, 50 per cent for Irish and 14 per cent for English and Welsh (Welsh alone 19 per cent), matching the comparative literacy ranking of England, Scotland, Wales and Ireland. Of those identifiably Cornish, four out of nine (44 per cent) made marks, perhaps reflecting the generally high illiteracy level in that county.[46]

Further analysis of the crew list samples corroborates the evidence of the parish registers for earlier in the century – that literacy at sea had, like that on land, a hierarchical structure. Whether a sailor was literate often reflected his position on board ship. The sample of crew lists of 1860–1 reveals all masters, carpenters and stewards signing their names and almost all boatswains. Similarly, the 1863 Sample A shows all masters, mates and stewards able to sign their names, and only seven (11 per cent) of 61 boatswains making marks, only seven (14 per cent) of 50 cooks and only one of 11 carpenters. This is hardly surprising, but points to the danger of regarding seafarers as a culturally homogeneous group.[47] Whether they were literate or not depended to some extent on their place of origin and their job on board ship, but there is no evidence to suggest that mariners were generally drawn from an illiterate sub-group of the working classes.[48] The examinations for Board of Trade certificates for masters and mates of certain types of vessel (see above), however defective in practice, at least ensured the possession of educational attainments far above those of mere basic literacy: a fact which must also have affected also aspirants to those positions. And at a more humble level, industrial-training, reformatory and other ships for preparing youths for the merchant navy were established in some ports from the late 1850s.

The age structure revealed in crew lists suggests that, aside from the ships' officers and those intending to become officers, most men did not make a lifetime career of the sea. Thus, of the crew members (excluding masters) in the 1863 Sample A of crew lists, 70 per cent were aged between 16 and 30, and a high proportion of those over 30 were mates and boatswains. In the 1863 Sample B (confined to seamen and boys) 73 per cent were below the age of 26.[49] Literary evidence supports the likelihood that many sailors took up land-based jobs after a few years at sea. The practice of interspersing occasional service at sea with land employment was also not uncommon.[50] The distinction between ordinary sailors and landsmen in the study of social attributes, including literacy, thus becomes blurred. Seaports must have included many non-sailors who had once served afloat.

So far not considered is the possible effect of the presence of Royal Navy and Marine personnel on local illiteracy levels, for there were concentrations of these men in such ports as Portsmouth, Gosport, Plymouth-Devonport, Chatham, Woolwich and Sheerness.[51] Such evidence as exists suggests that such men were, by the mid-century, quite as likely to possess basic literacy skills as other seamen. The results of a survey of the educational standards of some 57,000 men and boys in the Navy and Marines in 1865 is presented in Table 7. If it is assumed that only those who could 'write not at all' would have made marks on marriage, then a remarkably low level of illiteracy is on record – 15 per cent as opposed to a national level for grooms of 22 per cent making marks in 1865.[52] The Navy did, of course, have schools both aboard ship and in harbour, and however defective such facilities were – and they came in for much criticism – they cannot but have assisted in promoting basic literacy.[53]

Further evidence is provided by the Marine Society's registers of boys 'entered as servants in the King's ships'. Analysis of some years covered in these show that, over the years 1842 and 1843, 82 per cent of 143 boys (aged 14–18 and all of humble origin) were able to read and write, 5 per cent able to read only, and but 13 per cent possessed neither of those skills. Similar record of entries for the three years 1863, 1864 and 1865 (of 98 boys aged 13–16) gives 86 per cent able to read and write and 14 per cent illiterate.[54] Males in these age groups would on average have married about ten to a dozen years later, and comparison with the national levels of illiteracy in grooms (embracing all social classes) in 1855 (30 per cent) and 1875 (17 per cent)[55] suggests that entrants into the Royal Navy were less likely to have been illiterate than were men generally in their age-cohort.

Finally some further remarks may be made on other occupations associated with ports. On the one hand, many lowly jobs connected with docks, shipyards and harbours did not require literacy skills. Of London dock labourers Mayhew wrote in 1849: 'This class of labour is as unskilled as the power of a hurricane. Mere muscle is all that is needed.'[56] And indeed in the sample of forty-four parish registers made use of above, 41 per cent of the 49 'boatmen', 'bargemen', 'tidesmen', 'watermen', 'lightermen', 'caulkers', and the like, marrying in the period 1815–44, were illiterate, probably a considerably higher proportion than the national level for grooms. On the other hand the same sample records all customs officers, excisemen and coastguards as signing their names, while of 22 chandlers and victuallers whose marriages were recorded only two did not sign, and of 153 'shipwrights', 'shipbuilders' and 'ships' carpenters' only 8 per cent made marks.[57] Shipwrights (as opposed to some other men working in shipyards) are, indeed, likely to have possessed a sound education. Traditionally they served a long and rigorous apprenticeship.[58] And for those seeking apprenticeships in the royal dockyards at Deptford, Woolwich, Chatham, Sheerness, Portsmouth, Devonport and Pembroke in the mid-century there were civil service examinations covering the three Rs, grammar, composition, geography and mathematics, and after entry attendance followed at dockyard schools (open also to other young employees) where instruction was given in mechanics, hydrostatics, advanced mathematics, dynamics and calculations relating to the displacement and stability of ships. In practice such schools fell far short of aspirations but they clearly offered an education well above that of an ordinary elementary school.[59] As has been pointed out above, however, the category of 'shipwrights etc' used in the Appendix embraces many, including labourers, for whom literacy was not a necessity.

This study has been more exploratory than definitive. It has, however, pointed to the likelihood that in towns and districts associated with the sea in the nineteenth century, concentrations of certain land occupations associated with the pursuit and regulation of trade, the organization of

Table 7

*Educational standards of 57,308 petty officers, seamen
and boys serving in the Royal Navy and Marines, 1865*

Approx. % able to	Petty officers	Seamen	Marines	Boys	All
read					
well	75	61	51	70	61
indifferently	20	28	32	29	28
not at all	5	11	17	1	11
write					
well	65	52	40	61	50
indifferently	28	34	38	37	35
not at all	7	14	22	2	15

*Source: Statistical Return of Education . . . in 227 Ships, 10 Coast Guard Ships and 5
Divisional Barracks . . . P.P. 1867 XLIV, 347*

shipping and the building of ships tended to promote a lower incidence of
illiteracy than might otherwise have been so, and that such a tendency was
probably strengthened by the presence of bodies of seafarers. On the other
hand the presence of other sea navigation occupations – such as dock and
shipyard labourers, hemp manufacturers, sail makers and the like –
probably had a contrary effect. The existence of varying proportions of
different types of sea navigation occupations in individual ports will go
some way to explain the fact that illiteracy levels varied between maritime
districts, but in any particular case is unlikely to be the sole explanation –
for the districts contained also other people unconnected with the sea in
varying numbers and of differing types. There still remains the need for
historians to explain not only the like attributes of places apparently
basically similar, but also the reasons for difference. In this essay common
ingredients have been stressed, but each place will nevertheless have had
unique features. Sometimes influences other than those of the sea are
rather obvious – in Liverpool, for instance, the presence of large numbers
of unschooled and indigent Irish immigrants from the mid-century and of
factory workers must have affected the situation. In other places the
reasons for difference may not be so clear and there is scope for much more
work at the local level.

References

1 See especially, David Cressy, *Literacy and the Social Order: reading and writing in Tudor and Stuart England* (1980); R. A. Houston, *Scottish Literacy and the Scottish Identity: illiteracy and society in Scotland and northern England, 1600–1800* (1985); W. B. Stephens, *Education, Literacy and Society, 1830 –70; the geography of diversity in provincial England* (1987); David Vincent, *Literacy and Popular Culture: England 1750–1914* (1989); and works cited in these books.

2 W. B. Stephens, 'Literacy in England, Scotland, and Wales, 1500–1900', *History of Education Quarterly*, xxx (1990), and works cited there.

3 For arguments for and against, see citations in R. A. Houston, 'The development of literacy: northern England, 1640–1750', *Economic History Review*, 2nd series, xxxv (1982), 200–1; Stephens, *Education, Literacy and Society*, 269, nn. 1–2. And see, especially, R. S. Schofield, 'The measurement of literacy in pre-industrial England', in J. Goody (ed.), *Literacy in Traditional Societies* (1968), 314–15; Houston, *Scottish Literacy*, Chapter 5; Victor E. Neuburg, 'Literacy in eighteenth century England: a caveat', *Local Population Studies Magazine and Newsletter*, ii (Summer, 1969), 44–6.

4 Stephens, *Education, Literacy and Society*, App. D.

5 Stephens, *Education, Literacy and Society*, 42, 57 and *passim*.

6 See, e.g., M. Sanderson, 'Social change and elementary education in industrial Lancashire, 1780–1840', *Northern History*, iii (1968); Stephens, *Education, Literacy and Society*, 86–100; W. B. Stephens, *Regional Variation in Education during the Industrial Revolution, 1780–1870* (1973); W. B. Stephens, 'Illiteracy and schooling in the provincial towns, 1640–1870' in D. Reeder (ed.), *Urban Education in the Nineteenth Century* (1977).

7 Thomas A. Welton, *Statistical Papers on the Census of 1851* (1860). For the definition of 'sea navigation occupations' as used by Welton, see below.

8 Some of these districts (eg, Poplar, Stepney, St George-in-the-East) were notoriously poverty stricken (see L. Marks, 'Medical care for pauper mothers and their infants: poor law provision and local demand in east London, 1870–1929', *Economic History Review*, 2nd series, xlvi (1993), 519), yet returned illiteracy rates for grooms below the national level and in some cases respectable proportions of their populations at school (see Appendix). In London, however, dock labourers often included those in other trades who had fallen on hard times: many handloom weavers, for example, worked as dockers in spells of unemployment (G. Stedman Jones, *Outcast London* (1971), 101). Again comparison with the illiteracy rate of the metropolis as a whole – which, as might be expected of the hub of the empire and the seat of government, with its concentrations of the wealthy and the educated, was extraordinarily low (see Appendix) – is hardly appropriate.

9 R. S. Schofield, 'Dimensions of literacy, 1750–1850', *Explorations in Economic History*, x (1973), 209, *inter alia*.

10 'H.R.', 'Education of seamen', letter in *Albion*, 26 Feb. 1841 (copy in Liverpool

Record Office (Brown Library), ref. 374.21 EDU). I am grateful to Dr A. Kennerley of the University of Plymouth for drawing my attention to this.

11 See, eg, Robert Unwin, 'Literacy patterns in rural communities in the Vale of York, 1660–1840' in W. B. Stephens (ed.), *Studies in the History of Literacy: England and North America* (1983).

12 Stephens, *Education, Literacy and Society*, 20–1.

13 Deduced from Stephens, *Education, Literacy and Society*, App.F.

14 Unfortunately occupational information for brides is usually lacking.

15 D. Alexander, 'Literacy among Canadian and foreign seamen, 1863–1899' in R. Ommer and G. Panting (eds.), *Working Men Who Got Wet* (St John's, Newfoundland, 1980), 4. I am grateful to Professor Lewis R. Fischer of the Memorial University of Newfoundland for a copy of this essay.

16 S. Ville, 'Literacy in the merchant marine, 1788–1815', *Mariner's Mirror* lxviii (1982), 125–6.

17 See K. Matthews, 'Crew lists, agreements and official logs of the British Empire, 1863–1913, now in the possession of the Maritime History Group, Memorial University, St John's, Newfoundland', *Business History*, xvi (1974).

18 As cited in n. 15 above.

19 For literacy of sailors in the seventeenth and early eighteenth centuries, however, see R. A. Houston, 'Illiteracy in the Diocese of Durham, 1663–89 and 1750–62', *Northern History*, xviii (1982), 244–50.

20 Calculated from Ville, 'Literacy in the merchant marine', 125–6.

21 Schofield, 'Dimensions', 450.

22 W. Couth, 'Development of the town of Gainsborough, 1750–1850' (unpublished MA thesis, University of Wales, 1975).

23 See A. Kennerley, 'Navigation school and training ship: educational provision in Plymouth for the merchant marine in the nineteenth century' in S. Fisher (ed.), *West Country Maritime and Social History: some essays* (1980); D. G. Bovill, 'Education of mercantile mariners in the north east ports' (unpublished PhD thesis, University of Durham, 1987); A. Kennerley, 'The education of the merchant seaman in the nineteenth century' (unpublished MA thesis, University of Exeter, 1978). I am grateful to Dr Kennerley for lending me his MA thesis and for providing me with other information on the subject of seamen's education. See also citations in n. 26 below.

24 See, eg, N. Hans, *New Trends in Education in the Eighteenth Century* (1951), espec. 101–8; D. G. Bovill, 'The proprietary schools of navigation and marine engineering in the ports of the north east of England, 1822–1914', *History of Education Society Bulletin*, 44 (1989); C. Jeans, 'The first statutory qualifications for seafarers', *Transport History*, vi (1973), 258.

25 Cf. Ville, 'Literacy', 4, 33n.

26 N. Cox, 'The record of the Registrar General of Shipping and Seamen', *Maritime History*, ii (1972), 179. For the system of certification in detail, see Kennerley, 'Education of the merchant seaman'; Jeans, 'The first statutory qualifications'; T. W. C. Vasey, 'The emergence of examinations for British shipmasters and

H

216 W. B. STEPHENS

mates, 1830–1850' (unpublished PhD thesis, University of Durham, 1980); C. H. Dixon 'Seamen and the law . . . 1588–1918' (unpublished PhD thesis, University of London, 1981); Joseph Kay, *The Law Relating to Shipmasters . . .* (1875), vol. I. I am grateful to Mr A. W. H. Pearsall of the National Maritime Museum, Dr D. M. Williams of the University of Leicester and Dr A. Kennerley for some of these references and for information generally on Board of Trade certification, etc.

27 Board of Trade, Naval Department, *Notice of Examinations of Masters and Mates established in Pursuance of the Mercantile Marine Act, 1850* (1850), 4. Already serving and experienced officers, however, were provided with Certificates of Service without an examination.

28 Cox, 'Records of the Registrar General', 180.

29 Ex inf. Dr A. Kennerley.

30 Schofield, 'Dimensions', 450.

31 Schofield, 'Dimensions', 445, graph. Stephens, *Education, Literacy and Society*, App. D, gives 36 per cent for 1841.

32 For fishermen, see below.

33 Public Record Office, Board of Trade, Agreements and Crew Lists, ships 15474, 8219, 10097, 38880, 12102, 12188, 12135, 12708, 33060, 9293, 23541, 549, 5193, 3557, 32809, 32801, 2529, 4443, 10561, 17658, 17653, 35579, 39594, 14323, 5441, 20600, 26400, 16198, 15469, 10097, 16200. I am grateful to Dr David F. Mitch of the University of Maryland for providing me with transcripts of these records.

34 Alexander, 'Literacy among Canadian and foreign seamen', 17.

35 *Annual Report of the Registrar-General of Births, Deaths and Marriages for 1863*, P.P. 1865 XIV.

36 Kennerley, 'Education of the merchant seaman', 231–2.

37 Kennerley, 'Education of the merchant seaman', 231–2.

38 Cf. Alexander, 'Literacy among Canadian and foreign seamen', 6.

39 Table 5. Numbers recorded are, however, too small for firm conclusions.

40 See above.

41 West Devon Record Office, Plymouth, W 668T: *First Report of the Marine School* [of Liverpool] (1816). I am grateful to Dr Kennerley for drawing my attention to this.

42 'H. R.', 'Education of seamen' (see n. 10 above).

43 *Minutes of the Committee of Council on Education, 1853–4*, 923.

44 As last note, 926.

45 As n. 43, 909–13, 921–9.

46 By no means all places of birth were identifiable, so that these calculations do not embrace all sailors in the sample. N.B. 1863 Sample B, however, was confined to seamen born in Cornwall, Devon, Somerset and Dorset and showed very low illiteracy levels: see above.

47 A similar hierarchy was apparent in Canadian vessels: Alexander, 'Literacy among Canadian and foreign seamen', 28.

48 Alexander (cited in last note), 32 concluded similarly.
49 Kennerley, 'Education of the merchant seaman', 232.
50 See memoirs of seafarers calendared in J. Burnett, D. Vincent and D. Mayall (eds.), *The Autobiography of the Working Class*, vols. I and III (1984, 1989).
51 Welton, cited n. 7 above, 126.
52 Stephens, *Education, Literacy and Society*, App. D.
53 See, eg, *Report of the Royal Commission on the State of Popular Education*, P.P. 1861 XXI (pt. 1), 428–37.
54 National Maritime Museum, Greenwich: Records of the Marine Society, Registers of Boys entered as Servants in the King's Ships, MSY/0/14, 15. I am grateful to Dr Roger Morriss of the Museum for drawing my attention to these records. Unfortunately similar registers for boys apprenticed by the Society to the·merchant marine give no educational information.
55 Stephens, *Education, Literacy and Society*, App. D.
56 Henry Mayhew, *The Morning Chronicle Survey of Labour and the Poor: the metropolitan districts* (Caliban Books, 1981 edn.), vol. 1, 66.
57 The ships' carpenters here were probably sailors – but the categorization adopted in the marriage analysis forms used (see Table 5) places them with shipwrights and shipbuilders and they cannot be distinguished here.
58 P. L. Robertson, 'Technical education in British shipbuilding and marine engineering industries, 1863–1914', *Economic History Review*, 2nd series, xxvii (1974), 223.
59 *Royal Commission on the State of Popular Education* (as cited n. 53 above), 437–46.

Appendix

Illiteracy in census districts with at least 3 per cent of adult males in 'Sea navigation occupations', 1850s

Registration Districts	Notes (see below)	Numbers and percentages of men, 1851						Total men engaged about sea navigation		Percentage marriage marks, 1856			Percentage of population at school, 1851	Percentage marriage marks, 1856 (counties, and London)		
		Seamen	Pilots	Dock labourers, etc	Shipowners	Shipwrights, etc	Hemp manufacturers	Number	% of all men	G	B	T		G	B	T
Berwick		150	5	4	2	37	57	255	4.4	10	26	18	14	*Northumberland*		
Tynemouth		2,198	72	34	114	526	129	3,073	18.3	21	37	29	10	18	22	20
Newcastle		1,509	14	21	25	279	192	2,040	8.4	23	41	32	8			
South Shields		1,627	193	36	74	612	106	2,648	29.6	24	41	33	11	*Durham*		
Sunderland		2,725	192	155	155	1,944	348	5,519	30.9	26	44	35	10	27	44	36
Easington	(1)	387	42	46	5	25	12	517	9.2	35	62	49	11			
Stockton		1,502	147	301	47	336	170	2,503	17.1	24	39	32	12			
Whitby		449	18	2	51	143	58	721	13.6	17	27	22	11	*North Riding*		
Scarborough		235	6	1	39	82	39	402	6.4	19	30	25	12	20	29	25
Bridlington		185	1	3	5	8	13	215	5.4	19	29	24	13	*East Riding*		
Sculcoates	(2)	402	3	205	25	276	90	1,001	8.9	20	38	29	10	20	35	28
Hull		1,613	56	481	36	246	114	2,546	18.5	17	36	27	10			
Goole		215	5	97	4	53	18	392	10.8	26	37	32	10	*West Riding*		
Selby		82	0	2	4	25	36	149	3.5	27	38	33	13	29	51	40
Pontefract		174	0	0	6	38	43	261	3.4	35	44	40	10			
Thorne		89	0	7	4	20	34	154	3.5	27	40	32	9			
Gainsborough		145	1	12	0	36	100	294	4.0	25	34	30	12	*Lincolnshire*		
Caistor	(3)	142	10	344	1	38	17	552	5.7	28	40	34	10	29	34	32
King's Lynn		527	37	26	15	42	47	694	12.6	18	28	23	9	*Norfolk*		
Walsingham	(4)	177	15	3	4	36	24	259	4.6	43	33	38	13	40	38	39
Yarmouth		907	10	6	23	148	192	1,286	20.1	32	36	34	11			
Mutford	(5)	235	89	10	10	68	118	530	10.2	32	29	31	11	*Suffolk*		
Ipswich		346	12	39	7	116	37	557	6.6	20	26	23	11	43	39	41
Tendring	(6)	483	16	5	9	53	16	582	7.9	43	46	45	7	*Essex*		
Colchester		139	0	0	4	5	8	156	3.4	18	30	24	10	40	37	39

	( )															
Romford	(8)	137	0	0	18	32	35	222	3·4	37	34	35	10	*London* 12	20	16
Poplar		1,479	9	478	9	1,187	128	3,290	24·6	15	20	18	12			
Stepney		2,083	65	1,551	32	849	578	5,158	18·0	18	28	23	10			
St George-in-the-East		1,521	7	820	3	239	135	2,725	20·4	18	36	27	9			
Whitechapel		1,025	2	818	5	41	95	1,986	8·5	24	40	32	11			
Bethnal Green		100	1	472	2	10	202	787	3·5	24	44	34	12			
St Olave, Southwark		451	6	53	5	45	39	599	10·7	16	23	20	13			
Bermondsey		443	7	262	3	149	198	1,062	8·3	19	29	24	15			
Rotherhithe		791	3	88	4	409	82	1,377	26·7	8	16	12	13			
Greenwich		634	15	112	24	768	99	1,652	5·6	18	27	23	15			
Gravesend		217	81	28	4	37	12	379	8·9	21	21	21	12			
North Aylesford	(9)	88	0	0	4	155	7	255	5·6	26	32	29	11	*Kent (extra metropolitan)* 27	28	28
Medway	(10)	595	2	8	5	359	189	1,158	9·1	22	35	29	11			
Faversham		239	0	0	2	10	10	261	5·8	40	34	37	12			
Blean	(11)	360	0	2	2	31	8	403	11·0	30	26	28	11			
Thanet		799	6	20	0	81	36	943	12·5	14	19	17	10			
Eastry	(12)	518	60	0	1	14	21	613	9·1	28	26	27	13			
Dover		582	62	44	0	52	25	766	9·9	19	17	18	8			
Elham	(13)	255	2	15	2	15	11	298	5·8	25	19	22	13			
Rye		140	5	5	3	46	6	204	6·2	24	33	29	11	*Sussex* 26	23	25
Steyning	(14)	189	13	6	9	44	10	265	6·0	18	18	18	13			
Worthing		99	5	3	1	42	12	170	3·7	32	15	24	11			
Portsea Island	(15)	1,050	22	31	1	640	139	1,883	9·1	21	32	27	12	*Hampshire* 25	28	27
Alverstoke	(16)	223	0	7	1	106	20	357	6·1	27	42	35	9			
South Stoneham	(17)	118	6	1	1	35	0	161	3·9	22	21	22	11			
Southampton		668	18	276	6	285	24	1,272	14·4	15	19	17	13			
Isle of Wight		708	58	8	0	145	42	967	7·5	18	21	20	13			
Lymington		94	0	6	8	15	15	130	4·4	42	23	33	14			
Poole		361	17	18	6	87	57	548	17·2	29	27	28	13	*Dorset* 33	33	33
Weymouth		326	11	14	2	35	18	410	6·9	17	22	20	11			
Bridport		50	6	1	16	30	305	394	9·9	41	48	45	11			
St Thomas	(18)	259	29	4	47	57	67	432	3·6	21	24	23	9	*Devon* 26	32	29
Totnes	(19)	337	7	8	2	163	83	645	7·7	27	24	26	11			
Kingsbridge		126	3	2		47	20	200	3·8	25	32	29	9			

continued overleaf

Appendix *continued*

Registration Districts	Notes (see below)	Seamen	Pilots	Dock labourers, etc	Shipowners	Shipwrights, etc	Hemp manufacturers	Total men engaged about sea navigation Number	% of all men	Percentage marriage marks, 1856 G	B	T	Percentage of population at school, 1851	Percentage marriage marks, 1856 (counties, and London) G	B	T
Plymouth		878	25	52	21	149	153	1,278	9·1	22	36	29	8			
East Stonehouse		80	0	2	2	45	20	149	5·2	37	46	42	9			
Stoke Damerel	(20)	288	1	3	3	509	114	918	9·4	24	37	32	12			
St Germans		100	10	0	2	73	48	233	5·7	25	36	32	10			
St Austell	(21)	185	5	20	1	43	25	279	3·6	40	51	46	9	*Cornwall* 36	47	42
Truro		203	36	14	5	52	24	334	3·4	34	40	37	8			
Falmouth		754	20	23	3	81	51	932	17·1	26	32	29	11			
Penzance		322	15	15	10	116	66	544	4·5	33	48	41	11			
Scilly Islands		119	31	3	6	49	11	219	32·8	11	5	8	17			
St Columb		117	14	4	2	62	12	211	4·8	36	47	42	9			
Bideford		288	0	4	6	129	37	464	10·1	29	36	33	11	*Devon*		
Barnstaple		236	10	5	2	55	15	323	3·5	36	25	25	9	26	32	29
Bridgwater		216	16	10	5	35	24	306	3·6	40	43	42	10	*Somerset*		
Bedminster	(22)	251	32	18	5	180	87	573	5·9	22	30	26	9	33	36	35
Bristol		873	0	140	10	179	114	1,316	7·7	21	31	26	12	*Gloucestershire*		
Gloucester	(23)	190	7	36	1	57	47	338	3·7	25	24	24	10	26	31	29
Wirral		317	14	699	42	154	47	1,273	8·9	42	52	47	10	*Cheshire*		
Runcorn		60	1	85	1	99	33	279	4·1	27	47	37	11	32	52	42
Liverpool	(24)	6,965	99	5,854	57	1,257	463	14,695	20·1	16	27	22	9	*Lancashire*		
West Derby	(25)	1,453	77	1,392	40	1,247	630	4,839	13·1	26	44	35	12			
Fylde		170	4	10	1	25	75	285	5·1	26	44	35	14			
Whitehaven		782	0	35	18	221	107	1,163	12·9	29	44	37	11	*Cumberland*		
Cockermouth	(26)	640	2	33	15	304	54	1,048	10·7	19	29	24	12	17	30	24
England and Wales		64,097	2,400	17,919	1,526	19,338	14,296	119,576	2·5	29	40	35	10			

Sources to Appendix

Thomas A. Welton, *Statistical Papers on the Census of 1851* (1860); *Annual Report of the Registrar-General of Births, Deaths and Marriages for 1856*, PP 1857–8, XXIII; *Census of Great Britain, 1851. Education (England and Wales)*, PP 1852–3, XC.

Notes to Appendix

G = Grooms; B = Brides; T = all spouses.
Welsh districts (detailed by Welton) are not included here.

1. Includes Seaham.
2. Suburb of Hull.
3. Includes Grimsby.
4. Includes Wells, Blakeney.
5. Includes S. Yarmouth, Lowestoft.
6. Includes Harwich.
7. Includes Brightlingsea.
8. Includes Barking.
9. Includes Strood, Northfleet.
10. Includes Chatham, Rochester.
11. Includes Whitstable, Herne Bay.
12. Includes Deal, Sandwich.
13. Includes Folkestone, Hythe.
14. Includes Shoreham.
15. Comprises Portsmouth.
16. Includes Gosport.
17. Adjoins Southampton.
18. Includes Exmouth, Topsham.
19. Includes Dartmouth, Brixham.
20. Includes Devonport.
21. Includes Fowey.
22. Suburb of Bristol.
23. Includes Birkenhead.
24. Surrounding Liverpool.
25. Includes Fleetwood.
26. Includes Workington.

A Select Bibliography of works by Peter Gosden

I. SEPARATE WORKS

The Friendly Societies in England, 1815–1875, Manchester University Press, 1961, x + 262 pp. Reprinted in 'Modern Revivals in Economic and Social History' Series, Gregg, 1993.

The Development of Educational Administration in England and Wales, Oxford, Basil Blackwell, 1966, x + 228 pp.

Educational Administration in England and Wales: a Bibliographical Guide, Leeds, Institute of Education, 1967, 55 pp.

History for the Average Child, (with D. W. Sylvester) Oxford, Basil Blackwell, 1968, 89 pp.

How They Were Taught: Learning and Teaching in England 1800–1950, Oxford, Basil Blackwell, 1969, 229 pp.

The Evolution of a Profession: a Study of the Contribution of Teachers' Associations to the Development of School Teaching as a Professional Occupation. Oxford, Basil Blackwell, 1972, 372 pp.

Self-Help: Voluntary Associations in Nineteenth Century Britain, London, Batsford, 1973, viii + 295 pp.

Studies in the History of a University, 1874–1974, (ed. with A. J. Taylor) Leeds, E. J. Arnold, 1975, x + 318 pp.

Education in the Second World War: A Study in Policy and Administration, London, Methuen, 1976, vii + 527 pp.

The Development of an Education Service: The West Riding, 1889–1974, (with P. R. Sharp) Oxford, Martin Robertson, 1978, x + 273 pp.

The Education System since 1944, Oxford, Martin Robertson, 1983, xii + 227 pp.

Education Committees, (with George Cooke) London, Longmans, 1986, x + 166 pp.

The University of Leeds School of Education, 1891–1991, (ed.) Leeds, Leeds University Press, 1991, x + 161 pp.

The North of England Education Conference, 1902–1992, Leeds, Leeds University Press, 1992, vi + 137 pp.

II. ARTICLES

(A selection of some of the more important or more characteristic articles)

'General Studies in the Sixth Form', *Times Educational Supplement*, no. 2372, 1960.

'The Board of Education Act, 1899', *British Journal of Educational Studies*, vol. 11, no. 1, 1962, pp. 44–60.

'The BEd degree', *British Universities Annual*, 1968, pp. 115–122.

'The Report of the Royal Commission on Local Government and the Education Service', *Journal of Educational Administration and History*, 1969, vol. II, no. 1, pp. 49–53.

'Technical Instruction Committees', *Studies in the Government and Control of Education*, London, Methuen for History of Education Society, 1970, pp. 27–41.

'The Student Body', *Studies in the History of a University, 1874–1974*, Leeds, E. J. Arnold, 1975, pp. 43–81.

'The Early Years of the Yorkshire College', *Thoresby Society Miscellany*, 1976, vol. 16, part 3, pp. 209–229.

'The Origins of Cooptation to membership of local education committees', *British Journal of Educational Studies*, 1977, vol. XXV, no. 3, pp. 258–265.

'The rebuilding of the English school system, 1945–1955', *Education Research and Perspectives*, 1981, vol. 8, no. 1, pp. 67–76.

'Twentieth Century Archives of Education as Sources for the Study of Education Policy and Administration', *Archives*, 1981, vol. XV, no. 66, pp. 86–95.

'The Educational System of England and Wales since 1952', *British Journal of Educational Studies*, 1982, vol. XXX, no. 1, pp. 108–121.

'Recent developments in the study of the History of Education in teacher education courses', *Trends in the Study and Teaching of the History of Education*, London, History of Education Society, 1983, pp. 14–20.

'The governance of the education system', *University of Leeds Review*, 1983, vol. 26, pp. 25–43.

'National policy and the rehabilitation of the practical: the context', in D. Layton (editor), *The Alternative Road: the Rehabilitation of the Practical*, Leeds, Centre for Studies in Science and Mathematics Education, 1984, pp. 7–20.

'The role of central government and its agencies, 1963–82', in R. J. Alexander, M. Craft and J. Lynch (editors) *Change in Teacher Education:*

Context and Provision since Robbins, London, Holt, Rinehart and Winston, 1984, pp. 31–45.

'Education policy, 1979–84', in D. Bell (editor), *The Conservative Government 1979–84: an Interim Report*, London, Croom Helm, 1985, pp. 105–122.

'The Institute of Education and the Affiliated Colleges', (with M. S. Gosden), *University of Leeds Review*, 1988, vol. 31, pp. 61–72.

'Teaching quality and the accreditation of initial teacher-training courses', in V. A. McClelland and V. P. Varma, *Advances in Teacher Education*, London, Routledge, 1989, pp. 1–18.

'From Board to Ministry; the impact of the war on the education department', *History of Education*, 1989, vol. 18, series 3, pp. 183–193.

'Reflections from East of Offa's Dyke', in *The Welsh Intermediate Education Act of 1889: A Centenary Appraisal*, Cardiff, Welsh Office, 1990, pp. 81–96. Also published as 'Ystyriaethan o Du Dwyreiniol Clawdd Offa', *Deddf Addysg Ganolraddol Cymru 1889: Cloriannu Can Mlynedd*, Swyddfa Gymreig, 1991, pp. 81–96.

'The nationalising of Britain's universities, 1945–1965', *University of Leeds Review*, 1991, vol. 34, pp. 137–156.

'Public education in England 1839–1989: The Department and the governance of the system', in *1839–1989 Public Education in England, 150th Anniversary*, HMSO for Department of Education and Science, 1991, pp. 1–26.

'The James Report and recent history', in J. B. Thomas (editor) *British Universities and Teacher Education: a century of change*, London, Falmer Press, 1991, pp. 73–86.

'Die Entwicklung der Sparkassen in Grossbritannien', in Manfred Pix und Hans Pohl (editors), *Invention – Innovation – Diffusion: die Entwicklung des Sparkassengedankens in Europa*, Stuttgart, Franz Steiner Verlag, 1992, pp. 161–177.

'Le Développement des caisses d'épargne en Grande–Bretagne', in *La Diffusion de l'idée de caisses d'épargne au XIXᵉ siècle*, Paris, Les Editions de l'Epargne, 1993, pp. 193–214.

'Teachers and Teaching', *Education Review*, 1994, vol. 8, no. 1, pp. 31–35.

Notes on Contributors

PETER CUNNINGHAM wrote his PhD thesis on the Government Schools of Design under the supervision of Professor Gosden, and subsequently lectured at Westminster College, Oxford. His engagement with the training of primary school teachers and his work in Oxfordshire primary schools led to the publication in 1988 of *Curriculum Change in the Primary School since 1945* (Falmer Press). He is now Director of Studies in the History of Education at Homerton College, Cambridge, and is co-director of a Leverhulme funded project 'Professional Identity and the Training of Teachers in the Early Twentieth Century'.

JOHN DUNFORD is a lecturer in Educational Administration and Management at the University of Leeds. He was previously an Education Officer in several LEAs in Yorkshire. He is co-author (with Paul Sharp) of *The Education System in England and Wales* (1990). He also writes in the areas of educational law and the relationships between central and local government in the field of education.

EDGAR JENKINS is Professor of Science Education Policy, Deputy Director of the Centre for Policy Studies in Education, and Chairman of the School of Education at the University of Leeds. A chemistry graduate with a background in school teaching, he has written extensively about the social history and politics of school science education. He is the editor of *Studies in Science Education* and his books include *From Armstrong to Nuffield: Studies in Twentieth Century Science Education in England and Wales* (1979), *Technological Revolution? The Politics of School Science and Technology in England and Wales since 1945* (with G. McCulloch and D. Layton, 1985) and *A Magnificent Pile: A centenary history of Leeds Central High School* (1985).

DAVID LAYTON was Director of the Centre for Studies in Science Education from 1970 to 1982 and Professor of Science Education in the University of Leeds from 1973 until his retirement in 1989. His numerous publications in the social history and politics of science and technology education include *Science for the People* (1973), *Interpreters of Science* (1984) and, with Gary McCulloch and Edgar Jenkins, *Technological Revolution? The Politics of School Science and Technology in England and Wales since 1945* (1985). He co-directed the national evaluation of the TVEI curriculum (1985-88) and served on the Secretary of State's Working Group which formulated the original proposals for technology in the national curriculum of England and Wales.

DONALD LEINSTER-MACKAY, Associate Professor of Education at the University of Western Australia, has produced the only major academic book on Prep Schools, *The Rise of the English Prep School* (1984). His other publications include *The Educational World of Edward Thring* (1987), *The Educational World of Daniel Defoe* (1981), *Education and The Times: an index of letters to 1910* (in press), *Cross-Pollinators of English Education: Case Studies of Three Victorian School Inspectors* (1988) and *Alleyn's and Rossall Schools: The Second World War, Experience and Status* (1990). Professor Leinster-Mackay is in the process of completing a second book on prep schools entitled *Prep School Down Under* on which the chapter in this volume is based.

STUART MARRIOTT has worked in university adult and continuing education since 1965, first as an extra-mural lecturer in social psychology and subsequently in the study of education for adults as an academic subject in its own right. He has held positions in the Universities of Edinburgh and Leeds, and was appointed to the Chair of Continuing Education at Leeds in 1985. Social psychology provided the background to his evolving interest in organization theory, and this in turn took on an increasingly historical emphasis. Since 1980 his research and published work has been concerned with the historical evolution of institutions and policies in education for adults. Most recently this has taken on a comparative and 'intercultural' aspect involving collaboration with adult education specialists in Continental European universities. Professor Marriott is currently editor of the *Journal of Educational Administration and History,* and the monograph series 'Leeds Studies in Continuing Education'.

GARY McCULLOCH is Professor of Education at the University of Sheffield. He began his academic career as Research Fellow in Education at the University of Leeds, before taking up posts at the University of Auckland and later at Lancaster University. His publications include *The Secondary Technical School: A Usable Past?* (1989), *Philosophers and Kings: Education for Leadership in Modern England* (1991) and *Educational Reconstruction: The 1944 Education Act and the 21st Century* (1994).

PETER SCOTT is Professor of Education and Director of the Centre for Policy Studies in Education at the University of Leeds. He was Editor of *The Times Higher Education Supplement* from 1976 to 1992. Originally an Oxford historian, he spent two years as a visiting scholar at the Graduate School of Public Policy in the University of California at Berkeley while holding a Harkness Fellowship from the Commonwealth Fund of New York. He has honorary doctorates from the University of Bath and the

Council for National Academic Awards and is an Honorary Fellow of the University of Manchester Institute of Science and Technology. He is also a member of the Academia Europaea.

PAUL SHARP graduated in History in 1966 and has taught in secondary schools. He has completed MEd and PhD degrees and is now Senior Lecturer at the School of Education, University of Leeds. His PhD researched the role of the state in the provision of technical and vocational education in Victorian England. He has published widely in the history of education and on the contemporary educational system. He is the author of *The Development of an Education Service: The West Riding, 1889-1974,* (with Peter Gosden) (1978), *The Creation of the Local Authority Sector of Higher Education,* (1987), *The Education System in England and Wales* (with John Dunford) (1990) and numerous chapters and articles.

DR W. B. STEPHENS was until retirement Reader in the University of Leeds. He is currently an Honorary Lecturer in that University and Honorary Research Fellow at University College London. His numerous publications embrace seventeenth-century economic history, eighteenth- and nineteenth-century educational and social history, and the study of local history in England and the United States. He is a former Deputy General Editor of the *Victoria County Histories,* a founder editor of the *Journal of Educational Administration and History,* and at various times has been Research Fellow at the Newberry Library, Chicago, visiting lecturer at the University of Western Australia and visiting professor at the College of William and Mary in Virginia and at Brigham Young University, Utah.